VIRTUAL DECISIONS

Digital Simulations for Teaching Reasoning in the Social Sciences and Humanities

VIRTUAL DECISIONS

Digital Simulations for Teaching Reasoning in the Social Sciences and Humanities

Edited by

Steve *Cohen*
Tufts University

Kent E. Portney
Tufts University

Dean Rehberger
Michigan State University

Carolyn Thorsen
Boise State University

Routledge
Taylor & Francis Group
New York   London

First published by Lawrence Erlbaum Associates, Inc., Publishers
10 Industrial Avenue
Mahwah, New Jersey 07430

Transferred to digital printing 2010 by Routledge

Routledge

270 Madison Avenue
New York, NY 10016

2 Park Square, Milton Park
Abingdon, Oxon OX14 4RN, UK

Cover design by Kathryn Houghtaling Lacey

Library of Congress Cataloging-in-Publication Data

Virtual decisions : digital simulations for teaching reasoning in the social sciences and
    humanities / edited by Steve Cohen . . . [et al.]
        p.   cm.
    Includes bibliographical references and index.
    ISBN 0-8058-4994-7 (c : alk. paper)
    ISBN 0-8058-4995-5 (p : alk. paper)
    1. Simulation games in education.   2. Social sciences—Computer-assisted
instruction.   3. Decision making—Computer-assisted instruction.
4. Virtual reality in education.   I. Cohen, Steve, 1958–

LB1029.S53V57   2005
300'.71—dc22   2004060682
                                                                          CIP

Books published by Lawrence Erlbaum Associates are printed on acid-free paper,
and their bindings are chosen for strength and durability.

Printed in the United States of America
10 9 8 7 6 5 4 3 2 1

Contents

Preface

Every day, social decisions are made. Police decide to question suspects in a robbery. Members of congress speak in favor or against an expenditure citing any number of justifications. People decide to become romantically involved with one another. The number and kinds of decisions go on and on. What does it mean for students of social science to understand each and all of these decisions?

This book offers a way to begin answering this question and its implication for teaching and learning social science. The goal of this book is to advance the premise that having students understand social science through an examination of social decisions is a broad and meaningful paradigm for conceptualizing social science. It means adopting as a curricular goal having students understand how and why one decision is made instead of another. At face value the premise seems bold. How can examinations of social decisions form the basis of understanding social science? Ultimately that is a research question for those developing the methods and theories set forth in this book. However, there are some promising trends that point to the practicality and virtue of this approach.

Digital role-play simulations, the types described in this book, offer an opportunity to have students "experience decisions" in ways previously inconvenient, if not impossible. The opportunity to control and manipulate the simulations gives instructors the power to construct lessons designed to highlight features of decisions and decisions' contexts. Networked environments offer students a chance to contrast in detail their own decisions to those made by their peers. Realistic decision contexts reduce the effect of students' imagination and visualization, and direct them to carefully look at why their decisions might be different but still valid. Tools for describing "decision behavior" at the class level can help instructors illustrate how a range of decisions are possible and justifiable. Overall, using this framework means students learn to understand decisions from a reflective and comparative standpoint, rather than as an analytic outsider looking in. The immediate benefit of this approach is that students are more likely to see a social decision as one of many possible outcomes. The long term benefits should come from a paradigm that captures policy decisions from a sampling point of view with each student as a member of the sample. Using this approach allows teachers and researchers to bring tools for describing data to teaching social decisions.

The book is intended for scholars and educators. First and foremost, it is intended for social science instructors and those who develop curricula for social sciences. It offers opportunities to consider a new paradigm and pedagogy for teaching and conceptualizing social science. Digital decision simulations should also be useful for students and researchers in the fields of cognitive science, learning psychology, and social psychology. Many of the issues addressed involve knowledge representation, learning with images, and impediments to learning owing to limits in the ways we think.

The two parts of the book address different but complementary domains. The first part of the book considers research that highlights the learning challenges faced when trying to teach students about social decisions. Some of the research comes from social psychology, in particular work that addresses impediments to understanding complexity and variability. Other areas of research address problems students have understanding math and physics. Together, these two branches of research form the basis of the learning paradigm developed in the book.

The second part of the book offers a look at decision simulations. Each of the simulations is a role-play supported by a digital context. All these simulations could serve as the basis for a curricular unit on the complexity of social decisions. The chapters in the second part of the book offer a range of simulations, each with different learning goals. All the simulations, either in their entirety or in preview, are available on the Web. The final chapter offers a look at the future of digital decision simulations and their role in education.

ACKNOWLEDGMENTS

The book would not have been possible without support from the Spencer Foundation for a roundtable conference to consider the role of digital decision simulations in education. In addition, Tufts

University and Tufts Academic Technologies, directed by Barbara McMullen and David Kahle, supported the conference and the development of this book. Judy Gallagher and Abha Verma flawlessly organized the details of the conference. Anoop Kumar, Matt McVey, Ranjani Saigal, and the AT technical staff made sure the presentations went off without a hitch. The entire AT staff made sure no leftover food went to waste.

Lori Hawver at Lawrence Erlbaum Associates worked with us to produce the manuscript and did a wonderful job, keeping us on track and on time. Versions of the manuscript were reviewed by David Kahle and Durwood Marshall, and we thank them for their comments and suggestions.

Finally, projects like these take time away from families, and the support of our spouses and children was indispensable. Thanks to those whose decisions we try hardest to understand.

—Steve Cohen and Kent Portney
Medford, MA
June, 2004

About the Authors

Steve Cohen, Ph.D.
Senior Learning Technologist
Director, Center for the Assessment of Learning
  with Technology and Media
Tufts University

Ph.D., Psychology, Tufts University. Steve Cohen is Director of the Center for Assessment of Technology and Media at Tufts University. Dr. Cohen directed the development of instructional technology project for over 10 years, and has recently turned his attention to assessment of learning outcomes from instructional technologies. He is currently a Principal Investigator of the National Gallery of the Spoken Word Project (http://www.h-net.msu.edu/about/press/ngsw.html), assessment consultant to the Oyez! Project at Northwestern University (http://oyez.nwu.edu/), and the usability and learning outcomes assessment consultant to the Crime and Punishment/AMBER project at Tufts. (http://www.tufts.edu/tccs/at/people-at-at/scohen.shtml and http://www.tufts.edu/tccs/at/archives/at-features/center-for-assessment/)

Kent Portney, Ph.D.
Professor of Political Science
Tufts University

Ph.D., Florida State University, 1979. Kent Portney teaches courses in methodology, judicial politics, public administration, survey research, and environmental politics. He is the author of *Approaching Public Policy Analysis* (Prentice-Hall, 1986), *Sitting Hazardous Waste Treatment Facilities: The NIMBY Syndrome* (Auburn House, Greenwood Publishing Group, 1991), *Controversial Issues in Environmental Policy* (Sage Publications, 1992), and *Taking Sustainable Cities Seriously* (MIT Press, 2003). He is also the coauthor of

The Rebirth of Urban Democracy (Brookings, 1993), which won the American Political Science Association's 1994 Gladys Kammerer Award for the Best Book in *American Politics*, and the American Political Science Association Organized Section on Urban Politics' 1994 Best Book in Urban Politics Award; and he is the coeditor of *The Distributional Impacts of Public Policies* (St. Martin's, 1988). He also has written numerous journal articles and book chapters. His co-authored article, "Mobilizing Minority Communities: Social Capital and Participation in Urban Neighborhoods," appeared in *American Behavioral Scientist* (1997), and his article, "Environmental Justice and Sustainability: Is There a Critical Nexus in the Case of Waste Disposal or Treatment Facility Sitting?" appeared in *Fordham Urban Law Journal* (1994). Portney has held grants from the Ford Foundation, the National Science Foundation, and the Polaroid Foundation. He also received a 3-year grant from the U.S. Department of Education's Fund for the Improvement in Postsecondary Education (FIPSE) to support the development of *Crime and Punishment*, a multimedia simulation of the criminal sentencing process in the felony courts, which was featured at H-NET's Envisioning the Future conference. Professor Portney was recipient of the American Political Science Association's 1997 Rowman and Littlefield Award for innovative teaching in Political Science. He also received the APSA section on Computers and Multimedia Award for best instructional software. He is also cofounder of the Simulation Education and Research Group (SERG), an academic group dedicated to the advancement of digital decision simulations in the social sciences and humanities. His current research includes analysis of sustainable cities initiatives in the United States (http://ase.tufts.edu/polsci/fac_staf/kportney/portney.html)

Dean Rehberger, Ph.D.
Associate Director of Matrix
Associate Professor of American Studies
Michigan State University

Ph.D., University of Utah. Associate Professor at Michigan State University, and the Associate Director of MATRIX. Dean has been teaching online courses for several years and has run several faculty technology workshops for both MSU faculty members and African scholars. He has developed educational software for courses and several online educational sites and resources. His primary areas of research are the impact of the Internet on culture and the uses of Internet technologies in the classroom. He is project coordinator for several large archives projects including the NGSW and West African Archive Initiative. He is also coordinating a host of other Matrix projects (http://matrix.msu.edu).

Carolyn Thorsen, Ph.D.
Professor and Chair,
Department of Educational Technology
College of Education,
Boise State University

Ph.D., Utah State University. Carolyn is the Chair of the Educational Technology department at Boise State University's College of Education. She specializes in educational technology in all educational settings, and is a highly recognized scholar in the field. Among her publications is the book *Techtactics: Instructional Models for Education Computing* and the internationally delivered "Educational Technology Competency Examination." Additionally she is working with the Buck Institute for Education and the George Lucas Educational Foundation directing the design and implementation of a FIPSE funded Web site for teaching project based learning at http://edtech.boisestate.edu/FIPSE

Kenneth O. McGraw, Ph.D.
Professor of Psychology
University of Mississippi

Ph.D., University of Oklahoma. Ken McGraw received his undergraduate degree in English Literature from Washington and Lee University in 1966. Following 2 years in Tunisia with the Peace Corps, 2 years as a TEFL teacher in downtown Atlanta, and 2 years in Japan on a Fulbright Grant, he attended the University of Oklahoma where he received his Ph.D. in experimental psychology in 1976. Since then he has been on the faculty at the University of Mississippi where he is Professor of Psychology and L. Stacey Davidson Professor of Liberal Arts. His current research interests are in applied statistics and he is co-founder and project director of PsychExperiments. (http://psychexps.olemiss.edu/)

John E. Williams, Ph.D.
Assistant Professor of Psychology
University of Northern Iowa

Ph.D., University of Mississippi in 2002. John completed his clinical internship at the Durham VA in Durham, NC, and has been involved in PsychExperiments since 1997. Recent publications include "Equivalence of standard and computerized versions of the Raven Progressive Matrices Test" in *Computers in Human Behavior (forthcoming)*, "Review of computer-based test interpretation software for the MMPI-2" in *Journal of Personality Assessment (forthcoming)*, "The integrity of web-delivered experiments: Can you trust the data?" in *Psychological Science, 11*(6), 2000, 502–506, and "PsychExps: An online psychology laboratory" in Brinbaum, M. (Ed.), *Psychology Experiments on the Internet* (pp. 219–233). San Diego, California: Academic Press, 2000. http://www.psych.uni.edu/faculty/williams/

Jerry Goldman, Ph.D.
Professor of Political Science
Northwestern University

Ph.D., Johns Hopkins University. Goldman is co-developer (with Kent Portney and Steve Cohen) of the *Crime and Punishment* multimedia simulation of criminal sentencing. He was an early pioneer in legal field experiments and he conducted critical experiments in the 1980s on the IRB process. For the last 7 years, Goldman has been developing accessible digital resources on the United States Supreme Court. The OYEZ Project (funded by NEH and NSF) is a web-based multimedia relational database on the Court, its justices and constitutional decisions http://oyez.nwu.edu. The database contains upwards of 1,000 case abstracts, 800+ hours of oral arguments, and a QTVR tour of the Supreme Court building. With additional support, Goldman will add text-track searching capabilities with audio playback, making the OYEZ audio archive a simple resource to exploit for scholarly and instructional purposes. The OYEZ Project has won numerous awards including the 1998 Silver Gavel Award for New Media, the highest distinction conferred by the American Bar Association for works that improve public understanding of law. With additional support from NEH, Goldman (in collaboration with Mark Kornbluh at Michigan State University) is building "History and Politics Out Loud," a general WWW audio resource for American history and politics. (http://www.hpol.org) Goldman received the 1997 EDUCOM Medal for his contributions to computing and higher education. He is also the recipient (with Kent Portney) of the first Rowman & Littlefield Prize for Innovative Teaching in Political Science, which was awarded in 1997. (http://www.polisci.northwestern. edu/Faculty/americanpolitics.htm#goldman)

Sandy Simpson
Social Studies Teacher
Public Service Program
Dorchester High School
Boston (MA) Public Schools

Simpson teaches social studies to 10th and 11th grade students at Dorchester High School. The vast majority of the students in her classes are from poor backgrounds, and most are racial or ethnic minorities. Many of these students speak something other than English as their primary language. Sandy elected to have her students take part in the *Crime and Punishment* decision simulations as a test of how well the simulation would be received by secondary school students.

Robert Cavalier
Associate Teaching Professor
Department of Philosophy
Carnegie Mellon

Dr. Cavalier received his BA from New York University and a Ph.D. in Philosophy from Duquesne University. His interest in the convergence of computers and philosophy dates to the early 1980s, when he coauthored a CAI program to accompany Copi's *Introduction to Logic*. By the late 1980s he had joined Carnegie Mellon's Center for Design of Educational Computing (CDEC), where he became Executive Director in 1991. While at CDEC, he was co-principal in the 1989 EDUCOM award winner for Best Humanities Software (published in 1996 by Routledge as *A Right to Die? The Dax Cowart Case*). He also coauthored the CD-ROM *The Issue of Abortion in America* (Routledge, 1998). Dr. Cavalier is currently affiliated with Carnegie Mellon's Philosophy Department where he teaches numerous courses including Ethics and Political Philosophy. In 1996 Cavalier was designated "Syllabus Scholar" by Syllabus Magazine in recognition of his life long work with educational technologies. In 1999 he received an award for "Innovation Excellence in Teaching, Learning and Technology" at the 10th International Conference on College Teaching and Learning. In 2002 he was recipient of the H&SS Elliott Dunlap Smith Teaching Award. Cavalier's current interests involve developing Project PICOLA (Public Informed Citizen Online Assembly), a multimedia Internet tool for supporting deliberative democracy.

Lynn Miller, Ph.D.
Professor, Annenberg School for Communication
University of Southern California

Ph.D., Psychology, University of Texas. Interpersonal theory and research, especially concerning how people communicate in close interpersonal relationships. Recent work has focused on the role of communication with regard to the prevention of AIDS. She studies the use of computer simulations in social science research, evolutionary approaches to understanding communication problems. Research interests include using fuzzy logic for modeling sexual harassment perceptions and examining factors that affect, how at-risk populations process and react to AIDS-related, messages, using evolutionary approaches and connectionist models to understand communication processes. Grants: Director of Institutional Predoctoral Training grant; Principal Investigator of a number of past and current AIDS-related grants, all funded by the University-wide AIDS Research Program, State of California (total awards in excess of $400,000); PI—Centers for Disease Control Grant to study how ethnic minority women process AIDS-related messages ($920,920; $1.7 million). PI—NIMH grant on interpersonal interaction (Total Direct Costs: over $90,000); AT&T Equipment Grant ($125,000); Consultant, AIDS Interactive Video Project (NIMH); Co-PI: Interactive video consortium for Social Problems ($100,500). Co-PI—Harassment in the Corporate Community.

Stephen J. Read, Ph.D.
Chair and Professor of Social Psychology
Department of Psychology
University of Southern California

Ph.D., The University of Texas at Austin in 1981. He has been at USC in the Department of Psychology since 1984, and currently serves as Chair of the Department. Dr. Read's research specialty is social perception and causal reasoning in social interaction. Among the specific topics he is interested in are: the role of causal reasoning in the coordination of social interaction, specifically close relationships, the use of parallel constraint satisfaction systems to model social reasoning, and developing a comprehensive model of social perception and causal reasoning. His teaching specialties are Social Cognition and Research Methods. Dr. Read has received several federal grants. He is Principal Investigator on a National Science Foundation grant entitled "Explanatory Coherence in Social Explanation" and is Principal Investigator on a grant from the State of California entitled "Simulating Safer Sex: Interactive video HIV intervention." He is currently a coinvestigator on a training grant based on training students as behavioral science researchers focused on understanding risky sexual behavior. He is well known for his work on a knowledge structure approach to causal reasoning and the applications of this work to understanding behavior in close relations. Dr. Read has published widely on causal reasoning, analogical reasoning, and close relationships. He is currently a member of the Society for Experimental Social Psychology, the American Psychological Society, the Cognitive Science Society, the Society for Judgment and Decision Making, and the Society for Text and Discourse. (http://www-rcf.usc.edu/~read/)

Victor Asal, Ph.D.
Assistant Professor
Department of Political Science
State University of New York at Albany

Victor Asal received his MA from Hebrew University in International Relations and his Ph.D. at the University of Maryland, where he served as simulation developer for Project ICONS. He has taught or cotaught classes on negotiation including: Negotiations, Decision Making, and Political Simulations; Conflict and Conflict Resolution Between Israel and the Arab World; Managing Ethnic Conflict in Diverse Societies; and Conflict Transformation and Multi-Track Diplomacy. He has worked extensively with the International Communication and Negotiation project at the University of Maryland, creating several simulations. He has also led negotiation training for the Israeli Army and has taught International Relations and Negotiation courses for gifted and talented high school students. He is conducting research work for Ted Gurr on the Minorities at Risk project and with Jonathan Wilkenfeld on negotiation and mediation. His three primary research interests are: the study of ethnic conflict and terrorism, the strategies and tactics of international negotiation and how to effectively teach them; the relation of power and norms in the spread of the right to participate in inchoate and established democracies. (http://www.icons.umd.edu/about/index.html and http://www.albany.edu/rockefeller/pos/faculty/asal.htm)

John O'Looney, Ph.D., Ed.D.
Public Service Associate
Carl Vinson Institute of Government
University of Georgia

Ph.D., Ed.D., University of Georgia. Dr. O'Looney provides technical assistance in the areas of program evaluation and performance measurement, strategic planning, database development and management information systems, economic development, operation and service delivery reengineering, and sustainability planning. He is a trained mediator and has published extensively in areas of human service and information systems design, contract management, conflict resolution, economic development, and land-use policies. Dr. O'Looney is the author of five books: *Economic Development and Environmental Control, Redesigning the Work of Human Services, Outsourcing State and Local Government Services, Beyond Maps: GIS and Local Government Decision Making*, and *Emergency 911 Systems*. (http://www.cviog.uga.edu/fac_staf/olooney.htm)

Melissa Dodd, M.A.
Director of MyBPS
Boston (MA) Public Schools

M.A., Harvard School of Education. Melissa is currently the director of the MyBPS initiative for the Boston Public School System. MyBPS is the Boston Public School District's intranet portal that provides teachers, administrators, principals, and staff with access to the essential, everyday information and resources they need to enhance teaching and learning across the district. MyBPS is a vehicle that unifies all BPS constituents in the improvement of student achievement by using technology to deliver educational tasks.

Jim Blascovich, Ph.D.
Professor and Vice-Chair
Department of Psychology
University of California, Santa Barbara

Ph.D., University of Nevada at Reno. Dr. Blascovich takes a biopsychosocial approach to understanding the influence of interpersonal and interpersonal factors on motivation and performance as measured subjectively, behaviorally, and physiologically. His biopsychosocial model specifies differential patterns of cardiovascular responses associated with challenge and threat in motivated performance situations. He also codirects the Research Center for Virtual Environments and Behavior where he uses immersive virtual environments to study social influence processes. (http://www.psych.ucsb.edu/fac/blasc98.htm and http://www.psych.ucsb.edu/research/recveb/)

Jeremy Bailenson, Ph.D.
Assistant Professor
Department of Communications
Stanford University

Ph.D., Northwestern University. Dr. Bailenson spent 4 years at the Research Center for Virtual Environments and Behavior at the University of California, Santa Barbara as a Post-Doctoral Fellow and then an Assistant Research Professor. Bailenson's main area of interest is the phenomenon of digital human representation, especially in the context of immersive virtual reality. He explores the manner in which people are able to represent themselves when the physical constraints of body and veridically rendered behaviors are removed. Furthermore, he designs and studies collaborative virtual reality systems that allow physically remote individuals to meet in virtual space, and explores the manner in which these systems change the nature of verbal and nonverbal interaction. His work has been published in several academic journals, including *Cognitive Psychology, Discourse Processes, Personality and Social Psychology Bulletin*, and *PRESENCE: Teleoperators and Virtual Environments*, and his research is funded by the National Science Foundation. (http://communication.stanford.edu/faculty/bailenson.html)

THEORETICAL FRAMEWORKS

1

Practical Contexts and Theoretical Frameworks for Teaching Complexity with Digital Role-Play Simulations

Kent E. Portney
Tufts University

Steve Cohen
Tufts University

The world of instructional technology has altered the fabric of education over the last twenty years. Actual uses of instructional technology have not always lived up to their billing, often promising far more than they could ever deliver. Yet in recent years, the confluence of interest in the development and use of various kinds of role-play decision simulations with improvements in digital technologies has ushered in an era where simulations are finding their way into curricula and being used to address a wide array of teaching and learning challenges not previously possible. Advances in instructional technology have helped improve learning of advanced concepts in mathematics and statistics, and now advances in technology and learning theory are being applied to complex issues and concepts in the social and behavioral sciences and humanities. While instructional technology was once thought to be irrelevant to instruction of high-order concepts in the social sciences, this has changed. The development of various kinds of digital simulations has been a significant part of this change.

This volume is essentially about some of these changes. With this volume, our goal is to provide a foundation for understanding the uses of digital role-play decision simulations in curricula for the social and behavioral sciences. It provides documentation for some of the instructional contexts in which these simulations have been used, and introduces the theoretical foundations underlying their design and instructional use. The first three chapters of this volume provide an extensive overview of the background and foundational issues that apply broadly to the design and application of digital role-play decision simulations for understanding social decisions. It is part of the hypothesis put forward by this volume that the introduction of digital role play simulations into a carefully designed social science curriculum offers the potential for rethinking that it means to understand and research social decisions. Subsequent chapters present in-depth discussions of specific decision simulations that have been developed by social scientists and humanists, and used in research and instructional settings. The reader is left to consider whether simulation-based curricula proposed could improve how students and researchers think about social decisions. The purpose of this chapter is to provide the conceptual and definitional underpinnings that establish the need for such simulations and related curricula.

DIGITAL ROLE-PLAY DECISION SIMULATIONS

The focus of this volume is on a specific kind of simulation, the digital role-play simulation. In the social sciences, whether in the context of research or instruction, the term simulation is often used to refer to a variety of techniques used to mimic some social, political, economic, or psychological process. Here the focus is on specific types of simulations, and it is important to be clear about what we mean by digital role-play simulations. The role-play element is key. *In digital role-play simulations the student participates in the simulation rather than directing it.* In contrast, other simulations allow the user–students to play "God": users set parameters, start a simulation, and see what happens as events unfold over time.

While digital role-play decisions may be flexible, *the flexibility is not in the hands of the student.* The simulations discussed in this volume keep the control in hands of the instructor–mentor and require participation by the students. A student–user plays a crucial role by participating in the simulation and making one or more decisions that influence an outcome. The simulations may allow faculty and simulation administrators the flexibility to (systematically) modify the simulations and study how different contexts might influence decisions and student learning.

In many fields, analogous to case-based instruction and problem-based learning, role-play decision simulations have long been used as a legitimate instructional technique. Sometimes referred to as social process simulations, such techniques are often used where instructors believe there is something to be learned from taking part in a personal experience that resembles some similar real-life decision-making process. In the traditional form, these simulations provide students with the opportunity to make a decision or a series of related decisions where the decision topic and context are artificially created and controlled. Usually this consists of defining a number of different roles that students are assigned to play. The context is designed to constrain the decision in controlled ways, and the students playing the roles are usually free to interact in whatever way they wish within the constrained context. For example, an instructor might create a simulation of a government budgeting process where some students play the role of budget requestors, and other students play the role of budget approvers, perhaps to mimic the process of deciding federal agency budget requests by Congressional appropriations committees. Presumably, the specific tasks assigned to the students, the type of decisions that have to be made, and every other aspect of the simulation, are designed to teach students specific lessons about budgeting, the budgetary process, or both. One challenge in the creation of such simulations is to construct the simulation with enough realism to make it engaging and yet not so much that the central lessons are lost or difficult to find because of excessive complexity.

Based on the topic of the simulation and curriculum plan for supporting its use, specific lessons about decisions and decision making vary considerably. Sometimes simulations and related lessons focus on the impossibility or difficulty of making decisions in some areas, sometimes they focus on specific factors that influence decisions to be made one way rather than another. For example, a simulation could be designed to show that if one decision process is used, a particular decision is more likely to be made than if a different decision process is used.

This volume extends the focus from traditional role-play simulations into the digital world. Increasingly, digital technologies are being employed to create simulations for use in education, and the contention of this volume is that bringing technology into the equation has altered the general technique to make it more efficient and/or more effective in improving learning goals. The reasons underlying this contention will be explained in more detail over the next two chapters, with examples found in chapters five through ten. It is important at this point to be clear about what it means to bring role-play decision simulations into the digital world.

Digital role-play decision simulations are defined as social process simulations that are delivered using some form of digital technology. Earlier uses of technology for delivering simulations simply made accessible the same written materials and documents that might have been printed on paper and handed out in class. So frequently digital technology simply provides a mechanism for conveniently making accessible simulation materials that are stored on some digital medium, such as a DVD, CD-ROM, or even a floppy zip disk. Increasingly it means making the simulations accessible over the Internet or World Wide Web that, if nothing else, makes the distribution of simulation materials very efficient. More and more commonly it means developing digital video assets to help define the decision scenario and create the context in which the decisions are made. Moving well beyond the paper-and-pencil variety of simulations, digital simulations frequently try to improve upon the realism of the decision context by building truer pictures, or virtual environments, of the decision scenarios or elements of the decisions themselves.

Regardless of the mechanism for delivery, simulations invite a certain amount of interactivity as thought to be necessary in order to achieve the desired learning goals. Like any component of a curriculum, part of the job of a simulation is to engage students in the topic and learning process. In the traditional role-play simulation, students interact with each other in a classroom setting or immediately outside of class as they progress through the decision process. Sometimes the interactions are scripted and scheduled, and sometimes they are spontaneous. Usually such interactions are in person. In the digital world, this interactivity might simply represent interactions between individual students and a computer. Sometimes it reflects interactions between and among students in a class or in related classes using e-mail, chatrooms, bulletin boards, or other interactive communication mechanisms. Increasingly, as digital media become more and more sophisticated, such interactions include situations where the computer itself plays a virtual role in interacting with students. In chapters 5 through 10 there will be numerous examples where the computer has been designed to perform the interactions believed to be necessary to maximize achievement of learning goals.

To summarize, digital role-play decision simulations represent efforts to create synthetic or artificial decisions situations to teach students about the designated decisions or their underlying processes. They require that students play roles and participate in the decision and use digital technologies in order to deliver simulation materials and to facilitate some sort of interpersonal interactions.

WHY ROLE-PLAY SIMULATIONS ARE NEEDED: THEORETICAL FRAMEWORKS

Why do we go through the trouble of creating sophisticated role-play simulations to teach students about complex social decisions? We hope to illustrate why we believe understanding social decisions, such as prison sentences handed down by judges, or allocations of natural resources, or resolving value conflicts, to name a few, is so challenging both to teach and to learn. In the simplest terms, the problem stems from the challenge of appreciating the context in which the decision maker makes a social decision. *We suggest that unless you can put yourself in the shoes of the decision maker and understand the context in which the decision is made, you have not really understood the decision.* It is acquiring the detailed context, and the ability to understand a decision in light of this context, that is such a formidable educational challenge. We, as social animals, are not cognitively equipped to do this. Research in psychology suggests that there are cognitive filters in place that make it extraordinarily difficult for students to appreciate a decision context outside of themselves. In addition, social decisions are typically taught by books, teachers, or both, further removing the student from the context of the decision maker. The end result is a student who knows what decision was made, but does not understand the context that motivated the decision. The goal of this volume is to identify the genesis of this problem and offer a prescription for improving students understanding of social decisions. The prescription is the use of realistic multimedia-based simulations delivered in a sound instructional environment.

INTRODUCTION TO THE PSYCHOLOGICAL JUSTIFICATION
FOR DIGITAL ROLE-PLAY SIMULATIONS

For the most part, elements of the educational problem have been identified over the past 50 years, but have not necessarily been catalysts for developing and using simulations to teach social decisions. Since the cognitive revolution in the 1950s (Gardner, 1985), attention has been focused on what goes on inside our student's minds. It took the move to cognitive models of human thought to provoke interest in how people make decisions. Research in the area of judgment and decision making confirms that decision processes are complex. A social context brings an added dimension of complexity. Given this picture of social decisions, what is it we hope students will learn about social decision making? By what means can the chances of instructional success be improved?

While research on judgment and decision making has moved forward since the 1950s, it has not explicitly pointed to problems or suggested a need for improvements with the way students understand social decisions. In the present case, the origins of this volume come principally from three separate but related fields. First, it comes from research in math and science education. In that arena, a healthy part of the psychological and educational community has been concerned with how students are, or are not, learning math and science. Much of the research has focused on ideas in probability and physics that many students, and sometimes experts, find almost impossible to learn (as anyone who has taught statistics knows all too well). A key part of that research has focused on why certain ideas are so difficult to master, and much of the research points to limitations imposed by students' preexisting ways of thinking and their epistemology. We see that these kinds of limitations, or biases in thinking, play a similar role in students' inability to master the often-complex concepts that underlie many social decisions.

A second area of research comes from generative learning, an area of learning research that requires students to reconcile confusing ideas. This field looks at the improved memory for ideas when students experience an "aha" phenomenon. For example, when students see the sentence "the house became smaller when the sun came out" they are confused until they hear the word "igloo." This kind of experience results in durable semantic memory for the ideas, a form of transformation that helps students see the world in new ways. Often this kind of transformation is crucial for students to realize the limits of their own ways of understanding social decisions. Our experience suggests that when students participate in well-designed role-play simulations and related instructional contexts, they often experience the "aha" effect that helps them realize what a limited and biased sense of the decision context they had attributed to the decision.

A third area of research that helps justify the use of role-play simulations comes from the meaningful use of situations to anchor learning and multimedia to create the most intuitive, widely applicable, decision contexts. This branch of research points to the potential for creating contexts that root learning in virtual situations and mimic real life circumstances. A key part of the simulation approach is to improve the chance that learning, which takes place in an educational setting, will transfer to the real world. By creating contexts that inspire similar emotional, cognitive, and behavioral reactions to those experienced in real life, and permit students to focus all their cognitive resources on the decisions they will be making, the chance that students will actually understand and apply what they have learned improves.

Ideas from all three areas of research apply to how students come to understand social decisions, and decision making, as well. They form a set of building blocks for thinking about and designing simulations. Individual simulations designed to help address specific learning objectives may also draw on research from other areas of psychology and the social domain being modeled. The second half of this volume includes five examples of simulations used in curricula to teach social decisions. Each chapter considers in detail how subtle features of a simulation can incrementally improve education and address needs of particular students. However, the psychological foundations and motivations explored in this first chapter, spanning across all simulations discussed in this volume, come from these three strains of research. Each of these research areas deserves a closer look.

LEARNING FROM EDUCATIONAL CHALLENGES IN MATH AND SCIENCE EDUCATION

The challenge in teaching many critical ideas rooted in social decisions emerges from the same complex rubric that underlies teaching challenging concepts in mathematics and physical sciences. *The de-*

gree of information transfer found in traditional teaching methods (i.e., lecture and reading texts) is very often not suitable for helping many (perhaps even most) students move beyond their own <u>limits as learners</u> so that they can grasp the complexities of social decisions. Instructional methods for teaching social decisions require special attention to the mindset and predisposition that students bring to a topic or a course. As with teaching in the advanced sciences and mathematics, the challenge comes from the general tendency for students to utilize everyday, existing, ways of thinking and preserve predictability in the face of complex, counterintuitive ideas.

The challenge of teaching and learning in physics serves as an example. Many students develop what is termed a "naïve" physics that is useful for understanding observed physical behavior. Watching a Frisbee fly and then land does not suggest that a body in motion tends to stay in motion (Newton's 1st law). Yet, the naïve idea that physical objects in motion tend to come to a halt *is a useful heuristic for everyday life.* Without it, life would be very frightening indeed. Its usefulness makes it resilient and is even applied in circumstances where it does not belong.

In fact, in many respects, understanding social decisions may rate with Newtonian physics and probability as among the most difficult topics to teach in all of higher education. Taking into account the beliefs students bring to a course, both their genesis and their durability, is a key to teaching and learning in the sciences and math, and, we suggest social decisions as well. Research on the role of prior knowledge and biases in thinking in the learning process is abundant on the topic of math and science education. Prior knowledge and beliefs, and the role they play in learning, has been recognized as a key issue in teaching difficult subjects, in particular Newtonian Mechanics (Carey, 1986; Smith, diSessa, & Roschelle, 1993) and probability (Cohen & Chechile, 1997; Cohen, Smith, Chechile, Burns, & Tsai, 1996; Hammer, 1997; Konold, 1989; Pollatsek, Konold, Well, & Lima, 1984; Tversky & Kahneman, 1971, 1974). Students often come to class with preexisting ideas that are *inconsistent* with the formal, theoretical foundations in these two subjects, as the Frisbee example previously mentioned illustrates (Carey, 1986).

Only careful research and assessment will reveal the problems students have learning subjects like physics and probability. Simple declarative questions, such as "what is Newtons's 1ˢᵗ law?" are not likely to reveal any confusion. Most students are adept at answering these

Problem: The left side of the figure below shows a ball X, in motion. The ball slides down an incline, AB, then on a frictionless, horizontal, track BC. At C, the ball leaves the track. Ignoring air resistance:

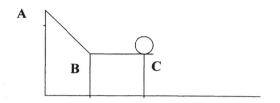

The speed of the ball on the horizontal track BC is:

F. Constant
G. Continuously increasing
H. Continuously decreasing
I. Increasing for a while, and constant thereafter
J. Constant for a while, and decreasing thereafter

FIG. 1.1.   Problem from an introductory physics diagnostic tool.

questions from memory and relish the sight of them on exams. Even basic homework and test questions, which students can often solve by rote, will not reveal a problem. The kinds of questions that illustrate that naïve ideas and the formal ideas do not coexist effectively are counterintuitive, and force students to use the formal ideas in unexpected ways. For instance, the problem in Fig. 1.1 is designed to expose misconceptions stemming from the mis-application of everyday experience to the world of physics. Notice that the problem states (in a classic information transfer style) that the ball is on a *frictionless, horizontal* track. Can this information catalyze students to appeal to a normative model of physics? Unfortunately, no. Knowledge of everyday experience is applied, and students typically choose B rather than A.

This misconceptions paradigm for addressing learning problems in math and the physical sciences emphasizes the interference of everyday heuristics and prior beliefs. It can be summed up in two principles: the need for, and resiliency of, prior beliefs brought to class by students; and the bias in thinking that can prevent the formal, normative principals of physics and probability from finding an appropriate place to live in a student's network of ideas.

APPLICATION OF MATH AND SCIENCE LEARNING
TO UNDERSTANDING SOCIAL DECISIONS

We see the same kind of impediments applying when students try to learn and understand social decisions. What kinds of cognitive mechanisms create a deep challenge for students trying to understand social decisions? A plausible set of answers come from research in *social* psychology. The psychologist Heider (1958, Ross & Fletcher, 1985) initially addressed this issue in his seminal work on social cognition and attribution theory. He hypothesized a fundamental drive in all people to reduce unpredictability. People, he suggested, are uncomfortable when faced with unpredictable outcomes. Rather than tolerate unpredictability, most people will attribute causes to events. There is comfort in having attributed causes to events, *even if the causes are wrong (i.e., have no empirical validity), are appropriate only in certain idiosyncratic settings, tell only part of a story, or are ideologically driven.* Inferring from Heider's work, most people will instantly attribute causes to events in an effort to reduce the unpredictability. He further hypothesized that once these attributions are in place, they are difficult to modify, *especially if modifications will reduce predictability.* What role does this fundamental drive to reduce unpredictability play in trying to help students acquire a complex understanding of a social decision? It is critically relevant as it acts as a filter and is responsible for framing knowledge about social decisions. It is one of the impediments to accommodating complex presentations in the social sciences and humanities.

Taking Heider at his word, not only does this drive impede students' ability to understand decisions as they are taught, but it has a more enduring influence as well. Most students will not begin a social science class *tabula rasa. Prior to class, students will have constructed a network of resilient beliefs about social issues resulting from a drive to reduce unpredictability.* They typically begin a course having had at least minimal exposure to the basic problems motivating a social decision, whether it addresses welfare reform, sex education, or siting of a landfill, to name but a few. The simple belief networks resulting from exposure to these topics are extremely difficult to modify and expand. The combined motivation to reduce unpredictability and the beliefs such cognitive filters put in place make it exceedingly challenging for students to acquire a complex picture of a social decisions. This educational challenge, in our eyes, is not unlike the challenge of having students learn to apply Newton's first law correctly when faced with a counter-intuitive problem.

Heider's postulate, and the students existing belief networks, are not the only impediments to learning about social decisions. A third mechanism that limits students' existing ability to acquire complex interpretations of social decisions tends to increase the likelihood students will assign blame and responsibility for decisions made by others rather than accommodate the complex circumstance that may have influenced a particular decision. *One reason why it is easy for students to quickly attribute erroneous causes and motivations to decisions is that the perceived agents of the causes are external and decontextualized with respect to the student.* This error in judgment is an example of a cognitive transaction originally identified as a fundamental *attribution error* (Ross & Fletcher, 1985), a principle that suggests that it is easier for people to assign blame and responsibility to those other than themselves. In more current research and cognitive modeling, the fundamental attribution error, along with Heider's postulate, is described more formally as part of connectionist networks that influence social perception, cognition and attributions (Read & Miller, 1998; VanOverwalle & Van Rooy, 1998). It plays a similar role to the cognitive mechanisms that interfere with learning physics and probability. These nefarious fraternal cognitive mechanisms, seen as interfering with learning probability and understanding social decisions, have followed similar developmental paths, becoming more developed and refined over the last 30 years. The probability heuristics that interfere with probabilistic reasoning (Tversky & Kahneman, 1971) helped lead to a science of misconceptions and their roles in cognitive architectures. Likewise, the fundamental attribution error is part of more formal models of cognition used to understand social reasoning. For the sake of simplicity the term fundamental attribution error will be used.

Appealing to mechanisms like the fundament attribution error, it would be more difficult to attribute and rely on causes like racism or incompetence if students themselves were the agents. It is clearly difficult to see yourself or your peers as racists or incompetents. Yet it is easy to see others this way. Faced with the need to attribute causes and reduce unpredictability, simple-minded attributions are readily available. These attributions play a critical role in helping students forge and maintain a tolerable cognitive balance. Without the attributions, students are faced with the difficult task of tolerating unpredictable behavior. Beliefs that play such an important role are difficult to change through instruction. However, that is where teachers must start. The argument here is that in teaching students about social decisions, teachers need to consider the kinds of *thinking processes* and *beliefs* that occupy students' minds in order to effectively design teaching methods and instructional approaches.

In summary, work in math and science has highlighted fundamental impediments to learning that make it difficult to clearly understand and apply concepts in physics and probability. We see students' ability to understand the complexity of social decisions suffering for similar impediments. The general problem stems from a cognitive bias that maximizes predictability at the cost of accommodating complexity, and the natural tendency of all people to fall victim to the fundamental attribution error. This problem is pervasive. The fundamental attribution error is in play whenever students are expected to learn about a concept or subject where they arrive to the task with resilient belief systems that have been put in place to simplify, and where they need to understand the decisions of actors and institutions to which they themselves do not belong. Topics and concepts with these properties are not difficult to identify in the social and behavioral science curricula. For example, any student faced with learning about political tolerance and related policy decisions will come to class with resilient belief networks, ripe to commit the fundamental attribution error. For the same reason, students may also misunderstand the web of beliefs and motivations behind a decision not to use a condom, or take more than a "fair" share of a precious natural resource. In short, the problem framework applies to a wide range of topics. We also expect our prescription will apply very broadly. Our prescription suggests that well-designed instructional simulations can help students understand and think through complex social decisions.

We realize that research in the field of social perception, social cognition, and judgment and decision making clearly paint a more complex picture than the one described here. Existing studies make clear that there are a variety of complex cognitive mechanisms at work in learning, and the learning challenges or impediments are many. This chapter tries only to illustrate in a broad way that biases, of which the fundamental attribution error is an important one in the use of decisions simulations, interfere with appreciating complexity. Individual chapters 5 through 10 of this volume provide more in-depth discussions of how specific research has been applied in developing and using the specific simulations described there. Each simulation has its own approach, and has its own underlying conceptions of how to deal with impediments to learning in their respective domains.

A THEORETICAL FOUNDATION FOR TRANSFORMING BELIEFS: THE GENERATION EFFECT

Taking into account the naïve beliefs students bring to a course, both their genesis and durability, is not a new idea in education. These naïve beliefs present challenges to teachers when they try to help students replace ideas inconsistent with formal, theoretical notions, or simply help them build on their prior understanding instead of replacing it (Strike & Posner, 1992). This latter case is especially informative for teaching about social decisions. The instructional goal is not to replace naïve beliefs for they certainly have a legitimate place in any network of beliefs. Rather, the goal is to *extend* and *reconfigure* each student's network of ideas and beliefs to include the potential of accommodating normative ways of thinking about social decisions. This kind of shift is analogous to moving from a naïve physics to a Newtonian model (Strike & Posner, 1992).

Yet how is this to be accomplished? Unfortunately, it is not easy to extend and reconfigure belief networks. As noted earlier, it often requires insight or "aha" experiences on the part of the student that their network is simply inadequate for explaining certain results. For example, students probably do not have a set of ideas ready to help them understand the idea that "the house got smaller when the sun came out." It is an idea that does not integrate well with your current ideas about the relationship between the size of houses and the sun. However, when this idea is followed by the word "igloo," the confusion disappears. In the search for clues to making social decision making understood more deeply, cognitive learning theory offers some assistance. Because of the expectation that learning about these topics resembles, in important ways, learning to decipher the problem of the relationship between the size of a house and the sun, the learning model framework advanced here borrows on the research on the generation effect (Soraci et al., 1994).

Research suggests that curricular approaches based on the generation effect offer key methods for helping students reconfigure their beliefs. At the heart of this effect is the result that students who *generate* their own responses to open-ended queries tend to have much better memory for responses than students who have the responses supplied for them (Soraci et al., 1994). For instance, students faced with the problem:

A stocky dog: B____X____R

show much greater retention of the response "boxer" when they themselves generate the letters to fill in the blanks than when the responses (the missing letters) are supplied for them. In addition, Chechile, and colleagues (1999) have recently demonstrated that memory for words such as "boxer" is enhanced if it is generated based on multiple variable meanings (e.g., a stocky dog, a prize-fighter) as opposed to multiple redundant meanings (e.g., a stocky dog, a canine). Robust generative learning advantages have been documented across a range of experimental contexts, including math problems (McNamara & Healy, 1995) and pictures (Peynir-cioglu, 1989). In all cases, generative enhancement requires an active, engaged participant.

Related research on "aha" effects suggests *that the order of the information plays a key role*. For instance, telling students the house became smaller when the sun came out followed by the word igloo results in much better memory than mentioning igloo first followed by the sentence. This suggests an unorthodox but theoretically based instructional design for superior learning. Put the student in an active learning environment in which he or she will first experience noncomprehension (or confusion), then directly experience a transition from noncomprehension to comprehension. This kind of process has been shown to work in other learning situations including tutoring (VanLehn, Siler, Murray, Yamauchi, & Baggett, 2003); students seem to learn best after they reach an impasse. While it may be best for students to resolve the confusion or ambiguity on their own, superior learning also occurs when the confusing sentence is proposed first and the key concept is subsequently revealed. This is important, since education often does not permit enough time for students to resolve as many puzzles as we would like them to.

This kind of learning process appears to be essential if students are really going to broaden their understanding of social decisions. An example from criminal justice is illustrative. Simply informing students that factors like deterrence or retribution influence criminal sentencing decisions will not help most students appeal to these ideas when confronted with the necessity of understanding issues of criminal sentencing. *Students may be able to recite these ideas on a test of recall, but they generally do not to avail themselves of these explanations when critically reviewing controversial decisions (Portney, Cohen, Soraci, & Goldman, 1999). Students must first appreciate the limited application of their preconceived ideas.* Only then will they be in a position to extend their understanding. Research demonstrates that once this kind of insight occurs it lasts. It is nearly impossible to return to a naïve way of understanding. You will always remember the word "igloo" follows "the house got smaller when the sun came out."

The generation effect is easily demonstrated and accomplished in a psychology laboratory. However, it is more challenging to bring about in an educational setting. It cannot be argued that the kind of black and white transformation triggered when hearing "igloo" will instantly happen when students work through a digital role-play simulation. *It is the feedback from their performance in the simulation, and the corresponding integration into the educational setting, that tends to help students see their limitations as learners.* There are a range of curricular approaches, depending on the domain, prior knowledge and beliefs. The approaches, and the motivation, will be developed and discussed in the chapter 2.

Ultimately, the key insight is for students to realize that they are potential decision makers themselves; that reducing complexity for the sake of comfort is paramount to giving the richness of a social decision short shrift. We expect that when students come to terms with the limits of their own way of seeing the world outside themselves, they will be receptive to the complex picture that they currently resist acquiring. Simulations, with the proper instructional setting, can be used to help students understand their limitations, as learners, via a profound generative experience. Research in the area of interactive multimedia points toward features that appear to bolster the effectiveness of digital role-play simulations.

SITUATED LEARNING CONTEXTS AS THE VEHICLE
FOR SIMULATIONS

The third area of research on which the digital decision approach rests is the work on situated learning and anchored instructions (Goldman, with the Cognition and Technology Group at Vanderbilt, 1990). The most important benefit here comes from the opportunity to situate and define a learning context (Brown, Collins, & Duguid, 1989; Brown & Duguid 2002; Collins, Brown, & Newman, 1989). Under the broad umbrella of situated cognition, the emphasis applied here is in creating a meaningful context (i.e., anchored the instruction). Learning out of context is problematic. For instance, students learning vocabulary outside of contexts in which it is used either never use that vocabulary, or demonstrate misuse of words when trying to integrate them into everyday conversations (Miller & Gildea, 1987). In the absence of a familiar context applications of learned material can suffer. Situated contexts have been shown to make a difference in many specific learning areas or domains. Students working in situated contexts show improvement in learning mathematics (Goldman, with the Cognition and Technology Group at Vanderbilt, 1993). Likewise, students with problems attending to the source of materials used (i.e., who is the author?, is it an original source?, interpretive work?, fact?, fiction?) when doing historical analyses (Wineburg, 2001) show improvement when learning the skill in a situated environment (Britt & Aglinskas, 2002; Britt, Perfetti, Van Dyke, & Gabrys, 2000). Using a situated context has been shown to help prepare students to write more effectively (Robertson, 2000), and role-play based simulations for discovering principles of economics have also proven to produce learning gains (Shute, Glaser, & Raghavan, 1989). The list of successful applications of situated cognition is even larger when focusing more on learning applications in the physical sciences and mathematics. The question now for this chapter is, given the empirical support for the role of situated learning contexts, what roles should digital delivery systems and multimedia play in curricula using decision simulations based on situated learning theory?

Clark (1994, 1985a, 1985b), in the early 1980s, made the case that the delivery medium used to bring lessons to students (teachers, computers, etc.), or the media used in a lesson (audio, video, etc.) made no difference in the success of the instruction. He maintained that any study that demonstrated a difference based on medium or method was missing the true reason for the measured improvement. Improvement could be due to a better lesson, the novelty of a new technology, or other spurious effects. The medium and the media, according to Clark, are not the cause for learning success. While Clark has been challenged to a modest degree by Kozma (1991), and by strong results of individual assessments and studies, the line Clark has drawn in the sand has not been an easy one to cross. Nor will this volume attempt to empirically challenge his position.

However, there are some important potential benefits to identify, especially in terms of the educational psychology of using digital simulations and their efficiency, that make the digital environment ripe for delivering role-play simulations. These benefits do not come simply by choosing a digital environment to deliver a simulation. *They come when the design and objectives of a role-play simulation are well suited to the features and options a digital environment can offer.* The following guidelines are offered for considering how to use digital delivery for instructional advantage. They rely on cognitive learning theory to help identify features of a simulation and related curriculum that can produce higher-order, more complex, thinking (Herrington & Oliver, 1999). At the very least it should be clear that there is probably nothing to lose by going digital; research suggest that moving from physical (i.e., real) learning environments to virtual worlds does not seem to produce any ill effects (Triona & Klahr, 2002). In addition, current research in educational psychology has helped to maximize investments in multimedia environments by empirically validating various dos and don'ts. For instance, Moreno (2000, 2002) and colleagues have helped demonstrate when avatars are useful for providing feedback in multimedia environments, and how to minimize interference by overusing sound.

In addition, research has been done that suggests cognitive load (i.e., the amount of mental effort a student needs to use in order to work through an instructional task) can influence learning outcomes (Cooper, 1998; Mayer, 1989; Mayer & Anderson, 1992; Mayer & Gillini, 1990; Mayer & Sims, 1994; Moreno & Mayer, 2002; Paas, 1992; Pierce, Duncan, Gholson, Ray, & Kamhi, 1993; Robins & Mayer, 1993; Sweller & Chandler, 1991). For instance, while discovery learning can be very effective, students who spend too much energy *learning how to use a tool to facilitate discovery* may not gain much in the way of content knowledge. All their thinking is directed in the wrong place—learning to use the tool. In effect, the medium can get in the way of the message. This kind of research has implications for simulation design. It is key that the simulation be easy and intuitive to use, or the mental energy will be misguided. Well-designed simulations can reduce cognitive load, offering students the opportunity to attend to cues already familiar from real world experience. For instance, in the criminal sentencing simulation described in chapter 5, when asking students to play the role of judge, having them role play in a full-motion video environment, a frame of which is depicted in Fig. 1.2, lets most students effectively use prior knowledge. If the design is not done well (i.e., does not reduce cognitive load), then a simple pencil and paper simulation, which requires students to read a case and render a sentence, might be more effective. Digital technologies now allow the creation of environments like the one in Fig. 1.2 that can easily be developed on typical desktop computers with off-the-shelf software.

These media-based simulated environments offer three other potential advantages over simpler environments that might use only text. To begin, by using video and audio of virtual simulation participants to convey ideas, the extent to which students supply the associated simulation features on their own should be greatly reduced.

FIG. 1.2.   A simulated courtroom from the *Crime and Punishment* simulation.

The media offers an element of environmental fidelity that makes it possible for instructors to assume that students (or subjects, if the simulation is being used to support research) have not imposed many of their own perceptions onto the decision context. With simulations that are based on paper-and-pencil exercises, for example, students are free to conjure images on their own and fill in gaps wherever they exist. Simulations that allow students to conjure their own voices, images of virtual participants or actors, or settings and contexts, would be expected to produce more variability in the instructional implementation. With so many potential variables at work, this may serve to complicate the achievement and measurement of learning outcomes. As a matter of learning research, it certainly makes it more difficult to account for learning outcomes based on particular features of the simulation.

Second, it may be the case that a student needs to think, behave (make a decision), or both, in a certain environment. For example, perhaps a learning challenge requires a student to learn how to negotiate emotionally charged interpersonal situations at school. That student is most likely to be successful if the teaching simulation mimics the school setting, where the student is placed in a decision-making context that comes as close to being like that encountered in real-life situations. Research on training simulations suggests that transfer is better when the real world context resembles the learning environments. Part of the learning is connected to emotions raised during the simulation, and is also captured in episodic memory of the event. Presumably, the memory resulting from a virtual simulation will be available and accessible to a student during the real experience at school.

Third, it is more convenient to account for individual differences in learning styles and aptitudes using digital delivery (Shute, 1992). Some students may need help learning to confront male students on the playground, while others might need to learn how to confront peers who are not following through on their end of a school project. The relative ease with which digital assets—video and audio—can be added or modified means that simulations can address these differences, and utilize different voices and videos to help prepare for different learning needs.

Finally, implicit in the delivery of digital-decision simulations is the networked world of the Internet and Internet2. The world of high bandwidth and high-speed connections provide opportunities for learning that could not be possible otherwise. Sometimes reliance on this networked world provides opportunities to connect and communicate, in real time, with people who are traditionally outside of students' immediate learning environments but who can play an enormously influential role in the learning process. For example, the *Project CONS* decision simulations, described in chapter 8, connect students at one university to students at other universities around the world. The *Crime and Punishment* simulation, described in chapter 5, relying on the Internet and Internet2, allows the centralized collection of simulation results from courses using the simulation anywhere, and facilitates comparisons among students within a class and across classes. If an instructor in Michigan would like to compare her class' results to those of similar classes in Texas, he or she can readily do so because the simulation's networked functions automatically collect, store, and aggregate students' decisions. Moreover, reliance on Internets makes it possible for large numbers of students to participate in the simulation simultaneously without degradation of the simulation quality. In the absence of Internet2, larger numbers of students using the simulation at one time often means greater wait times and slower interactions, both of which could certainly interfere with the learning experience. Of course, the Internet also provides access to instructional materials on a broad scale, often permitting instructors to use materials developed far away with minimal investment of time and resources. These are but a few examples of how reliance on the networked world makes possible learning experiences with digital simulations that have never before been possible.

TOWARD A NORMATIVE THEORY OF UNDERSTANDING SOCIAL DECISIONS

Underlying our approach to teaching and learning social decisions is the idea of a normative model for understanding decisions; understanding and applying particular decision contexts is key. This appeal to a normative model comes from work in math and science education. In the areas of physics and probability, there are well-developed normative models, and the idea of a misconception, or concept that does not integrate easily into preexisting knowledge structures, is clear. When students (and experts) consistently overestimate the representatives of a sample, it is easy to appeal to probability and sampling theory in order to demonstrate that students' knowledge does not conform to an accepted normative model.

In the social sciences and humanities, it is not so easy. Applying a normative approach to understanding social decision is more difficult. There usually is no well-accepted, normative, model of what it means to understand a social decision. Nor does a normative model based on context lend itself to the kinds of precise, mathematically neat models that predict physical and probabilistic phenomena.

However, the normative model proposed here is paramount to helping students acquire a complex picture of a social decision, one that extends beyond their own point of view. *It is the complex set of interpretations, as well as the context of the decision maker, which is the social decision.* If students are to understand the decision itself, they need to be able to move beyond their limits as learners, just as a physicist must at some point reconcile formal Newtonian mechanics and the heuristics that take you through everyday life. Research in the area of social psychology makes clear that we crave simplicity and tend to see decisions by others very differently than we see ourselves. The limits, by definition, make it impossible to understand the decision. Our goal in using and developing digital roleplay simulations is to help students intuitively move beyond these limits and consider decisions in the social contexts where they have their impact.

THE REMAINDER OF THE VOLUME

In the subsequent three chapters, an effort is made to present, in some detail, the reasons why virtual decision simulations must be considered an important part of teaching and learning in the social sciences and humanities. The following chapters are divided into two sections. The first section focuses on the central conceptual issues surrounding the need for, and use of, virtual decision simulations to teach about complex concepts in the social sciences and humanities. Chapter 2 presents an explanation of the curricular role for understanding social decisions, highlighting the need and opportunity for virtual decision simulations to make a significant contribution. Chapter 3 discusses, in some depth, the limitations of more traditional approaches to teaching about social decisions. This chapter presents the argument that traditional didactic methods often fall short of producing the desired learning outcomes, and they do so because they fail to confront the kinds of impediments described earlier and discussed in chapter 2.

Chapter 4 provides an overview of some of the work that has been accomplished to make social process simulations readily accessible to teaching and learning communities nearly everywhere. It discusses the *PsychExperiments* project at the University of Mississippi. Chapters 5 through 10 provide detailed presentations of digital role-play decision simulations that have already been developed and used in instruction. Chapter 5 discusses the *Crime and Punishment* simulations, developed by Portney, Cohen, and Goldman, where students play the role of criminal court judges who must make decisions about the severity of sentences for convicted felons. The main purpose of this simulation is to allow instructors to address issues of race, gender, and other differences in criminal sentencing. Chapter 6, by philosopher Cavalier, focuses on efforts by Carnegie Mellon University philosophers in applied ethics, to use digital role-play simulations so that students will learn how to engage in the resolution of ethical conflicts through negotiation and mediation. Chapter 7 presents a simulation, created by two psychologists (Miller and Read) from the University of Southern California, which came about as the result of efforts to find ways of teaching gay men how to engage in safe sex.

Chapter 8 provides a comprehensive look at *Project ICONS*, the effort of political scientists and others at the University of Maryland to simulate a variety of international conflict situations. Students play the roles of world leaders, and engage in efforts to resolve specific conflicts in cross-national or cross-cultural settings. Chapter 9, by O'Looney and Dodd, discusses efforts at the Carl Vinson Institute of Government at the University of Georgia, to create complex simulation experiences for disaster control decision makers. The simulation places the student in the role of an emergency management official who must make numerous rapid decisions in response to a natural or human-made disaster. Chapter 10 pushes the technology to its limits when it discusses the use of immersive virtual decision environments. Based on the work of Blascovich, a psychologist at the University of California at Santa Barbara, such environments go far beyond the presentation of decision environments on a computer screen when they attempt to create true virtual reality. Instead of watching digital video depicting the process of walking into a room that is part of the decision context, imagine actually walking into a simulated room. Such immersive environments represent the direction that digital role-play decision simulations will move in the future.

Taken together, these simulations represent instantiations of the general approach to digital role-play decision simulations for teaching and learning about complex decisions. They cross different disciplines, and they seek to address important and complex decision areas that have proven resistant to more traditional didactic approaches. Each simulation has its own specific learning goals, and uses its own underlying learning theory. Yet together they represent a fundamentally different opportunity for teaching and learning whose potential is only beginning to be realized. Chapter 11, written by an expert on instructional technology from Boise State University, provides a summary of this potential and directions that digital role-play simulations are likely to take in the future.

REFERENCES

Britt, M. A., & Aglinskas, C. (2002). Improving students' ability to identify and use source information. *Cognition and Instruction, 20*(4), 485–522.

Britt, M. A., Perfetti, C. A., Van Dyke, J., & Gabrys, G. (2000). The sorcerer's apprentice: A tool for document-supported history instruction. In P. Stearns, P. Seixas, & S. Wineburg (Eds.), *Knowing, teaching and learning history: National and international perspectives* (pp. 437–470). New York: New York University Press.

Brown, J. S., Collins, A., & Duguid, P. (1989). Situated cognition and the culture of learning. *Educational Researcher, 18*(1), 32–41.

Brown, J. S., & Duguid, P. (2002). *The social life of information*. Cambridge, MA: Harvard University Press.

Carey, S. (1986). Cognitive science and science education. *American Psychologist, 41*(10), 1123–1130.

Clark, R. E. (1994). Assessment of distance learning technology. In E. L. Baker & H. F. O'Neill, Jr. (Eds.), *Technology assessment in education and training* (pp. 63–78). Hillsdale, NJ: Lawrence Erlbaum Associates.

Clark, R. E. (1985a). Confounding in educational computing research. *Journal of Educational Computing Research, 1*(2), 137–148.

Clark, R. E. (1985b). Research on student thought processes during computer-based instruction. *Journal of Instructional Development, 7*(32), 2–5.

Cohen, S., & Chechile, R. A. (1997). Probability distributions, assessment, and instructional software: Lessons learned from an evaluation of curricular software. In I. Gal & J. B. Garfield (Eds.), *The assessment challenge in statistics education* (pp. 253–267). Amsterdam: IOS Press.

Cohen, S., Smith, G. E., Chechile, R. A., Burns, G., & Tsai, F. (1996). Impediments to learning probability and statistics identified from an evaluation of instructional software. *Journal of Educational and Behavioral Statistics, 21*(1), 35–54.

Collins, A., Brown, J. S., & Newman, S. E. (1989). Cognitive apprenticeship: Teaching the crafts of reading, writing, and mathematics. In L. B. Resnick (Ed.), *Knowing, learning, and instruction: Essays in honor of Robert Glaser* (pp. 453–494). Hillsdale, NJ: Lawrence Erlbaum Associates.

Cooper, G. (1998, December). *Research into cognitive load theory and instructional design at UNSW.* Sydney, Australia: University of New South Wales.

Gardner, H. (1985). The *mind's new science: A history of the cognitive revolution.* New York: Basic Books.

Goldman, S. R. (1990). Anchored instruction and its relationship to situated cognition. *Educational Researcher, 19*(6), 2–10.

Goldman, S. R., with the Cognition and Technology Group at Vanderbilt. (1993). The Jasper series: Theoretical foundations and data on problem solving and transfer. In L. A. Penner, G. M. Batsche, & H. M. Knoff, & D. L. Nelson (Eds.), *The challenges in mathematics and science education: Psychology's response* (pp. 113–152). Washington, DC: American Psychological Association.

Hammer, D. (1996). Misconceptions or p-prims: How might alternative perspectives of cognitive structure influence instructional perceptions and intentions? *Journal of the Learning Sciences, 5*(2), 97–127.

Heider, F. (1958). *The psychology of interpersonal relations.* New York: Wiley.

Herrington, J., & Oliver, R. (1999). Using situated learning and multimedia to investigate higher-order thinking. *Journal of Educational Multimedia and Hypermedia, 8*(4), 401–421.

Konold, C. (1989). Informal conceptions of probability. *Cognition and Instruction, 6*(1), 59–98.

Kozma, R. B. (1991). Learning with media. *Review of Educational Research, 61*(2), 179–211.

Mayer, R. (1989). Models for understanding. *Review of Educational Research, 59*(1), 43–64.

Mayer, R., & Anderson, R. B. (1992). The instructive animation: Helping students build connections between words and pictures in multimedia learning. *Journal of Educational Psychology, 84*(4), 444–452.

Mayer, R., & Gillini, J. (1990). When is an illustration worth ten thousand words? *Journal of Educational Psychology, 82*, 715–726.

Mayer, R., & Sims, V. (1994). For whom is a picture worth a thousand words? Extensions of a dual-coding theory of multimedia learning. *Journal of Educational Psychology, 86*, 389–401.

McNamara, D. S., & Healy, A. F. (1995). A procedural explanation of the generation effect: The use of an operand retrieval strategy for multiplication and addition problems. *Journal of Memory and Language, 34*, 399–416.

Miller, G. A., & Gildea, P. M. (1987). How children learn words. *Scientific American, 257*(3), 94–99.

Moreno, R., & Mayer, R. E. (2000). A coherence effect in multimedia learning: The case for minimizing irrelevant sounds in the design of multimedia instructional messages. *Journal of Educational Psychology, 92*, 117–125.

Moreno, R., & Mayer, R. E. (2002). Learning science in virtual reality multimedia environments: Role of methods and media. *Journal of Educational Psychology, 94*, 598–610.

Moreno, R., Mayer, R. E., Spires, H., & Lester, J. (2001). The case for social agency in computer-based teaching: Do students learn more deeply when they interact with animated pedagogical agents? *Cognition and Instruction, 19*, 177–213.

Paas, F. G. W. (1992). Training strategies for attaining transfer of problem-solving skill in statistics: A cognitive load approach. *Journal of Educational Psychology, 84*(4), 429–434.

Peynircioglu, Z. F. (1989). The generation effect with pictures and nonsense figures. *Acta Psychologica, 70*, 153–160.

Pierce, K. A., Duncan, M. K., Gholson, B., Ray, G. E., & Kamhi, A. G. (1993). Cognitive load, schema acquisition, and procedural adaptation in non-isomorphic analogical transfer. *Journal of Educational Psychology, 85*(1), 66–74.

Pollatsek, A., Konold, C., Well, A. D., & Lima, S. D. (1984). Beliefs underlying random sampling. *Memory & Cognition, 12*, 395–401.

Portney, K., Cohen, S., Soraci, S., & Goldman, J. (1999). From analog to digital: Teaching about criminal sentencing with technology. In D. G. Brown (Ed.), *Computer enhanced learning: Vignettes of best practice from America's most wired campuses* (pp. 178–183). Winston-Salem, NC: Wake Forest University Press–Scientific Division.

Read, S. J., & Miller, L. C. (1998). On the dynamic construction of meaning; An interactive activation and competition model of social perception; In S. J. Read & L. C. Miller (Eds.), *Connectionist models of social reasoning and social behavior* (pp. 27–69). Mahwah, NJ: Lawrence Erlbaum Associates.

Robertson, J. (2000). *Effectiveness of a virtual role-play environment as a preparation activity for story writing.* Unpublished doctoral dissertation.

Robins, S., & Mayer, R. (1993). Schema training in analogical reasoning. *Journal of Educational Psychology, 85*, 529–538.

Ross, M., & Fletcher, G. (1985). Attribution and social perception. In G. Lindzey & E. Aronson (Eds.), *Handbook of social psychology* (Vol. II, 3rd ed., pp. 73–118). New York: Random House.

Shute, V. J. (1992). Aptitude treatment interactions and cognitive skill diagnosis. In J. W. Regian & V. J. Shute (Eds.), *Cognitive approaches to automated instruction* (pp. 15–47). Hillsdale, NJ: Lawrence Erlbaum Associates.

Shute, V. J., Glaser, R., & Raghavan, K. (1989). Inference and discovery in an exploratory laboratory. In P. L. Ackerman, R. J. Sternberg, & R. Glaser (Eds.), *Learning and individual differences: Advances in theory and research* (pp. 275–326). San Francisco: Jossey-Bass.

Smith, J., diSessa, A., & Roschelle, J. (1993). Misconceptions reconceived: A constructivist analysis of knowledge in transition. *Journal of the Learning Sciences, 3*(2), 115–163.

Soraci, S. A., Franks, J., Bransford, J., Chechile, R., Belli, R., Carr, M., & Carlin, M. (1994). Incongruous item generation effects: A multiple-cue perspective. *Journal of Experimental Psychology: Learning, Memory, and Cognition, 20*(1), 67–78.

Strike, K. A., & Posner, G. J. (1992). A revisionist theory of conceptual change. In R. A. Doschl & R. J. Hamilton (Eds.), *Philosophy of science, cognitive psychology, and educational theory and practice* (pp. 147–176). Albany, NY: SUNY Press.

Sweller, J., & Chandler, P. (1991). Evidence for cognitive load theory. *Cognition and Instruction, 8*(4), 351–362.

Triona, L. M., & Klahr, D. (2003). Point and click or grab and heft: Comparing the influence of physical and virtual instructional materials on elementary students' ability to design experiments. *Cognition and Instruction, 21*(2), 113–147.

Tversky, A., & Kahneman, D. (1971). Belief in the law of small numbers. *Psychological Bulletin, 76*, 105–110.

Tversky, A., & Kahneman, D. (1982). Judgment under uncertainty: Heuristics and biases. In D. Kahneman, P. Slovic, & A. Tversky (Eds.), *Judgement under uncertainty: Heuristics and biases* (pp. 3–20). Cambridge, England: Cambridge University Press.

VanLehn, K., Siler, S., Murray, C., Yamauchi, T., & Baggett, W. B. (2003). Why do only some events cause learning during human tutoring. *Cognition and Instruction, 21*(3), 209–249.

VanOverwalle, F., & Van Rooy, D. (1998). A connectionist approach to casual attribution. In S. J. Read & L. C. Miller (Eds.), *Connectionist models of social reasoning and social behavior* (pp. 143–173). Mahwah, NJ: Lawrence Erlbaum Associates.

Wineburg, S. (2001). *Historical thinking and other unnatural acts*. Philadelphia: Temple University Press.

2

Teaching with Digital Role-Play Simulations

Dean Rehberger

In chapter 1, an effort was made to provide a foundation for motivating the use of role-play simulations, particularly with an eye toward arguing that such simulations represent useful and effective means for teaching and learning about fairly complex issues in the social sciences and the humanities. Much of that discussion focused on the empirical and theoretical basis for the decision simulation itself; much less attention was focused on the broader context in which simulations are, or should be, used. In this chapter, an effort is made to explicate the characteristics of the broader context, to examine the inter-play between the decision simulation itself and the curricular setting, and to begin outlining what would seem to be some of the more important pragmatic issues instructors face in using digital decision simulations in class. Based on research focusing on simulations more generally, on instructional technology, and a wide array of experiences, this chapter makes an attempt to provide guidance. This chapter will outline a basic instructional design for using simulation in the curriculum.

THE INSTRUCTIONAL CONTEXT FOR SIMULATIONS

In the classic work, *Being Digital* (1996), on the utopian expectations of the digital future, Nicholas Negroponte writes longingly about the possibilities of computer-based simulations for changing the face of education. For Negroponte, these simulations offer students a rich and complex way to play, explore, and build, and in the process acquire knowledge that helps them to know more and to apply their knowledge in their everyday lives. He writes:

While a significant part of learning certainly comes from teaching—by good teaching and by good teachers—a major measure comes from exploration, from reinventing the wheel and finding out for oneself. Until the computer, the technology for teaching was limited to audio-visual devices and distance learning television, which simply amplified the activity of teachers and the passivity of children. . . . The computer changed this balance radically. All of a sudden, learning by doing became the rule rather than the exception. Since computer simulation of just about anything is now possible, one need not learn about a frog by dissecting it. Instead, children can be asked to design frogs, to build an animal with frog-like behavior, to modify that behavior, to simulate muscles, to play with the frog. (p. 199)

Although Negroponte explains well the value of simulations for learning, his description also appears, at face value, to participate in a McLuhanesque technological determinism in which the medium becomes the agent for social change, or at least learning improvement and change. It is easy to lose the point about the value and necessity of good teaching; so much emphasis is on learning and discovery. Negroponte seems to be telling us that we only need to give students computers and simulations and they will learn.

Even when looking more carefully at the message and examples he offers—a kind of reading often needed to cut through Negroponte's popularizing of the digital era—the curricular responsibilities are easy to overlook. When he explains MIT's LEGO/Logo project that allows students to control LEGO constructions with a simplified Logo computer program, he describes how one student experimented in moving a block structure with an off centered engine. After many failed experiments, the child found that he could get the blocks to move along "a squiggly line he had drawn on a large white sheet of paper." Negroponte goes on to explain:

The child became a hero. Teachers and students alike asked how his invention worked and looked at his project from many different perspectives, asking different questions. This small moment of glory gave him something very important: the joy of learning. (p. 198)

In this situation, the learning does not simply take place in the triangle between child, software, and hardware but in the context of the class as a whole: the child explains and demonstrates his work to the class.

Is this a success attributable to the integration of digital technologies in education? For the student hero almost certainly. More is learned by "the student hero" than mechanics. The joy of learning was also a lesson learned. However, in spite of the richness of Negroponte's report, some legitimate questions are left. How many failed experiments can students tolerate before getting discouraged and giving up. Did many classmates give up? Did the classmates who joined in and asked questions develop the same insights as our hero? Could (more) students have enjoyed the same success if they had been prepared more effectively by the teachers and mentors? The questions are not aimed at challenging the potential benefits of constructivist learning and the epistemological paradigm it manifests. Rather, it is intended to emphasize the point that we need to learn how to maximize the benefit of instructional contexts if we are going to see Negroponte's vision fulfilled.

It is worth dwelling on Negroponte's examples to begin this chapter because it demonstrates well the slipperiness of talking about using digital role-play simulations. Popular computer games like *SimCity* (http://simcity.ea.com/), *Sid Meier's Civilization* (http://www.civ3.com/), *Roller Coaster Tycoon* (http://www.rollercoaster tycoon.com/), *The Sims* (http://thesims.ea.com/), *The Oregon Trail* (http://www.isu.edu/~trinmich/Oregontrail.html), and others cloud the picture even more. These games, among others, are marketed as simulations and allow users to adopt various roles to negotiate the fate of the social order created within the program. They can be played at individual computer stations or in online environments; they can be played alone or in groups. They are used as games for friendly competition or pleasure, and as educational role-play simulations in classrooms around the world (Frye & Frager, 1996).

That is why the term *digital decision role-play simulation used in education* is preferred over *educational role-play digital decision simulation*. For educators the definition of a digital role-play simulation is not found in the object alone but in the context as well. In fact, a complementary emphasis placed on how to best use role-play simulation in education is as important as defining precisely what a digital role-play simulation is. Negroponte's example of students making frogs is pointing at something more than play and games, escaping its own claims of technological determinism. The children are designing animals with "frog-like" behavior and stimulating muscles. To do so, the children would need to have some significant amount of *prior knowledge* about frogs. To focus on building frogs that replicated real frogs and to identify their behaviors and muscles also implies that the children are doing so in a context of a discipline, perhaps biology, which values these skills and knowledge. That is to say, as with the LEGO/Logo example, the frog simulation implies the importance of the educational context. In the example of the frog simulation, the child has adopted the role of biologist and is studying the frog within the context of the discipline. Yet unlike the traditional classroom, at least some children are learning actively to apply their knowledge through their engagement with the simulation.

To limn a model for teaching educational role-play simulations in the classroom, several levels or aspects of context in which these simulations are used must be explored. From previous research on using technology based environments to support exploratory and experimental learning it is clear that the educational benefits are not necessarily distributed equally (Cohen, 1998; Corno & Snow, 1986; Gay, 1986; Mayer, Heiser, & Lonn, 2001; Rose & Meyer, 2002; Shute, 1992; Shute & Glaser, 1990; Shute, Glaser, & Raghavan, 1989; Shute & Regian, 1993). And while some ideas may be rather straightforward to conceptualize, acquired step by step (Case & Berieter, 1984), many others do not become acquired in a straightforward way (see chap. 1). For these more elusive ideas, teachers need to know how to help students accommodate new ways of seeing the world. Students need to be primed, have their prior knowledge assessed, ready to adopt new beliefs. The remainder of the chapter deals with activities and considerations that have been key to the use of simulations in learning. The next section identifies differences (in degree) between games and simulations. This is important because while both can be used in the curriculum for similar purposes, the subtle differences between games and simulations may require teachers to consider alternative strategies for integrating them into a lesson. After looking at the differences, the remainder of the chapter will focus on four issues central to using role-playing simulation in the classroom.

GAMES AND SIMULATIONS

To better understand better the application of role-play simulations in an educational context, and to begin outlining stages for teaching with simulations, it is important to establish distinctions between games and simulations where it is possible. In *Designing and Evaluating Games and Simulations* (1992), Margaret Gredler does an excellent job of creating a detailed taxonomy for games and simulations that clearly distinguishes the two genres from the perspective of the designer and evaluator. For Gredler, games, on the one hand, are distinguished by three major characteristics:

1. [A] game is a world unto itself that is determined by its own particular set of rules that are not replications of real life. . . .
2. [T]he paraphernalia used in a game and the consequences prescribed by the rules may be a vast combination of objects and events that may enable a player or team to defeat one's opponents. . . .
3. [A] game involves winning by taking any course of action allowed by the rules to thwart or defeat other players. . . . (p. 13)

She concludes that games are primarily based on creating a fantasy world defined by rules and competition. The point is not that games are not educational but that they support a different kind of learning and learning goals that focuses on practicing, refining, and exploring relationships between known ideas.

Simulations, on the other hand, have a more complex learning function that allows students to explore the application of knowledge in more complex and ambiguous situations. For Gredler, simulations can be defined by five major characteristics:

1. Simulations are problem-based units of learning that are set in motion by a particular task, issue policy, crisis, or problem. The problems to be addressed by the participant may be either implicit or explicit, depending on the nature of the simulation.
2. The subject matter, setting and issues inherent in the simulation are not textbook problems or questions in which answers are cut-and-dried and determined quickly.
3. Participants carry out functions associated with their roles and the settings in which they find themselves.
4. The outcomes of the simulation are not determined by chance or luck. Instead, participants experience consequences that follow from their own actions.

5. Participants experience reality of function to the extent that they fulfill their roles conscientiously and in a professional manner, executing all the rights, privileges, and responsibilities associated with the role. (p. 16)

Gredler's outline of a simulation is based in part on the work of Ken Jones (1984, 1987), which makes a strong case that the primary focus of simulations is on replicating reality. Participants must take their roles seriously and inhabit their roles in a professional manner to create what he calls the "reality of function." Indeed, one of the primary allures of contemporary digital technologies is that they offer simulation designers greater ability than ever before to create highly realistic decision situations that make it easier for students to "suspend reality" and ultimately to play their roles in situated contexts. The sense "realness" created by simulations can be one of the greatest appeals for students (Moseley, 2001).

Gredler's definions are informative because they begin to outline a model for using role-play simulations in education and the importance of the educational context. Boiled down to their basics, games are defined by two primary characteristics: rules and competition. In contrast to games, simulations are based on very different characteristics: roles and fidelity to reality. *This is not to argue that these are hard and fast categories into which we can easily fit different software packages; rather, the distinction should be seen more as poles of a continuum of context and use.* An instructor can, after all, take any tools and media—pencil, paper, text, images, games, word processors, databases—into a classroom and cobble together an educational role-play simulation for her students (or a game). *What is essential for instructors is how they shape and model the simulation so that it focuses their students on roles and fidelity rather than rules and competition.*

TEACHING AND LEARNING WITH ROLE-PLAY SIMULATIONS

When considering digital decision simulations as a principal vehicle of instructions, four areas stand out as essential for maximizing the utility of the simulation and related lesson: Readiness, Roles, Reaction, and Reflection. Each of these stages or aspects relate to how digital decision simulations are actually used: what must be present before the simulation begins; how the role-play should progress; and what happens when the role-play is over. Although most of this discussion approaches these issues as though these aspects are squarely contained in the instructional context (such as the classroom), they often reflect a type of interaction or inter-play between the design of the simulation itself and the way it is used. In other words, the simulation may, depending on how it is designed and what its pedagogical goals are, facilitate positive results in these areas. Alternatively, the simulation may require the instructor to explicitly address these areas. In any case, they provide a convenient way to describe important elements that need to be considered in the process of using (or deciding to use) a digital role-play simulation.

Stage 1: Readiness

Readiness entails several different levels of preparation for both students and instructors. To begin, student's beliefs about media and instructional method can influence how much they learn when their education is delivered by computer or video and uses uncommon methods like simulation (Laurel, 1993; Snow, 1989). For example, if the presentation reminds users too much of television, the content may seem suspect (Karimi, Laurel, Oren, & Don, 1989). Likewise, students who have suffered the long term effects of a mostly didactic education may have come to believe that they only need to experience a lecture to fully understand a topic. Some may not seem to see the need for the alterative form of education. These kinds of prior beliefs and knowledge are essential to manage as beliefs about the domain addressed by the class and simulation. Addressing these beliefs is not simple; like naïve beliefs in the area of physics, probability, and social decision they will be resilient. Role-play has been shown to be an effective warm-up for writing and other learning exercises as well (Robertson, 2000); perhaps it is an effective warm-up exercise for role-play? Under this hypothesis, one option for addressing this kind of prior knowledge impediment is to have some students *play the role* of a teacher and explain complex roles and behavior to other students *without modeling or role-play*. This exercise might lead some students to understand what a role-play can contribute to their own learning.

Another way to bridge the readiness gap is to make constant connections among the course content, the course learning goals, and the simulation. This can best be done by making explicit course learning goals in discussions before and after the simulation and by encouraging students to make links between course content and readings and their experiences in the simulation. Schmidt (2003), for example, argues that implementing his web-based economic decision simulations, students learn best when the important economic concepts of the course are explicitly linked to students' activities in the decision simulation. Often the simplest way this can be done is to note directly on the syllabus the key concepts and readings needed to help prepare for the simulation. Yet as Schmidt notes, the role-play simulation typically provides an abundance of opportunity for the instructor to connect interactively the course's concepts and the content of the simulation (Schmidt, 2003, pp. 158–159).

On a more basic level, students must understand how the digital role-play simulation operates, the steps they will be expected to take, and the time limits imposed on the simulation. This kind of preparation is akin to orienting subjects to their tasks and responsibilities in a research study (Campbell & Stanley, 1963; Keppell, 1991).[1] Researchers, or their assistants, describe the experiment in detail without giving away the purpose of the research to subjects. They often have subjects try one or more trials as a warm-up. The same strategy should work in classes to reduce the influence of factors that interfere with student learning and make a reflection stage more challenging. Warm-up can sometimes best be done by demonstrating the simulation in class or in the computer lab with clearly defined instructions followed by having students do one or more trials on their own.

Effective educational role-play simulation requires that students have specific knowledge about the topic to participate in the simulation. It is important at this point that we do not confuse this concept of necessary knowledge with the concept of prior knowledge and biases introduced in chapter one. If the topic is about adjudicating student conflicts in a dorm, some prior knowledge about the roles and protocols is essential. Students will bring assorted and varied baggage to the simulation that will influence their decision making (the kind of baggage that digital role-play simulations are to help students examine). These simulations rarely teach students the basic

---

[1]In experiments, of course, it is possible for the experimenter to carefully define and choose the subjects who will participate. Such is not the case for teachers.

subject matter but are designed to enhance and augment the participants' knowledge while helping them to apply what they have already learned in class. Studies suggest that the better students are prepared for the simulation, the more it will run smoothly, require less instructor intervention, and help students to apply knowledge that they have learned (Hmelo et al., 2000). Similarly, the better students are prepared for the simulation, the more they will invest in their roles, the situation, and the outcome; they will also experience less stress and enjoy the process more.

Preparation is the key because without some knowledge of the situation and the role, it cannot appear real for the student. Ultimately, when *readiness* is at hand then "fidelity and roles" are improved. It is, after all, hard to act like a cowboy if one knows nothing about how a cowboy looks, acts, or works. Often students will also come to a role with conflicting ideas because of prior knowledge and biases developed before a specific course, particularly when they are asked to be politicians or lawyers. And, of course, students will never be expected to have a complete grasp of a subject to participate since it is a learning experience, and often people who make analogous decisions in the "real world" themselves have incomplete knowledge. Indeed, sometimes one of the pedagogical goals of a given decision simulation is to facilitate an understanding among students that decisions are very often made with less information than the decision maker would prefer.

Finally, readiness implies establishing a particular kind of class in which learning goals are explicitly addressed, active learning is valued, and student voices are central. For students to take the step of actively imagining themselves as inhabiting a real role in a professional manner and to experience the consequences of their decisions, they are required to invest themselves in the class and feel a sense of ownership for their learning and the class. If the students have a sense that the simulation is to lead to prescribed answers and "correct" results rather than one of open ended exploration, they are less likely generate their own responses and consequently to examine and reconfigure their networks of beliefs

Stage 2: Roles

It may seem strange to separate "roles" as a stage or aspect when teaching with role-play simulations. It is true that the readiness stage (discussed above) and the reaction and reflection stages (to be discussed shortly) all deal in some fashion with the roles that students (and instructors) play in digital decision simulations. Yet as the name "role-play" implies, the "role" is central to the experience and success of the simulation, and thus, special care and consideration needs to be given to it. The ability for students to imagine themselves performing the roles and taking seriously the fantasy created by the simulation is one of the strongest motivating factors of successful simulations (Alessi & Trollip, 2001).

The "roles" aspect involves ensuring that student participants in any simulation develop some prior understanding of the various players and perspectives that the simulation calls for—their own roles and those of others. The roles stage can often be the most awkward part of the simulation. While students may be very familiar with the general idea of role playing because it permeates every part of their culture and entertainment, the traditional role for students in the classroom is that of "student." Some can find it difficult to escape this role and end up either adopting the role they have already established in class or performing as they believe the teacher would want them to perform. This is particularly true if students participate in more passive and didactic learning situations; they can sometimes find it uncomfortable to step outside of their prescribed role.

Helping students meet the challenge of playing a role is the charge of the both the simulation and the instructor. With respect to the simulation the interface can make a strong difference. For example, decision simulations require students to enter into virtual decision-making processes; it helps if the interface of the simulation matches their expectations of what to do and how to behave in the role (Laurel, 1993; Norman, 1988). Some interfaces may be better at bringing about this match than others. Simulations that use a direct manipulation (i.e., direct manipulation over objects in the simulation rather than through syntax) will more effectively engage students in the simulation (Schniederman, 1987) and implicitly emphasize the role. For example, students playing the role of a judge will be better off banging a virtual gavel to stop a trial than clicking cancel. The gavel suggests authority in a way a button push does not. If the topic addressed by the simulation is dry, or students do not have a well developed and coherent mental model of topic to bring to the role play, a dramatic (Laurel, 1993), direct manipulation interface offers real benefits.

Teachers also need to directly address expectations for the roles and nonobtrusively monitor student behavior during the simulation. Failure to address role expectations can lead to greater stress for students and, in some cases, overdramatic renditions of their roles (Hill & Lance, 2001). It is also important to address roles and students' feelings about their performance directly during debriefing. Too often, instructors focus on the actions and decisions made during the simulation at the expense of considering the role, and yet focusing on the role and the feelings the student have had during and after the performance is an important part of the understanding and learning about their experience as a whole. After all, the focus of decision simulations is on the act of making choices and behavior in particular contexts.

Stage 3: Reaction

The reaction stage defines the space of the simulation. If students are properly prepared, the reaction stage is often the most fun and satisfying part of the simulation for students, but it can be the most difficult stage for instructors who are new to using technology (Baker, Gearhart, & Herman, 1994). During the simulation, instructors must adopt several roles that can be counter to their main role as teacher and can often be contradictory. The instructor or simulation administrator sets the parameters of the role for the student. However, once the simulation is started, the instructor must carefully choose how to proctor the role-play. If the (chief) learning goal is to help students understand the role and the context itself (as it might be in a training application), instructor intervention is important. Teachers can participate in the class as a "guide on the side," anticipating students reactions, and offering instruction and insight when necessary. This kind of instructor participation can help students come to terms with features of the roles and complexities of decisions. It is as if the student is an apprectice. The instructor should play the role of a facilitator or a manager, who works by questioning, counseling, and encouraging without "telling" students how to behave (unless the student behavior disrupts the simulation for other students or violates clearly articulated rules). To do this effectively often requires the teacher to be an unobtrusive monitor of students' "needs, feelings, and frustrations."

Alternatively, if the goal is to let the students immerse themselves in the role and gain insight through reflection after the simulation, instructors need to allow the students to act and react based on their prior knowledge and the situation, and thus avoid "leading" or "guiding" students into making the proper decisions.

If the simulation is run over several class periods or completed by students outside of class, it can be helpful to give students ten minutes at the end of class to discuss problems and issues with the simulation and the technology. With longer running simulations, students should also be encouraged to keep journals or logs recording their feelings and experiences. If the digital simulation allows the simulation administrator to view collected data, it can be helpful for the instructor to monitor student input to monitor if data is being inputted properly, and to monitor if students are having problems with the simulation content or technology. This is especially important when a simulation calls for extended written answers from students because it may be important to discuss the content and level of detail expected. It is important, however, that during the timeframe of the simulation that both students and instructors avoid making judgments about roles, actions, or decisions. Similar to the readiness stage, the process of running a simulation can be less taxing if the instructor has fostered an active learning environment and student-centered classroom throughout the course.

Stage 4: Reflection

Reflection is an essential part of every cognitive learning theory. It offers students a way to understand what they have learned, share it with others, and apply it to other situations and their lives. It is at this point that students become aware of the fullest range of the consequences of their behaviors in the simulation. They get to raise their awareness of what they did, why they did it, and often how what they did affects simulation outcomes (Lederman, 1984). The Reflection stage is often the most critical for students (Boud & Walker, 1991). It is the time they have to step back from their experience and think, question, write, share, connect, and apply what they have learned (Thatcher, 1990). After the role-play portion of the simulation is completed, it is good to discuss the experience as a class. Often it is best to begin the discussion by allowing students to describe their experiences and feelings. Afterward, during a reflection of the substance of the simulation and results, students often come to terms with the meaning of their decisions and instructors can locate the "aha" moments. Traditionally this stage is called the "debriefing," but this term can often be misleading for students because it can conjure images of interrogations and being instructed not to divulge classified materials. The term also reflects the traditional simulation acted out by participants who then move on to discuss orally their simulation and respond to questions. For these reasons, reflection tends to be seen as a stage that only happens at the end of the simulation. In classes that use digital role-play simulations, however, instructors often have the technical facilities and collected data to have students do a variety of reflective activities during and after the simulation. Thus there can be several levels to this stage in which debriefing is an important final step but reflection is key to all stages.

Reflections can be either student centered or (more) instructor guided depending on the learning goal. In some cases the learning is not straightforward; instead it requires a sustainable reevaluation of a topic in light of the results of a simulation. The learning goal here is typically a new way of thinking and an ability to dynamically change how topics and ideas are interpreted (Spiro, Coulson, Feltovich, & Anderson, 1998). Examples might include a new way to interpret a historical event and the ability *reinterpret it when new facts come to light*. Or it may include an examination of experimental results as compared to student expectations when considering the outcomes of physics experiments (Thornton, 1998). In the case of social decision simulations, it may be examining group results and behavior and considering how they frame a context for understanding social decisions (see chapter 3). In all three of these instances the reflections probably require more than an open-ended constructivist based view approach. The instructor has lead the students to insights.

For more straightforward learning goals the options for reflection increase. Instructor led reflections can identify key elements, moments, and turning-points and then analyze these and the experience as a whole. The instructor may want to introduce data or observations in order to assist students in the identification and analysis. A key part of the discussion is to guide (coach or nudge) students toward generalizing their experience in the larger context of the discipline and to make connections to course concepts, content, and readings (Ciodo & Flaim, 1993).

For larger classes or for simulations that use collaborative groups, it is often best to begin by having small group discussions before moving to the whole class. One of the best things to do, however, before initiating a class discussion is to have students reflect on their experiences in writing. This allows students time to digest their experience and outline their thoughts. As with many parts of the simulation process, this is often best if done as an informal assignment. Often letting students do free writes (writing as fast as they can and as much as they can during a timed period, usually 10 to 15 minutes) facilitates this reflection. Instructors can often guide the free writes with open-ended prompts or questions; journal writing or written interviews with group members are also possibilities. Online threaded discussions can be one of the best ways to elicit reflections from students both during and after the simulation. Done in and outside of class, having students write in an electronic forum lets them post their thoughts and react to other student posts. The online forum then becomes a record that can be brought into class and threads can be used as points of departure during the debriefing discussion. This can be particularly effective in larger classes and for students who often do not enter into class discussions. Threaded discussions allow students to carry the discussion forward with their group, into other assignments, and, most important, get feedback from their peers. A good assignment is to have students move from these informal writings to a more formal writing. In doing so, students can continue the reflection process and produce materials that can be assessed. In the end, while discussing the simulation is always an excellent idea, having students write about their experiences often constitutes an important step in maximizing the conceptual learning from the simulation and transferring their knowledge to other experiences and materials in the course (Patranek, 1994, 2000).

Finally, one of the most important steps in the reflection process is for instructors to assess and reflect on their use of the educational role-play simulation in the course. Did the simulation help support learning goals for the course? Were the students prepared to play their roles? Did the students treat the simulation as a game or as a serious event? Was the time allowed for the simulation adequate? Were students able to handle the technology? How could the post-simulation discussion be improved? How could better connections be drawn between the simulation and other class materials? These are only a few of the questions instructors should consider after completing the simulation exercise. As with any new addition to a course, instructors need to assess honestly its use and what revisions need to be made for next time the simulation is used.

Motivation is one primary key to learning, and computer-based simulations have been demonstrated to be both motivating and satisfying for students as learning tools (Mosley, 2001). Simulations offer students the four relevant factors of motivation: challenge, curiosity, control, and fantasy (Malone, 1981; Malone & Lepper, 1987). While simulations ask students to use knowledge in new ways, the challenge is mitigated and made reasonable by their familiarity with the medium and role-playing. Although simulation administrators set control limits of what students can do, they have the power to imagine themselves in roles that gives them the power to make decisions and face the consequences. In other words, digital role-play simulations offer instructors that rare moment in education where students can be challenged within disciplines in ways that will excite and motivate them to discover and learn more. It is a balancing act that lets them bring parts of their world and comfort zones in contact with the rigorous (and often ambiguous and complex) ways decisions are made in the social sciences and humanities.

One of the basic impediments to the use of digital simulations in class is not the students' insecurity with the technology, but the instructor's. It is not uncommon today for students to be more technologically adept than their instructors. Sadly, because of institutional shortcomings, instructors who use digital simulations often end up supporting themselves. Not only is this limiting in terms of the number of faculty (and courses) that use simulations, it also places what some might suggest is an unreasonable burden on those instructors (especially instructors of large classes) who take on the extra challenges. Yet instructors who are perhaps not as technologically adept as others can often develop strategies to compensate. One final strategy, then, that can be used—especially in large classes that are unable to meet in computer labs for the simulation—is to form groups that have at least one or two members who have extensive computer experience or expertise. This can often be enhanced by having a group of these students, who self-select as capable computer users, run through the digital simulation before the rest of the class does. These students can then help by acting as proctors or helpers when the students first use the simulation in or outside of class.

CONCLUSION

Working through the stages of the educational role-play simulation and the strategies for incorporating technology in courses can help instructors to develop a good plan for incorporating simulations in their course. While it is true that instructors could use a variety of digital materials to construct a role-play simulation, it would not necessarily be the best use of their time. And while it is true that any role-play simulation can be used as a game or a simulation, good digital role-play decision simulations, as defined in the opening chapters and like those presented in the second half of this volume, are designed to enhance and encourage the reality of function and the four stages of an educational role-play simulation. Moreover, they are often designed to meet the needs of particular contexts and methods of delivery from college courses, to professional training workshops, to video kiosks and from the Internet, to CD-ROMs, to virtual-reality goggles. The key issue here is to think of digital role-play decision simulations as tools that can be used to enhance a course based on active and cooperative learning, but the context must be set if the tool is to be used successfully with students.

This chapter reviewed some of the nuts-and-bolts issues associated with using digital role-play decision simulations in the social sciences and humanities. Along the way, it also raised some issues that need to be explored in more detail. Early in the chapter, the idea was introduced that the context in which digital role-play simulations are used—the educational or curriculum context—represents an important element in determining the extent to which the simulation will likely produce effective learning results. This specific issue is elaborated on in chapter 3.

REFERENCES

Alessi, S. M., & Trollip, S. R. (2001). *Multimedia for learning: Methods and development*. Boston: Allyn & Bacon.

Baker, E., Gearhart, M., & Herman, J. (1994). Evaluating the Apple Classrooms of Tomorrow. In E. L. Baker & H. F. O'Neill, Jr. (Eds.), *Technology assessment in education and training*. Hillsdale, NJ: Lawrence Erlbaum Associates.

Boud, D., & Walker, D. (1991). *Experience and learning: Reflection at work*. Deakin, Victoria, Australia: Deakin University Press.

Campbell, D. T., & Stanley, J. C. (1963). *Experimental and quasi-experimental designs for research*. Chicago, IL: Rand McNally.

Case, R., & Bereiter, C. (1984). From behaviorism to cognitive behaviorism to cognitive development: Steps in the evolution of instructional design. *Instructional Science, 13*, 141–158.

Chiodo, J., & Flaim, M. (1993). The link between computer simulations and social studies learning: Debriefing. *Social Studies, 84*, 119–121.

Cohen, S. (1998). *A detailed assessment of a novel approach to curricular software for teaching statistics*. Unpublished doctoral dissertation.

Corno, L., & Snow, R. E. (1986). Adapting teaching to individual differences among learners. In M. Whittrock (Ed.), *Handbook of research on teaching* (3rd ed.). New York: Macmillan.

Cranton, P. (1994). *Understanding and promoting transformative learning*. San Francisco: Jossey-Bass.

College students' use of the Internet. (2002). *Findings of the Pew Internet & American Life Project*. (http://www.pewinternet.org/reports/)

Freiermuth, M. R. (2002). Connecting with computer science students by building bridges. *Simulation & Gaming: An International Journal, 33*, 299–315.

Frye, B., & Frager, A. M. (1996). Civilization, Colonization, SimCity: Simulations for the social studies classroom. *Learning and Leading with Technology, 24*, 21–23.

Gay, G. (1986). Interaction of learner control and prior understanding in computer assisted video instruction. *Journal of Educational Psychology, 78*(3), 225–227.

Gredler, M. E. (1992). *Designing and evaluating games and simulations: A process approach*. London, Kogan Page.

Hill, J. L., & Lance, C. G. (2002). Debriefing stress. *Simulation & Gaming: An International Journal, 33*, 490–503.

Hmelo, C. E., Nagarajan, A., & Day, R. S. (2000). Effects of high and low prior knowledge on construction of a joint problem space. *The Journal of Experimental Education, 69*, 36–56.

Jones, K. (1984). Simulations versus professional educators. In D. Jacque & E. Tipper (Eds.), *Learning for the future with games and simulations* (pp. 45–50). Loughborough: SAGSET, Loughborough University of Technology.

Karimi, S., Laurel, B., Oren, T., & Don, A. (1989). *Evaluation guides. A user testing study*. Apple Computer Technical Report.

Jones, K. (1987). *Simulations: A handbook for teachers and trainers*. London: Kogen Page.

Keppel, G. (1991). *Design and analysis: A researcher's handbook*. NJ: Prentice Hall.

Laurel, B. (1993). *Computers as theatre*. Reading, MA: Addison-Wesley.

Lederman, L. C. (1984). Debriefing: A critical reexamination of the postexperience analytic process with implications for its effective use. *Simulation & Games: An International Journal, 15*, 415–431.

Lepper, M. R., & Chabay, R. W. (1985). Intrinsic motivation and instruction: Conflicting views on the role of motivational processes in computer-based education. *Educational Psychologist, 20*, 217–230.

Malone, T. W., & Lepper, M. R. (1987). Making learning fun: A taxonomy of intrinsic motivations for learning. In R. E. Snow & M. J. Farr (Eds.), *Apptitude, learning, and instruction: III* (pp. 223–253). Hillsdale, NJ: Lawrence Erlbaum Associates.

Mayer, R. E., Heiser, J., & Lonn, S. (2001). Cognitive constraints on multimedia learning: When presenting more material results in less understanding. *Journal of Educational Psychology, 93*, 187–198.

Moseley, W. G. (2001). Computer assisted comprehension of distant worlds: Understanding hunger dynamics in Africa. *Journal of Geography, 100*, 32–45.

Negroponte, N. (1996). *Being digital.* New York: Vintage Books.

Norman, D. (1988). *The psychology of everyday things.* New York: Basic Books.

Petranek, C. F. (1994). A maturation in experiential learning: Principles of simulation and gaming. *Simulation & Gaming: An International Journal, 25*, 513–523.

Petranek, C. F. (2000). Written debriefing: The next vital step in learning with simulations. *Simulation & Gaming: An International Journal, 31*, 108–118.

Robertson, J. (2000). *Effectiveness of a virtual role-play environment as a preparation activity for story writing.* Unpublished doctoral dissertation.

Rose, D., & Meyer, A. (2002). Teaching Every Student in the Digital Age: Universal Design for Learning. Association for Supervision & Curriculum Development.

Rogoff, B. (1990). *Apprenticeship in thinking: Cognitive development in social context.* New York: Oxford University Press.

Schofield, J. W. (1995). *Computers and classroom culture.* Cambridge; New York: Cambridge University Press.

Schmidt, S. J. (2003). Active and cooperative learning using web-based simulations. *The Journal of Economic Education, 34*(2), 151–167.

Shute, V. J. (1992). Aptitude treatment interactions and cognitive skill diagnosis. In J. W. Regian & V. J. Shute (Eds.), *Cognitive approaches to automated instruction* (pp. 15–47). Hillsdale, NJ: Lawrence Erlbaum Associates.

Shute, V. J., & Glaser, R. (1990). A large scale evaluation of an intelligent discovery world. *Interactive Learning Environments, 1*, 51–77.

Shute, V. J., Glaser, R., & Raghavan, K. (1989). Inference and discovery in an exploratory laboratory. In P. L. Ackerman, R. J. Sternberg, & R. Glaser (Eds.), *Learning and individual differences: Advances in theory and research* (pp. 275–326). San Francisco, CA: Jossey-Bass.

Shute, V. J., & Regian, W. (1993). Principles for evaluating intelligent tutoring systems. *Journal of Artificial Intelligence and Education, 4*(2), 245–271.

Snow, R. E. (1989). Aptitude-Treatment Interaction as a framework for research on individual differences in learning. In P. L. Ackerman, R. J. Sternberg, & R. Glaser (Eds.), *Learning and individual differences: Advances in theory and research* (pp. 13–59). New York: Freeman.

Spiro, R. J., Coulson, R. L., Feltovich, P. J., & Anderson, D. (1998). Cognitive flexibility theory: Advanced knowledge acquisition in ill-structured domains. In V. Patel (Ed.), *Proceedings of the 10th Annual Conference of the Cognitive Science Society.* Hillsdale, NJ: Lawrence Erlbaum Associates.

Thatcher, D., & Robinson, J. (1990). 'Me The Slow Learner—a case study.' *Simulation/Games for Learning.*

Thatcher, D. (1990). Promoting learning through games and simulations. *Simulation and Gaming, 21*(3), 262–273.

3

The Curricular Role for Understanding Social Decisions

Steve Cohen
Tufts University

Simulations, especially the digital decision simulations examined in this volume and accessible on the web, have merit as research and training applications. As research applications, they offer a context for studying human behavior, thinking and learning. Simulations provide a controllable and replicable context for carrying out experiments, especially in circumstances when it is unethical, undesirable, or impossible to place research subjects in the real world context. It would be unconscionable to have research subjects make real decisions about euthanasia (see chapter 6) and perhaps undesirable to have them make binding decisions in international negotiations. As training applications, digital decision simulations are intended to help people learn how to work through the complexities of different contexts, be it a courtroom (see chapter 6), or a bedroom (see chapter 7), and make decisions. Typically the people using the simulations are the same people who would be expected to make this type of decision in the real world, often as part of a job. The simulations offer a chance for them to learn how to approach a range of different circumstances they might face. They help users experience and appreciate the dozens of decisions and factors that influence how real world events might reach a conclusion. These simulations are training applications, designed and used for teaching people who will someday need to make similar decisions in a real world setting. In some cases they are used to teach people who are making the decisions for themselves (i.e., using a condom). In other cases simulation users are learning to manage complex situations, like environmental disasters or criminal processes.

This volume, however, is about using the simulations for a different purpose. The goal is to repurpose these simulations and use them to teach students about complex concepts in the social sciences and humanities. These students may never actually make the decisions in the real world that they are required to render in the simulations, nor use the simulation to conduct research. The simulations are there to help them develop intellectually and understand the contexts in which decisions are made. Ultimately, using digital role-play simulations in the context of a well-designed curriculum offers a unique window into a variety of complex concepts that permeate the core of the social sciences. Digital role-play simulations offer an exciting and effective mechanism for teaching social science and related concepts through a complex examination of social decisions.

Simulations have been used to help students develop both complex ideas in domains and, relatedly, their concept of themselves (Bers, 2001; Resnick & Wilensky, 1998; Shute & Glaser, 1990; Shute & Regian, 1993). However, as explained in chapter 1, integrating these two is difficult; there are unique challenges that interfere with students' ability to conceptualize both how they understand social decisions and what it means to understand a social decision. While there is a constructivist and generative theory guiding the learning paradigm proposed here, the focus is ultimately a learner-centered approach (Hay & Barab, 2001). The goal is for each student to develop a window into his or her own process for understanding decisions. It builds on the general approach to teaching with simulations discussed in chapter 2, with emphasis on roles and reflection.

Ultimately we are suggesting a complex, two-part process. The first part involves utilizing a training or research simulation where students can play the role of a decision maker. The simulations themselves allow students to walk a mile in the shoes of those who make complex social decisions. The role needs to be one where the decisions made have meaningful connections to the policies and theories addressed in a class. For instance, the role might be of a community member if the policies addressed in class are about public health behavior in a community. If the course is about sentencing, the role can be that of a judge. If the course deals with conflict resolution, the role of a resident assistant in a dorm would be meaningful.

This first part of the instructional model anchors the decision in a real context and creates an opportunity for students to work through a decision process and confront the details required to reach a decision. However, using the simulations alone would not likely be sufficient to help students acquire a durable and transferable sense of the complexities of social decisions, policies, and their implementation (Bereiter, 1995; Campione & Brown, 1990; Goldman, 1993b; Tripp, 1993).

The second part requires a careful review of the range of decisions made by students. In the model suggested here, role–play is followed by a class-based, instructor-led examination of how and why each student decision differs. This discussion is a specialized approach to reflection and is the province of the classroom and instructor (Nuthall, 2000). The goal is to help students move beyond their anchored experience in an isolated role-play. Students need to accommodate the range of decisions made by their peers as legitimate and perhaps not too different from their own. Through this process students begin to understand how their own perspective might limit the sense of possible (or reasonable) outcomes that a policy might need to address. Once they reach this point, they will be in a better position to see how their own perspectives might limit their ability to investigate real world policy decisions and program implementations. Out of the process come students who better understand how complex policy, policy processes, and policy implementation really can be, as in the Crime and Punishment simulation discussed in chapter 6. Students who have had this kind of education may well be in a better position to research policy decisions than those who have learned about policy using traditional classroom-based methods.

This chapter describes a particular paradigm and its associated working hypotheses about how to develop students' capacity to implicitly analyze and understand social decisions using digital role-play simulations and coordinated curricula. The approach comes from an examination of how simulations described in this volume have been used in higher education. It represents an important step toward understanding how to help students accommodate the complex circumstances and variables that motivate and determine social decisions particularly as they are made in the real world. This promises to offer distinct learning advantages over traditional approaches to teaching social science.

SHORTCOMINGS OF TRADITIONAL APPROACHES

For the most part, and perhaps with some notable exceptions, social science is taught from the outside looking in. Walking a mile in the shoes of a decision maker is not a standard part of a social science curriculum. Indeed, perhaps as a logical extension of behavioral approaches to social science research, the traditional way of teaching in the social sciences starts with an effort to have students understand existing research or perspectives concerning an issue or subject. Rarely do students have the benefit of being part of the social rubrics they study. Stated another way, the most important concepts that are taught in the social sciences are not normally thought of as applied concepts; rather they are thought of as abstract ones. This is especially true when the topics include government, public policy, private sector economics, criminal justice, and other related issues. (In many cases, like criminal justice, it may be desirable that students do not experience first-hand the social institutions and processes they study.) Rather, students learn about the abstract theories and research on the practice of social science as a body of knowledge outside the realm of their own experience. Students learning about international negotiations, at least initially, are not normally part of real negotiating teams with the interests and possible survival of a nation-state in their hands. Nor do students learning about American health policy participate in making decisions about specific public health issues, such as how to deal with the spread of infectious diseases.

In the social science research endeavor, the dominant idea is that we learn about decisions from objectively observing the decisions of others. But as a method for teaching and learning the underlying concepts of the social sciences, this research approach may not be adequate. Many students may not be ready to examine the results of objective social science analysis. Helping student develop an empirically based epistemology is an issue for students in the social sciences, as well as the natural science (Hammer & Schifter, 2001; Schommer-Aikins, 2002; Schommer & Walker, 1995). As outsiders looking in, students are prone to evaluate social decisions from their own, sometimes very limited and perhaps self-serving, perspectives. It is not hard to imagine any number of topics central to social science education that may not be taught well using traditional classroom based approaches to learning. By and large, topics are treated in ways that are abstracted from the social world and brought to students by way of lecture and example. This approach, which is referred to here as didactic, does not involve challenging and developing students' untutored ways of thinking. In short, didactic learning approaches create a wall of separation between students and the actual contexts in which decisions are made. Without participation (and ultimately the opportunity to reflect on it), students do not learn how they themselves influence their own understanding of social issues (see chapter 1).

The problem with this abstract, noncontext specific, approach to learning has been well documented. Perhaps the most recent influential work in this regard has been by Brown, Collins, and Duguid (1989), and more recently by Brown and Duguid (2002). Their work focused on what they call situated cognition, which effectively argues that all learning takes place within the context of a particular culture. Moreover, it argues that description of decision contexts presented to students from the perspective of objective outside observers creates inert knowledge, and is inadequate to create true understanding of the decisions or their contexts. In other words, it suggests that knowledge acquired outside the context in which it is used is not likely to be terribly useful. Other research reinforces the arguments made by Brown and others (Clancey, 1994; Vygotsky, 1976), and suggests more effective ways for creating durable learning experiences. Instead of an abstract, classroom-based, approach to learning, they suggest what they call an apprenticeship model for learning. This model prescribes that people who are relatively new to a type of decision (i.e., apprentices) should be placed in a decision context along with more experienced decision makers from whom the apprentice can learn. The apprenticeship provides a salient context, well suited to learning and practicing the skills, knowledge, and nomenclature of a specific body of knowledge and expertise. Although the apprenticeship approach may not be applicable to all kinds of decision situations, it does represent one approach to situated learning in order to overcome the limits of didactic approaches. Under the umbrella of the situated cognition model comes a prescription for context in learning, as well as recognition of distributed cognition; that notion that concepts, skills, and ideas do not reside exclusively in an individuals mind but are distributed across members of communities (Lave & Wenger, 1990).

Pragmatically, it is very difficult to design curricula that take full advantage of all that is implied by situated cognition. However, instructional designs based on some of the more salient aspects of the situated cognition model, notably the anchored instruction approach, have been developed. Following on the situated cognition model, anchored instruction utilizes context-based scenarios in order to root learning (Cognition and Technology Group at Vanderbilt, 1990). Anchored instruction usually focuses on creating particular learning environments, especially learning environments that are fundamentally different from those that would be associated with didactic approaches. Such learning environments essential represent efforts to root problem-based learning in particular contexts that represent closer approximations to real world decision contexts than could be achieved in didactic learning environments.

One example of curricular materials developed on the basis of anchored instruction comes from the Cognition and Technology Group at Vanderbilt University, 1990, (Bransford et al., 1990), which took a lead in developing context based learning scenarios. Early applications of the anchored instruction model addressed problems in learning mathematics. Perhaps most prominent among the efforts developed by this group is the Jasper Woodbury series (Goldman, 1993a) designed to provide a context for groups of fifth-grade children to work through math problems. In this series, rather than introduce and teach abstract math subjects as separate bodies of knowledge outside everyday problems, video-based scenarios were used to create problem contexts. Some scenarios required students to create equations around intuitive problems like filling a gas tank for a boat ride. The mathematics became anchored in contexts simulated by videodisc. There was a social component to the instruction as well. Students watched the video together, discussed the situation, and developed a way to work through simulated problems. Students' prior knowledge about the context (knowing phrases like mile per hour, familiarity with boats and prior experience planning trips) became part of the instructional setting and a context-inclusive way of characterizing mathematics problems emerged.

The digital role-play simulations presented in this volume address a similar educational need in the social sciences: the need to help students recognize the detailed, situated processes involved in rendering the decisions. The very design decisions themselves that go into creating the role-play simulations add an implicit situated component. The simulations themselves offer insight into the details and implications of a social decision that are nearly impossible to convey in a lecture or book about the topic. For example, students working through the sentencing simulation *Crime and Punishment* (see chapter 4) will get a sense of the details involved in a sentencing hearing even if they were not training to be a judge in criminal court. The details come in the form of a defendant's facial expression, in-depth information about the defendants past criminal history, and the description of guidelines for serving up a sentence. Students who experience the simulated sentencing process come away with a deeper understanding of how difficult it is to balance the multiple attributes of the case—the defendant's characteristics, the facts of the case, and the differing justifications for the criminal sanction. Likewise, an instructor who assigns the *ICONS* simulation (see chapter 8) to students in her course would likely find that students come away with a sense of what it means to negotiate an international issue. Groups of students, each playing representatives of a different nation, must react to how their peers decided to settle a conflict which involves several stakeholders with many interests. Presumably, experiencing the collective consequences of their actions is certainly different than learning second-hand about the process of multiparty negotiations, as experienced by others in the past. Case studies, for example, represent a frequently used method of teaching in this way.

Both anchored instruction and situated cognition have important prescriptions for learning in the mathematical, natural, and social sciences. In many ways they offer the foundation for a digital role-play based curriculum for the social sciences. The emphasis is on the development of contextualized knowledge and the role contextual knowledge plays in decisions. However, there is an important issue to consider before jumping ahead and embracing digital role-play based purely on the merits of anchored instruction and situated cognition. Situated cognition prescribes an apprenticeship model with the goal of offering an apprentice access to expertise, real world complex problems, and a unique learning context. The emphasis is on developing the knowledge and expertise required to solve problems in a particular domain. In other words, situated cognition would seem to work best when the goal is focused on how make the learning curve associated with making decisions less steep than it otherwise would be. This is a worthwhile goal, one suited to internships and training. However, the emphasis of the digital decision simulation-based approach proposed here is to help students develop an abstract, generalizable, perspective of social science without severing it from its roots in decision contexts. The goal is to help students move beyond situated cognition (Bereiter, 2000) and help them acquire mental models (Gentner & Stevens, 1983) of social science that they implicitly use to interpret decisions in the social sciences. This goal requires an educational approach that addresses the challenge of helping students move beyond the limitations of their own individual perspectives and their own experiences and transfer their learning to new decisions and decision contexts.

MOVING BEYOND THE SITUATED DECISION CONTEXT TO A MODEL OF COMPLEXITY

The curriculum approach proposed here utilizes a carefully managed discussion with very specific learning goals—to help students acquire a mental model of complexity, variability, and unpredictability that they can use to interpret social decisions. This mental model, steeped in variability and complexity is not acquired easily (Falk & Konold, 1997; Konold, 1989). Instructors who do not recognize the complexity run the risk of reducing the length and quality of the instruction and leaving students with only a partial understanding of the topic (Hmelo, Holton, & Kolodner, 2000). It takes some insight on the part of the student, insight that their own way of seeing the world is restrictive and is difficult to progress beyond. It means moving beyond simple characterizations like good and bad decisions or stupid and smart decisions and beyond the situated model acquired during the role-play (Berieter, 2000). It is similar to problem-based learning where instructors have a sense of the complexity of the problem and take students to a meaningful conclusion (Kolodner et al., 2003). However, it requires a rigorous approach to guided learning, beyond discovery and student-centered learning, based first in generative learning and insight.

The first opportunity for insight usually comes when the instructor, after assigning students to participate in a role-play decision simulation, presents the student's decisions to the class as a whole.[1] It requires on the part of the instructor (or researchers) a sense of the kind of transition taking place in the minds of the students (Roth,

---

[1]This is not a simple task. Not all students read graphs easily. Conveying the range of differences between student decisions requires careful consideration of visual displays (Cohen, Smith, Chechile, Burns, & Tsai, 1996).

2001). This exercise changes the idea of a social decision from a single event to a multiple outcomes event. Presenting results to students in a class implicitly introduces to students a sample space of possible decisions. Based on the particular decision simulation used, decisions may be made either by students playing role that they themselves might play in their community (in the case of using a condom (see chapter 6), or judging a jail-house line-up (see chapter 10), or by students playing participants in government (judges, negotiators, etc.). The students' decisions are all rendered during experience with an identical decision context. There can be no strong arguments by the students that differences in decisions are due to subtle but import differences in the decision context. The question becomes how did so many different decisions result from a group of relatively similar students? This exercise is nearly impossible to accomplish by studying real world political decisions. Every political actor is steeped in a unique context.

The goal of the instructor is to help students see the complexity and gradations of variability in the decisions; to see over a set of decisions made by peers how, why, and where they are different, and, in fact, maybe not so different. Having students begin to recognize this complexity is a step in helping them move beyond simple-minded, yes/no, and good/bad characterizations of decisions made by others. It is basically a six degrees of separation lesson: our decisions may not be as different as they appear to be.[2] The goal of the teacher is to disaggregate the decisions (and their meanings) with the help of the students who rendered them.

In some cases the outcome of the simulation makes this lesson relatively simple to teach. A sentencing simulation like *Crime and Punishment* offers the choice of months in prison as a primary outcome (or dependent variable). This outcome is effective for teaching complexity because there is typically a great deal of variability. Students can choose between 10 and 60 months. Natural questions about complexity emerge. Is there really a meaningful difference between 30 and 31 months? Motivations for alternative sentences are easy to identify since there is a true range of different outcomes. In the case of choosing to use a condom, identifying an outcome to begin class discussions on variability might not be so simple. It is certainly possi-

---

[2]Based on the idea that we are all connected by six or fewer stages of circumstance or acquaintance.

ble to begin discussions on the most obvious outcome: whether or not a condom was used. This can be useful but by itself may not capture or introduce complexity. It is a binary outcome. There are only two choices, yes or no. An alternative might be to capture as an outcome how the date ended: Did the student leave early, choose not to have sex, have unprotected sex, etc. A number of categories can be designed to capture and convey complexity. Simulations that offer the option of creating outcome variables for review can make a difference in the lesson offered in the classroom. This is an area where digital decision simulations can offer a real and clear benefit over alternatives; the results are relatively easy to gather and use in class. Simulations which include options to create alternative outcomes take this advantage a step further. Otherwise instructors have to account for this in advance by asking students to define their final decision based on predesignated categories.

The examples of sentencing and condom use offer one opportunity to make the point of about complexity. In both cases the most evident significant outcome of the *Virtual Sex* and *Crime and Punishment* simulations becomes the fulcrum for a lesson. However, a second level of analysis is also useful, one focusing on the steps students went through to render their decision. Almost every decision a student makes is somehow the aggregate of several supporting decisions. Student decisions about using a condom might be seen as the aggregate of choices made along the way: reactions to feedback offered by the simulation, attraction to the actors in the simulations, etc. The same may be said for the other simulations as well. This kind of lesson presents the decisions as a kind of binomial process. At each juncture in the simulation students can choose a direction that makes one kind of outcome more likely than another. The lesson introduces students to the number of dimensions associated with the decisions. This is the level of complexity we hope students will appreciate when examining real world social decisions. It involves recognizing the dimensions of policy decisions before evaluating them.

CONSTRUCTING MENTAL MODELS OF A DECISION PROCESS IN A SOCIAL SETTING

As mentioned in the previous section, the role-play simulations in this book permit students to play two different kinds of roles. In some cases, like project ICONS (see chapter 8), or *Crime and Pun-*

ishment (see chapter 5), students play the role of a decision maker who is part of a political institution. The student may play the role of a judge or negotiator. Students participating in this kind of simulation can learn about the variability associated with decisions by policy makers, members of the judicial branch, and other social institutions. In other simulations, such as *Virtual Sex* (see chapter 6) or the Eye Witness Identification simulation (see chapter 10), they are playing the role of community members, often taking on roles they may some day play, like making decisions about whether to use a condom, or which suspect in a police line-up may be the one who was observed as the perpetrator at the scene of a crime (chapter 10). Each of these role-plays leads to a different but complementary model of social reasoning.

The following model below, depicted in Fig. 3.1, illustrates the kind of mental model we hope a student acquires when the curriculum utilizes a simulation of decision maker that is part of a political institution. The model uses the example of a student playing the role of a sentencing judge. The range of decisions made by students during the role-play (center box) serves as an estimate of the distribution of legitimate decisions for a particular sentencing hearing (or perhaps several sentencing hearings). The students' decisions, when disaggregated and analyzed in class (top), offer a connection to the decision context and individual differences between students (Snow, 1989) that influence the decisions. For instance, students us-

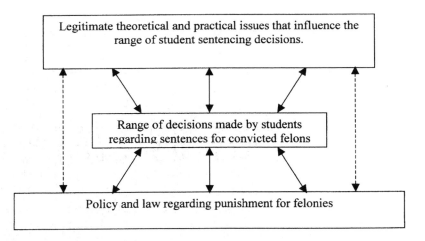

FIG. 3.1. Mental model from playing the role of a judge as decision maker.

ing *Crime and Punishment* have access to sentencing guidelines. They are a part of the simulated decision context and may be a factor in some of the decisions. Some students may take these guidelines more seriously than others. A discussion about the high and low sentences, as well as central tendencies, can anchor the role of sentencing guidelines in the student's memories of their role-play. Guidelines would be a (theoretical) factor influencing the distribution of student decisions.

Finally, the box on the bottom indicates the instructors appeal to the law and policy that governs real world sentencing decisions. The dashed arrows on the outside suggest an emerging mapping between the variability of decisions made by peers (top) and the law–policy that mandates real world sentencing decisions (bottom). The model shows development of capacity to implicitly consider social decisions without severing the connection to the simulation.

Figure 3.2 shows the development of a similar mental model for curricula requiring students to role-play a witness trying to identify a suspect in a police line-up. The simulation conveys the decision contexts. The simulation itself might be experimentally manipulated to illustrate factors that influence decisions (see chapter 10). The set of outcomes produced by students is an estimate of a legitimate set of possible outcomes from eyewitnesses (center box). The distribution of outcomes puts teachers in a position to disaggregate the results. Factors that influence the decision might include the properties of

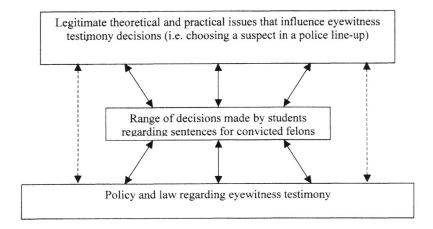

FIG. 3.2. Mental model acquired form from role playing a constituent.

the decision context, differences in how guidelines are interpreted, individual differences in students' backgrounds, etc. A careful explication of these factors should help students see the complexity and unpredictability of what at face value might be interpreted as a simple yes or no decision. Finally the bottom box shows the connection to the theoretical and abstract policies and guidelines that govern eyewitness testimony. The dashed arrows on either side of the model suggest the development of a relatively nonsituated mental model. Both models are similar in structure in that they depict a set of relationships between the decisions rendered by students in a simulated environment and a broader set of nonsituated issues.

One final point is in order. The use of two different examples is for more than just illustrative purposes. It is to suggest that the complexity acquired by students playing the role of a sentencing judge might be different than those playing a role where they are required to offer eyewitness testimony. In the former case, students are playing roles they are not likely to play in their lives. The decision contexts are truly foreign to them. Their perceptions of those roles, and the ideas they bring to the simulation and the class, may be very different than the ideas they bring to a role they may play some day as a member of a community or during a romantic interlude. For now it is an open question whether the mental models acquired while plating different roles might function in different ways.

EXPECTED DEVELOPMENTS

The working hypothesis regarding the benefit of a digital decision-based curriculum is in its infancy. The previous models are simple. Over time more sophisticated models will be used that capture changes in thinking brought about by role-play based curricula. The simulations found in the subsequent chapters of this volume offer encouraging support for the learning model suggested here. Several show learning benefits within the decision context itself, and others suggest the development of the kinds of nonsituated learning predicted.

Still, the theories underlying the use of digital decision simulations are young, and they raise many more questions than they answer. The simulations here can be used in a number of social science courses. How many role-play simulations and classroom discussions will it take before students acquire the skill to dissect decisions and accommodate complexity? Research has shown that the number of times students work through a simulation influences the learning outcomes (Megarry, 1979), and that an effort to carefully integrate several decision simulation across a curriculum could lead to a more robust learning result (Clark & Linn, 2003). Each simulation described here is not likely to be used more than once by a student, so the benefit of repetition will need to come from a coordinated curriculum. This is a project we hope to see develop, along with an assessment of learning over time.

How would learning from a curriculum that utilized these simulations be assessed? The mental models students are expected to develop may be subtly expressed. Asking students direct questions about the details of the simulations would not likely help to ascertain whether their implicit interpretations or understandings of social decisions have changed (Brown, Campione, Webber, & McGilly, 1992; Clark & Linn, 2003; Pelligrino, 1988). Evidence from assessments of students' conceptualization of physical systems suggests that those who acquire a deep conceptual understanding of physical systems from computer animations or simulations tend to recall fewer concrete details about the simulation. Consequently, asking students about the details they recall may not offer a measure of their cognitive development. The same may be true here. Blascovich (see chapter 10) describes the use of nonintrusive measures, and this likely is the best way to proceed. These measures gauge students' reactions in ways that do not utilize a planned, thought-out response. Instead they require a candid reaction to a decision in a nontesting situation.

The curricular model described in this chapter does make some demands on the design of digital decision simulations. Perhaps the most important demand is on the character of the decision made. If instructors are essentially required to disaggregate and look at the various components of the decisions rendered by their students, students have to be asked to make fairly complex decisions. For example, in the *Crime and Punishment* simulation, students do not render a simple binary decision (jail or no jail), but the number of months, a continuous variable with variability well suited to a lesson on complexity. Other dimensions of the decision include whether the defendant should also be subject to supervised probation, and if so, for how long, whether fines, restitution, or both should be ordered, and whether some sort of alcohol abuse, drug abuse, or domestic abuse counseling should be included as part of the sentence. Even binary decisions, like whether to use a condom, can be made complex by considering the stage of the simulation at which a decision is made, the pathway through role-play, etc. Without these factors it will be difficult to have students see the complexity and six degrees of separation that connects seemingly different decisions.

Finally, why use decisions as a center of gravity for a social sciences curriculum? Students in the social sciences are implicitly taught that objectively observing decisions of others is the way to learn. The assumption invites didactic approaches to teaching. There is some merit in abiding by this assumption, but only after students have acquired the ability to see the trees through the forest. The complexity of social decisions is difficult to convey through objective analysis of a decision from the outside looking in (see chapter 1). Decisions are suitable both for situated role-play simulations and, when made in parallel by a class full of students, analytic techniques typically used for examining samples and making inferences to larger populations. In this approach to teaching, decisions ultimately become (complex random) variables; each decision is only of many possible outcomes. This framework offers students a way to implicitly understand any decision as one of many, including their own.

REFERENCES

Bereiter, C. (1995). A dispositional view of transfer. In A. McKeogh, J. Lupart, & A. Marini (Eds.), *Teaching for transfer: Fostering generalization in learning* (pp. 21–34). Hillsdale, NJ: Lawrence Erlbaum Associates.

Bereiter, C. (2000). Situated cognition and how to overcome it. In D. Kirshner & J. A. Whitson (Eds.), *Situated cognition: Social, semiotic, and psychological perspectives* (pp. 281–300). Hillsdale, NJ: Lawrence Erlbaum Associates.

Bers, M. (2001). Identity Construction Environments: Developing personal and moral values through the design of a virtual city. *Journal of the Learning Sciences, 10*(4), 365–415.

Bransford, J., Sherwood, R., Hasselbring, T., Kinzer, C., & Williams, S. (1990). Anchored instruction: Why we need it and how technology can help. In D. Nix & R. Spiro (Eds.), *Cognition, education, and multimedia: Exploring ideas in high technology* (pp. 163–205). Hillsdale, NJ: Lawrence Erlbaum Associates.

Brown, A. L., Campione, J. C., Webber, L. S., & McGilly, K. (1992). Interactive learning environments: A new look at assessment and instruction. In B. R. Gifford & M. C.

O'Conner (Eds.), *Changing assessments: Alternative views of aptitude, treatment and instruction* (pp. 121–211). Norwell, MA: Kluwer.

Brown, J. S., Collins, A., & Duguid, P. (1989). Situated cognition and the culture of learning. *Educational Researcher, 18*(1), 32–41.

Brown, J. S., & Duguid, P. (2002). *The social life of information.* Cambridge, MA: Harvard University Press.

Campione, J., & Brown, A. (1990). Guided learning and transfer: Implications for approaches to assessment. In N. Fredericksen, R. Glaser, A. Lesgold, & M. Shafto (Eds.), *Diagnostic monitoring of skill and knowledge acquisition* (pp. 141–172). Hillsdale, NJ: Lawrence Erlbaum Associates.

Clancey, W. J. (1994). *Situated cognition: How representations are created and given meaning.* In R. Lewis & P. Mendelsohn (Eds.), *Lessons from learning* (pp. 231–242). Amsterdam: North Holland.

Clark, D., & Linn, M. C. (2003). Designing for knowledge integration: The impact of instructional time. *Journal of the Learning Sciences, 12*(4), 451–493.

Cognition and Technology Group at Vanderbilt. (1990). Anchored instruction and its relationship to situated cognition. *Educational Researcher, 19*(6), 2–10.

Falk, R., & Konold, C. (1997). Making sense of randomness: Implicit encoding as a basis for judgment. *Psychological Review, 104*, 301–318.

Gentner, D., & Stevens, A. L. (Eds.). (1983). *Mental models.* Hillsdale, NJ: Lawrence Erlbaum Associates.

Goldman, S. R. (1993a). The Jasper series: Theoretical foundations and data on problem solving and transfer. In L. A. Penner, G. M. Batsche, H. M. Knoff, & D. L. Nelson (Eds.), *The challenges in mathematics and science education: Psychology's response* (pp. 113–152). Washington, DC: American Psychological Association.

Goldman, S. R. (1993b). Anchored instruction and situated cognition revisited. *Educational Technology, 33*(3), 52–70.

Hammer, D., & Schifter, D. (2001). Practices of inquiry in teaching and research. *Cognition and Instruction, 19*(4), 441–478.

Hay, K. E., & Barab, S. A. (2001). Constructivism in practice: A comparison and contrast of apprenticeship and constructionist learning environments. *Journal of the Learning Sciences, 10*(3), 281–322.

Hmelo, C. E., Holton, D. L., & Kolodner, J. L. (2000). Designing to learn about complex systems. *Journal of the Learning Sciences, 9*, 247–298.

Kolodner, J. L., Camp, P. J., Crismond, D., Fasse, B., Gray, J., Holbrook, J., Puntambekar, S., & Ryan, M. (2003). Problem-based learning meets case-based reasoning in the middle school science classroom: Putting learning by design into practice. *Journal of the Learning Sciences, 12*(4), 495–548.

Konold, C. (1989). Informal conceptions of probability. *Cognition and Instruction, 6*(1), 59–98.

Lave, J., & Wenger, E. (1990). *Situated learning: Legitimate peripheral participation.* Cambridge, UK: Cambridge University Press.

Megarry, J. (1979). Monitoring. *Simulation/Games for Learning, 9*, 170–177.

Nuthall, G. (2000). The role of memory in the acquisition of and retention of knowledge in science and social studies. *Cognition and Instruction, 18*(1), 83–139.

Pelligrino, J. (1988). Mental models and mental tests. In H. Wainer & H. I. Braun (Eds.), *Test validity*. Hillsdale, NJ: Lawrence Erlbaum Associates.

Resnick, M., & Wilensky, U. (1998). Diving into complexity: Developing probabilistic decentralized thinking through role play environments. *Journal of the Learning Sciences, 7*(2), 153–172.

Roth, W.-M. (2001). Situating cognition. *Journal of the Learning Sciences, 10*(1&2), 27–61.

Schommer-Aikins, M. (2002). An evolving theoretical framework for an epistemological belief system. In B. Hofer & P. Pintrich (Eds.), *Personal epistemology: The psychology of belief about knowledge and knowing* (pp. 103–118). Hillsdale, NJ: Lawrence Erlbaum Associates.

Schommer, M., & Walker, K. (1995). Are epistemological beliefs similar across domains? *Journal of Educational Psychology, 87*(3), 424–432.

Shute, V. J., & Glaser, R. (1990). A large scale evaluation of an intelligent discovery world. *Interactive Learning Environments, 1*, 51–77.

Shute, V. J., & Regian, W. (1993). Principles for evaluating intelligent tutoring systems. *Journal of Artificial Intelligence and Education, 4*(2), 245–271.

Snow, R. E. (1989). Aptitude-treatment interaction as a framework for research on individual differences in learning. In P. L. Ackerman, R. J. Sternberg, & R. Glaser (Eds.), *Learning and individual differences: Advances in theory and research* (pp. 13–59). New York: Freeman.

Tripp, S. D. (1993). Theories, traditions and situated learning. *Educational Technology, 33*(3), 71–77.

Vygotsky, L. S. (1978). *Mind in society*. Cambridge, MA: Harvard University Press.

II

SIMULATIONS IN USE
AND IN PROGRESS

4

PsychExperiments: A Web-Based Resource for Enhancing Science Training Through Simulation

Kenneth O. McGraw
University of Mississippi

John E. Williams
University of Northern Iowa

Despite being the most technologically advanced nation in the world, the United States fights a continual problem in educating the broad spectrum of students about science. There is rampant confusion over basic distinctions between science and pseudoscience, so much so that surveys find that the average person believes Intelligent Design to be a theory with the same standing as evolutionary theory (Rennie, 2002). Even though the adjective scientific is very widely used in our culture, an NSF survey found that nearly 70% of Americans (NSF, 2002) could not adequately explain what it means to study something scientifically. This general lack of scientific literacy can be fought in the classroom, but it is fought best in the laboratory where students are given the opportunity to simulate the activities of research scientists by posing a question, collecting data, analyzing the data, and then forming an answer to the original question using the data and their analysis as empirical support.

Our contribution to this volume, therefore, begins with two assumptions. The first concerns the initial knowledge state of students and the second concerns the learning strategy best designed to move students from their initial state to the goal state. The initial knowledge assumption is that students begin their studies with little appreciation for how science differs from nonscience. In particular, they lack the capacity to discriminate scientific, empirically based claims from nonscientific, rationalistic, and commonsense claims. The learning strategy assumption is that the best way to teach students about science as an epistemological enterprise is to offer them opportunities to play the role of scientist by participating in the formation of empirical questions, the design of investigations that seek to answer the questions, the analysis of data from the investigations, and the reporting of results in ways that stop short of any unwarranted inference. The goal of our project, therefore, has been to extend opportunities for undergraduates to play the role of research scientists, but in our particular case, this has been limited to the roles of cognitive, social, and behavioral scientists.

The technology dependent project we have been involved in since 1997 is *PsychExperiments* (http://psychexps.olemiss.edu), an online psychology laboratory that offers interactive experiments, data collection, and data analysis. Like any laboratory, the site is an instructional resource. The site does not offer instructions or lessons, just tools. That is, instructors can use it in their classes to add a laboratory component to their instruction, but it is not built as a stand-alone with tutorials.

The experiments at the site are of two types: research experiments and laboratory experiments. Research experiments are ones posted by individuals, including undergraduate students, who want to collect their own data using a project of their own design. Undergraduates who have used our site in this way were typically collecting data for a class or thesis project. We have assisted students in developing their projects in the form of experiments or surveys and then we have posted them at our site where they benefit from a secure, reliable server, a preconfigured database, and preexisting generic scripts for writing and retrieving data from the database. Laboratory experiments are experiments that have been designed by us and other faculty to address questions that are of special interest in undergraduate psychology instruction. Table 4.1 gives a list of the laboratory experiments available Fall 2003 along with a brief description.

WHAT'S NEW AND WHAT'S NOT

Before providing a more extensive description of *PsychExperiments*, it is important to note that although the site is functionally and technologically novel, what it offers faculty and students is in many

TABLE 4.1
Laboratory Experiments at *PsychExperiments, Fall 2003*

Experiment	Description	Developer
Be a juror	A study of susceptibility to eyewitness testimony	Mark Mitchell, Clarion University
Covert attention	A study of the effects of attentional priming on response time	Ric Topolski, Augusta State University
Dichotic listening	A study of hemispheric specialization that measures whether sounds heard in the right or left ear are identified most accurately	PsychExperiments team
Facial recognition	A study of false memory that has implications for the validity of eye witness testimony	PsychExperiments team
Implicit association test	Measures the subtle effects of racial stereotypes on speed of categorization	PsychExperiments team
Infant communication	Measures individual differences in the ability to classify infant cries into pain, hunger, and pleasure categories	Martha Arterberry, Gettysburg College
Learning and memory	A study of a learning paradigm known as transverse patterning	Debra Titone, McClean Hospital & Harvard Medical School
Lexical decision	A study of the spreading activation theory of memory	Dawn Blasko, Penn State Erie
Line motion	A study to determine the time and speed parameters that determine when line motion will be misperceived as proceeding from an attentional focus rather from the actual origin	PsychExperiments team
Maze	Trial and error learning experiment	Shawna Regan, Univ. of Alaska
Mental rotation	Measures the effect of angle of rotation and type of decision on the speed of the decision	PsychExperiments team
Mirror drawing	A motor learning task in which the effects of cursor movements are reversed to simulate the task of copying a figure while observing one's hand in a mirror	Zhe Chen, Univ. of Mississippi
Mueller-Lyer	The effects of fin angle on the magnitude of a simple line illusion	PsychExperiments team
Numerical memory	Compares auditory and visual memory on a digit-span task	Will Sharp, Univ. of Mississippi
Object location memory	Compares males and females in their ability to recall the location of objects	Kathy Flannery, St. Anselm College
Perception of gender	Determines participants' ability to use facial information to discriminate males from females	Bill Wilson, Gettysburg College

(Continued)

TABLE 4.1

(Continued)

Experiment	Description	Developer
Phonemic transformation	Shows that pure vowel sounds are perceived to have verbal forms that are stable over time	Magdalene Chalikia, Moorhead State University
Pitch memory	Measures the accuracy of auditory memory of tones differing in pitch	*PsychExperiments team*
Poggendorff illusion	A study of the effects of line separation and length of line segments on the misperception of collinearity	*PsychExperiments team*
Ponzo illusion	Measures the magnitude of the Ponzo line illusions	*PsychExperiments team*
Reaction time visual	Measures reaction time to a visual stimulus	*PsychExperiments team*
Reaction time auditory	Measures reaction time to an auditory stimulus	*PsychExperiments team*
Self-reference	Compares memory for words that are evaluated using questions that elicit semantic or orthographic analysis	Gary Levine, Edinboro University
Social balance	Permits the test of a strong theory of social balance theory, one that makes quantitative predictions about the degree of liking between two people in a triadic relationship where the degree of liking in two of the three dyads are specified	Michael Birnbaum, Cal. State, Fullerton
Lateralized stroop experiment	Measures response time on a task that requires identifying the font color used in displays of color words (blue, red, green, yellow)	*PsychExperiments team*
Word recognition	Measures the ability to recognize words presented briefly in the right and left visual fields	*PsychExperiments team*

senses conventional. Long before *PsychExperiments*, psychology faculty provided students with resources for doing research. Laboratory courses, for example, are a near universal requirement for a psychology major. In these courses, students routinely complete one or more empirical investigations and report their results in a style acceptable for scientific communications. In addition to required laboratory courses, there are often opportunities for semester-long research in the form of capstone courses and undergraduate thesis programs. These research opportunities are often facilitated by prebuilt software that presents stimulus materials on a computer screen and then records users' responses. Students can select one of these tools and adapt it to the needs of their specific project. In one sense, therefore, *PsychExperiments* offers via the Web what was already offered locally. It offers prebuilt software and a means of recording responses made to the stimuli the software presents. The most direct analog to *PsychExperiments* from conventional technology are the experiment packages that were sold for laboratory use by commercial vendors such as CONDUIT in the early 1980s. Current products include Psychology Software Tools (http://www.pstnet.com) package for PCs called MEL and Cedrus Corporation's (http://www.cedrus.com) cross-platform product known as SuperLab LT. These packages offer stock programs that provide similar research opportunities to the experiments listed in Table 4.1.

What, then, is new in *PsychExperiments* that makes research simulation more prevalent in the psychology curriculum than before? To begin answering the question requires identifying the holes in the traditional means for offering research opportunities to students. One is that local resources and time demands have restricted the opportunities actually offered undergraduates. That is, even when faculty believe passionately in the important role that would be played by having students perform scientific research, they are not able to offer the experience, or do so to a lesser degree than they would like, because they are blocked by inadequate resources, time, or both.

The Local Resource Constraint

Inadequate resources in the form of equipment and space characterize smaller, less well-funded schools. Such schools may have a class of 15–20 students prepare all semester for a single semester-ending project on which all the students participate using equipment of their own manufacture. Another model is for students to work in small teams on a question of their choosing or, in some cases, to work alone on a unique question. Laboratory package software might not be used because of the expense, which typically runs about $35 per student.

The Time Constraint

In addition to the limitations on equipment and space that prevent poorly funded schools from offering more extensive opportunities for their students to play the role of behavioral scientist, all schools experience the time constraint. The length of a semester or a quarter is the same at all schools, no matter their size or financial status. Laboratory courses, independent research classes, capstone classes, or other classes (e.g., honor's thesis) all must fit within the 10-week to 15-week limit set by academic terms. This time constraint seriously limits the questions that can be addressed meaningfully with data, particularly in behavioral science where data are collected in series from a number of research participants, each of whom must be scheduled to participate during hours the laboratory is open. When one adds to data collection the time required to prepare the apparatus or other materials to be used in the research, many research endeavors are simply not feasible. The small data sets that result when there is inadequate time is compounded at small schools where there are relatively few participants available for use in the research.

In light of these problems with the conventional approaches to providing opportunities for students to play the role of scientist, the value of *PsychExperiments* begins to emerge. Even small, underfunded schools have Internet-connected computers students can use. These can be anywhere and certainly do not have to be in a classroom. This means that offering a laboratory course or research experience is feasible without local resources, so long as one is willing to restrict the research questions to those that can be addressed with current Web technology. This means research is limited to questions that can be addressed using human subjects through the delivery of multimedia stimulus materials to elicit user interactions measurable via a mouse or keypress. Familiar applications are having users make ratings, enter text responses, or move objects and, then, having the software record the speed or accuracy of these activities.

The time problem that confronts all undergraduate researchers is not eliminated by *PsychExperiments*, but it is greatly reduced. Traditional investigations require making measurements one subject at a time. This can be tedious work and it seldom adds anything substantial to the learning experience. Web-based experiments can be run on computers in parallel. Because data can be collected in parallel without the physical oversight of an experimenter, the data collection phase of an experiment can take just a day or two, depending on the recruitment method for participants. A number of the classes that use *PsychExperiments* are held in computer laboratories. Here, all the students in a class can participate in an experiment simultaneously, submit, and then download their data. This means that it is easy to have students participate in an experiment, then view and discuss their results as an in-class exercise.

The Small Research Pool Constraint

The speedy data collection that characterizes Web-based experiments makes it possible to achieve datasets quickly, but when the available subject pool is small, the dataset will be too, despite the speedy collection. This observation points to a major advantage of Web technology for research over conventional lab-based research—the subject pool is vast. One may argue over whether it is representative and how to achieve representative samples via the Web (O'Neil & Penrod, 2001; Reips, 2000), but there is no denying the size of the subject pool. In that access to Internet computers will only grow, one could say the subject pool is infinite. Unlike the relatively homogeneous subject pools on campuses, it is multilingual, multicultural, multiaged, and pluralistic in every other way one can imagine. It even includes the special populations that are frequently of interest to psychologists. A University of Mississippi undergraduate was able to complete an honor's research project concerning the cognitive performance of Prader-Willi clients in a local retardation facility by having them participate via the Web in the Stroop experiment at *PsychExperiments*. Mike Marcell at the College of Charleston has published a paper on individuals with Down's syndrome using the same approach. Since individuals from these special populations are often not concentrated in one geographical location, the Web offers an ideal method for reaching them.

Although the potential subject pool for any Web-based experiment is infinite, practical considerations of recruitment greatly restrict the number of people who will actually initiate and then complete a data session at a Web site. So the actual pool and potential pool are different. The actual pool consists just of those who visit the Web site and learn of the opportunity to participate or those who are recruited through traditional means by the researcher. At *PsychExperiments*, the actual pool consists primarily of the students currently taking psychology classes from instructors who have signed up to use the site. These instructors can be contacted via a listserv to which they are automatically added when they enroll at the site. In this way, a student at Mississippi College in tiny Clinton, Mississippi, was able to get 138 volunteers for a research project just 2 weeks before she presented the results at a regional psychology convention.

In addition to having a large pool of subjects potentially available for any new project, the cumulative database at *PsychExperiments* offers access to the data of everyone who has ever participated in one of the experiments. For some of the more popular experiments, the database holds in excess of 5,000 entries (see Table 4.2). These will only grow. Datasets of this size offer totally novel research opportu-

TABLE 4.2
Number of Experiment Sessions by Experiment and Academic Year

	Academic Year					
Experiments	1999 2000	2000 2001	2001 2002	2002 2003	2003 2004	Totals
Be a juror				539	689	1228
Covert attention	96	500	779	702	835	2912
Dichotic listening	7	238	214	222	269	950
Facial recognition	299	226	165	399	414	1503
IAT race				1155	425	1580
Infant communication				183	94	277
Lateralized stroop	463	1021	742	2026	940	5192
Learning and memory		260	367	729	267	1623
Lexical decision	1	206	660	1021	463	2351
Line motion	322	491	276	328	97	1514
Maze	2	322	306	546	415	1591
Mental rotation	1013	1231	1265	1722	1206	6437
Mirror drawing		41	544	1681	915	3181
Mueller Lyer	427	467	330	680	862	2766
Numerical memory		110	340	260	145	855
Object location memory	119	310	196	172	7	804
Perception of gender	15	1566	2035	1866	1145	6627
Phonemic transformation			78	132	118	328
Pitch memory	55	80	188	379	313	1015
Poggendorff	334	400	618	499	1160	3011
Ponzo	66	319	553	608	1272	2818
Reaction time color	478	939	1072	868	924	4281
Reaction time sound	182	153	96	146	135	712
Self-reference	568	1395	2330	1211	756	6260
Social balance				187	108	295
Word recognition	511	644	657	370	1128	3310
	4958	10919	13811	18631	21819	**70138**

nities. Among them are the possibilities of investigating phenomena that have small but reliable effects, effects that are represented in between subject differences (e.g., gender, cultural, or experiential effects), and effects that are found in multiway interactions of variables. Another novel opportunity is the chance to work with datasets large enough to permit more complex statistical analysis than small datasets.

In conclusion to the question of what's new and what's not, *PsychExperiments* in part is just old wine in a new bottle. On the laboratory side, there are a number of experiments that can be conducted using prebuilt software that interfaces with a database from which students can extract data. This much is old in that students at many campuses have had laboratory experiment packages to use since the early 1980s. Using these packages did depend on students or departments being able and willing to buy the software, and it depended too on having sufficient local resources to buy and house computers for students to use. These requirements excluded students at many small campuses. Nonetheless, if *PsychExperiments'* only innovation were Web-delivery of free software, it would not be offering substantially new opportunities for students to have the experiences that best enable them to discover the distinction between science and nonscience. The real innovations, therefore, come in the speed of data collection, which helps overcome the time constraint on undergraduate research projects, and in the size of datasets, which overcomes the problem of inadequate subject pools.

A DESCRIPTION OF *PSYCHEXPERIMENTS*

PsychExperiments is software, hardware, and people. The software core consists of the laboratory and research experiments programmed in Authorware, the SQL-Server database that stores the data, the ActiveServerPage scripts that write and retrieve data, and a visual basic for applications (VBA) macro that renders data to an Excel workbook and provides some data analysis. The hardware core is a secure, reliable server with hot swappable drives and power backup. The people are the developers and the users, who include all the faculty and students who have contributed both experiments and data to *PsychExperiments*.

The Experiment Software

Conducting experiments via the Web requires having software that can be executed in different browsers. Free software that meets this requirement includes HTML, Java, JavaScript, and VB Script. Commercial options include Macromedia's Authorware, Flash, and Director. Authorware was chosen for use at *PsychExperiments* because it was powerful enough to support the programming requirements of experiments (e.g., obtaining user input via mouse and keyboard entries, animation, video and audio stimulus presentations, user control of screen objects, and excellent event timing), easy enough to learn that developers did not have to be full-time programmers, and affordable because of generous academic pricing ($300–$350 depending on vendor).

Authorware's ease of learning derives largely from the graphical user interface, which is a set of icons representing different functions that can be placed on a flowline in the order in which they are to be executed. This interface provides a picture of what happens in an experiment. Figure 4.1, Panel A, is a screen shot of the icons that are used to create a tachistoscopic display—a brief stimulus display. The picture is quite literal in that it consists of a display icon that contains the image to be placed on the computer screen, a wait icon programmable in milliseconds that specifies how long the image is to be retained on the screen, and then an erase icon that removes the image from the screen. In order to keep the icons that make up an experiment in readable form, they can be grouped in holders called map icons. Map icons are used to hold the pieces that make up an experiment. The three icons that provide the tachistoscopic presentation, for example, can be grouped into one map called tachistoscope. Figure 4.1, Panel B, shows how maps are used to provide a visual display in a complete experiment. Our experience in using and teaching Authorware gives evidence that experiments that might take days to create using code that is written line by line according to strict syntactical rules can take just hours in Authorware, primarily because of the intuitive graphical interface.

The SQL-Server Database

Options for storing the results from experiments are myriad. The simplest is to write data directly to a textfile to which each new participant appends data. For more flexibility, a database is needed.

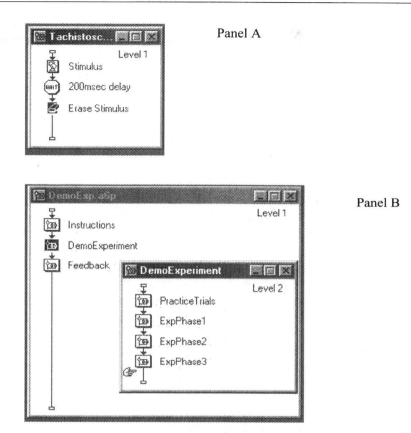

Panel A

Panel B

FIG. 4.1. The graphical user interface in Authorware provides a visual representation of the components of an experiment. In Panel A, the program used to produce a tachistoscopic display is represented by an icon for the display (the stimulus), an icon for the time the display is to remain on the screen (200 msec), and an icon that erases the display when the 200 msec delay is up. Icons are executed top to bottom along the flowline. Panel B shows the graphical display representing a complete experiment. The icons in this display are all map icons, which are used to hold the many components of an experiment. Using "map" icons, one can organize functional icon groups like "Tachistoscope" into meaningful parts of the experiment and then label these parts appropriately.

They range from low-end, easy-to-use databases like Access to high-end applications like Oracle or MS-SQL-Server. In keeping with the development principle of adopting tools that would not require including IT specialists on the development team, we began with Access but moved up to SQL-Server, because it supports simultaneous database users and is capable of storing large amounts of data. Access has a practical limit of 25 simultaneous users and begins to respond slowly to input and output requests when the data tables become exceedingly large. Although SQL-Server is a high-end application, it is relatively easy to migrate from Access to SQL-Server. The SQL-Server database has been in place since Spring of 2001 and has performed admirably.

The ASP Scripts

Writing data to databases on a server from a client computer requires a program or script that reads the data and places it into the predefined fields of the database. CGI scripts written in Perl are commonly used to perform this task in many database applications. However, in keeping with our desire to avoid solutions that would require additional training, we decided to use VB Script as the programming language for our database application. VB Script is not very different from VBA, which we were already using to create Excel macros, and it can be used to create Active Server Pages that run on Windows 2000 servers to provide server-side programming. To perform the initial task of taking data from Authorware experiments and placing it in appropriate tables in the database, we developed one generic ASP script. It serves as the intermediary between the Authorware experiment and the SQL-Server database. When an experiment participant chooses to submit data from an experiment, the data is transmitted to the ASP script, which verifies the integrity of the data, formats it, opens a database connection, and places the data in the database. The ASP script serves an important purpose in screening the data it receives for proper formatting and preventing the inclusion of rogue SQL commands inserted by possible hackers looking for security weaknesses.

The VBA Macro

When data are downloaded from the *PsychExperiments* server, a second generic ASP script writes them to a comma-delimited text file. Information needed to interpret the entries in the text file appear in html pages for each experiment. The pages are available via the instructor's only link on the *PsychExperiments* home page.

The comma-delimited files begin with four preliminary lines that are needed by the VBA macro, then the data follow. To perform analyses of the data, users can open the raw data that begin in Line 5 using the analysis tool of their choice, which might be a spreadsheet or a statistics program such as Systat or SPSS, or they can first use the downloadable VBA macro that is a program that reads the entries in the textfile, writes them to pages of an Excel workbook using one page per research subject, performs some descriptive analysis of the data for each subject (e.g., means and standard deviations for each value of variables that were manipulated within subjects), and then creates an overall summary page with summary data for each subject including any subject information that was gathered by the experiment (e.g., gender, age, academic major, race, etc.), descriptive statistics for each cell in the primary design (which can include between as well as within subject variables), and a line or bar graph portraying means and their standard errors for the primary research design. This analysis is not exhaustive because it breaks the data down according to a prespecified design (given in Lines 3 and 4 of the textfile). Yet it provides a quick way to begin more complex analyses.

In that data editing is important whenever there are outliers among the data values, the Excel spreadsheet produced by the VBA macro is editable. For example, if a subject's data contain aberrant values, the values can be deleted or changed following whatever conventions have been adopted for data editing. Once changed, the subject summary statistics are updated both on the subject page and on the summary page of the workbook.

Hardware

Delivering experiments via the Web requires a computer set up as a server, which requires special software. However, the software is easy to use and install. The hard part is attaining reliability and security for the server once it is set up. Until 2001, the *PsychExperiments* server was a standard desktop running NT and NT Server. In 2001, we were awarded equipment money from NSF with matching funds from the University of Mississippi to acquire a high-end server and house it along with other campus servers in the IT Computing Center. This facility has excellent physical security, power backup, and cooling. The computer has hot swappable components and automatic data backup to a separately housed tape backup system. As more and more instructors and students have come to rely on our site to deliver experiments on demand to multiple simultaneous users, the hardware support we now enjoy has been essential. Although, Web sites such as *PsychExperiments* could be run from much cheaper machines and in less secure settings, the current setup will allow *PsychExperiments* to grow without substantial hardware updates for the foreseeable future.

Data security and integrity are a vital concern when hosting experiments and collecting data from a Web site. *PsychExperiments* addresses these concerns by a combination of software and hardware tactics. For example, the antivirus software is kept current; VB scripts are used to analyze incoming data for inclusion of rogue SQL commands; routine database backups and logging and investigation of anomalous access attempts are performed. As mentioned, the hardware components provide redundant power backup and there is a fail-safe in the advent of hard drive failure. In addition, physical access to the server is restricted to only a few authorized administrators and kept behind multiple security checkpoints.

People

PsychExperiments was launched by the authors, who are psychologists, and electrical engineer Mark Tew, but from the start the development plan was for a communal site, a collaboratory—to use the term coined by NSF. The initial site funding, which was from FIPSE, allowed us to conduct on-campus workshops for 60 faculty to train them in the use of Authorware for developing experiments. Half of them were able to complete projects based on this training and have contributed experiments to the site. Admittedly though, a 3-day workshop by itself can only be an introduction to skills that are quickly lost with lack of use. For this reason, we have developed interactive training materials (McGraw & Tew, 2003) on CD-ROM that can be used in lieu of workshops or as a supplement to them. Our hope is that these materials will allow more students and faculty to contribute projects to the site. After all, the use of prebuilt software is very constraining on research questions. The question must be adapted to the tool. Yet when one is able to design one's own tool, there is no constraint.

While it may sound somewhat unrealistic to think that students and faculty engaged heavily in their disciplines can actually take the time to develop programming skills needed to develop novel programs, we have found that many novel programs can be built quickly and easily from parts of existing programs. This has proved to be another nice feature of Authorware. For this reason, we give free access to the Authorware code for experiments at *PsychExperiments*. We encourage others to take the code, modify it meet their needs, and then resubmit the modification for use. Illustrating the usefulness of this approach, Martha Arterberry of Gettysburg College was able to quickly assemble a very popular experiment on gender perception using existing code for a choice reaction time study, and Mitchell Metzger from Penn State-Sonoma put together a novel research experiment on face recognition using our study of false memory (Facial recognition in Table 4.1) as a template.

ASSESSMENT: HAS *PSYCHEXPERIMENTS* MADE A DIFFERENCE IN STUDENT LEARNING?

We must begin with the acknowledgment that the data are not in on student learning. We can point to usage figures, satisfaction ratings, narrative comments, and other feedback we have received but the acid test has not been conducted. We do not know whether *Psych-Experiments* has actually allowed students to ask questions they could not otherwise have asked using conventional technology and tools. We do not know if they have engaged in more simulation than they otherwise would have. We do not know if the simulations using *PsychExperiments* have been more beneficial than others they might have experienced. The data we do have come from a survey of 919 students who have used the site in their classes. The survey was conducted by soliciting evaluations using a splash screen that appeared at the end of each experimental session during November 2002 and April 2003.

Summary data from the survey of 919 students appears in Table 4.3, which gives the number of respondents making the choices "strongly agree," "agree," "neutral," "disagree," and "strongly disagree" in answer to six questions and the number answering yes and no to three others. The table also reports the percent who chose either strongly agree or agree on the first six items and the percent answering yes on the remaining three.

TABLE 4.3
Survey of Undergraduate Students Who Have Used *PsychExperiments*

	Strongly agree	Agree	Neutral	Disagree	Strongly disagree		Percent agree or SA
My educational experience this semester has been enhanced by use of resources provided by *PsychExperiments*.	121	361	362	41	34	919	52.45%
My understanding of course material has been enhanced by use of resources provided by *PsychExperiments*.	103	369	353	65	29	919	51.36%
My interest in course material has been enhanced by use of resources provided by *PsychExperiments*.	144	420	290	44	21	919	61.37%
The experiments I participated in were well designed.	286	482	116	19	16	919	83.57%
PsychExperiments gave me the opportunity to participate in more experiments than would otherwise have been available to me at this institution.	308	384	187	24	15	918	75.38%
I found using *PsychExperiments* to be more convenient than other options for participating in experiments.	378	313	189	23	15	918	75.27%
	Yes	No					Percent yes
Did you download data from *PsychExperiments*?	404	515				919	43.96%
Did you use the Excel macro from the site to analyze data?	267	650				917	29.12%
Did you have any frustrations or unusual difficulties in using *PsychExperiments* this semester?	100	817				917	10.91%

The first three questions asked whether using *PsychExperiments* had enhanced the student's educational experience, understanding, or interest in course materials. A little over half the students reported enhanced education experience and understanding and 61% reported enhanced interest. An item that gets closer to the mission of *PsychExperiments* was "*PsychExperiments* gave me the opportunity to participate in more experiments than would otherwise have been available to me at this institution." A third reported strong agreement with this item and an additional 42% agreed. Three-fourths of the students, therefore, reported that *PsychExperiments* was a resource that increased their opportunity to participate in scientific experiments beyond whatever opportunities existed locally. Participation in an experiment is not the same as playing the role of experimenter, however, so we need to follow up this question with one that addresses what students did with the data. The question "Did you download data?", which was endorsed by 44% of the respondents begins to get at this but is somewhat ambiguous because in some cases the classroom instructor performs the download and then passes the data on to students for analysis. The same problem exists with the item about the Excel macro, because instructors could have used the macro and then passed the results to students. The survey conducted during the next academic year will be adjusted to correct for these problems. In addition, we will add items to measure more directly the extent to which students use the site to fully simulate the role of a scientist—that is, to ask a question, gather data that address the question, analyze the data to determine what answers can be statistically justified, and then report the results in an acceptable scientific report.

The survey and usage data verify that *PsychExperiments* is used primarily by smaller schools. We infer from this that they use *PsychExperiments* because there is no local alternative for providing their students with comparable research experiences. Instructors responding to our survey all reported being at schools with fewer than 10,000 students. More convincing on this point is the actual list of schools given in Table 4.4 that were signed up to use the site in Spring 2004. Going through the list shows that small, regional institutions predominate. Another reason to believe that *PsychExperiments* enhanced the resources of institutions to offer students opportunities to participate in research is that 81% of the students responding to our survey reported that they participated in experi-

TABLE 4.4
Institutions with Classes Registered as Users
of *PsychExperiments* in AY 2003–2004

Colleges & Universities

Acadia University
Adams State College
Adrian College
American College Dublin
Anderson University
Arkansas State Univ.
Auburn University Montgomery
Augusta State Univ.
Barry University
Berkley College
Bethel College
Blinn College
Bluffton College
Birmingham Southern College
Bolton Institute
Boston College
Bournemouth University
Bramcote College
Bridgewater State
Brookdale Community College
Brown University
Cabrini College
California State Polytechnic University
California State University (Sacramento)
California State University (San Marcos)
Campbellsville University
Carl Sandburg High School
Carnegie Mellon University
Carroll College
Central Lakes College
Centre College
Cloud County Community College
Cheltenham and Gloucester College of Higher Education
Chowan College
City College of New York
City University of Hong Kong
College of Charleston

College of Mount St. Vincent
College of Southern Idaho
Colorado College
Columbia College
Columbus State Univ.
Columbus State University
Concordia College
Cumberland College
Curtin University of Technology
Deakin University
Delaware County Community College
De La Salle University (Manila)
Delta State University
Denison University
Dominican University of California
Eastern Michigan University
Eastern Nazarene College
East Stroudsburg University
Edinboro Univ.
Eisenhower High School
Emory and Henry College
Emporia State University
Escuela Campo Alegre
Ewha W. Univ.
Fachhochschule Kaiserslautern
Fayetteville State University
Færøernes Gymnasium
Føroya Studentaskúli
Florida International University
Florida State University
Francis Marion University
Franklin County High School
Fullerton College
George Fox University
Georgetown University
George Washington University

Georgia State University
Georgia Tech
Gettysburg College
Glendale Community College
Goddard College
Grand Valley State University
Grant MacEwan Community College
Guilford College
Gustavus Adolphus College
Hamline Univ.
Hanover College
Harriton High School
Havering
Hillside High School
Hofstra University
Holy Family College
Humboldt
Illinois State University
IUPUI
Indiana Univ.
Indiana University East
Inter University Centre
International Baccalaureate program
International Islamic University
James Madison University
Jefferson College
Jefferson Sci and Tech
Jim Hill High School
John Brown University
John Carroll University
Juniata College
King George V College
Lake Forest College
Lafayette College
Lehigh University
Le Moyne College
Lincoln Southeast High School
Lindsey Wilson College
Lomo Linda University
London Central High School
London Guildhall University

(Continued)

TABLE 4.4
(Continued)

Colleges & Universities

ouisiana College	Park University	St. Norbert College
oyola Marymount University	PennState	Stockholm University
acArthur High School	PennState Erie	Suffolk County Community College
adonna University	PennState Shenango	SUNY (Buffalo)
ay UM Workshop, OTH	Piedmont College	SUNY (Brockport)
ercer University	Plymouth State College	SUNY (Plattsburgh)
ercy College	Pomona College	SUNY (Potsdam)
ichigan Tech University	Poplar Springs Elementary School	Syracuse University
iddle Tennessee State	Pueblo School for Arts and Sciences	Tarlac State University
iddlesex University	Rancho Buena Vista High School	Texas AM Univ. (Kingsville)
illsaps College	Roland Park Country School	Texas Christian University
ississippi College	Rhodes College	Texas Tech University
issouri Western State	Ruamrudee International School	The American School Foundation of Monterrey
olloy College	Rice University	The New Atlanta Jewish Community High School
onmouth University	Rio Hondo Community College	Trent University
ontclair State University	Rochester Inst. of Tech.	Trinity College of Graduate Studies
ontgomery County Community College	Rollins College	United States Air Force Academy
oravian College	Sackville Community College	Universidad Catolica Argentina
orris Brown College	Salem State College	Universidad de Malaga
ount St. Mary College	Sampson Community College	Université de Moncton
ount Saint Vincent University	San Jose State U.	U. of Alaska Anchorage
ount Union College	San Jose State University	U. of Arizona
urdoch University	Sayville High School	U. of Baltimore
eenah High School	Scott Community College	U. of Cambridge
eumann College	Seminole Community College	U. of Calgary
ewnan High School	Shawnee State University	U. of California (Riverside)
ichols School	Silver Lake College	U. of Cincinnati
imitz H.S.	Sofia University	U. of Connecticut
orth Central College	Sonoma State University	U. of Dayton
ortheast Junior College	South Dartmoor Community College	U. of Denver
ortheastern University	Spelman College	U. of Fribourg
orthern Arizona U.	Spring Hill College	U. of Georgia
orthern Kentucky U.	SPJC	U. of Guelph
orthwest College	St. Andrews Presbyterian College	U. of Huddersfield
ccidental College	St. Anselm College	U. of Indiana
klahoma City U.	St. Bonaventure U.	U. of Iowa
hio Dominican College	St. Cloud State U.	U. of Joensuu
hio State University		U. of Kent at Canterbury
hio University		U. of Kiel
acific Lutheran University		U. of Liege
acific Lutheran Univ.		
acific Union College		

(Continued)

TABLE 4.4
(Continued)

Colleges & Universities		
U. of Liverpool	U. of Rhode Island	U. of Wisconsin (Superior)
U. of Louisiana (Monroe)	U. of San Diego	U. of Wisconsin (Whitewater)
U. of Massachusetts	U. of San Francisco	U. of York (UK)
U. of Minnesota (Duluth)	U. of Southern Indiana	U. of Zambia
U. of Mississippi	U. of Southern Maine	Wabash College
U. of Nebraska at Lincoln	U. of South Florida	Washington College
U. of Newcastle	U. of Southhampton	Washington State University
U. of New Hampshire	U. of Sunderland	Wellesley College
U. of the North	U. of Tasmania	Weston College
U. of North Alabama	U. of Texas Austin	Western Kentucky University
U. of North Carolina (Ashville)	U. of The Basque Country	Willamette University
U. of North Carolina (Wilmington)	U. of Westminster	Winona State University
U. of Nothumbria at Newcastle	U. of Wisconsin	Wittenberg University
U. of Puget Sound	U. of Wisconsin (Parkside)	Wollongong University
U. of Queensland	U. of Wisconsin (Rock County)	Worcester University College
	U. of Wisconsin (Stevens Point)	York College of Pennsylvania

ments at *PsychExperiments* using computers that were not located in their psychology department. Of these, better than half relied on private computers; the remainder used public computers available at their institutions. Only 12% used computers in psychology departments exclusively. Not surprisingly then, three-fourths reported positively on the survey item that asked about the convenience of *PsychExperiments* relative to other options for participating in experiments.

Based on the results of the student survey, we are somewhat optimistic that *PsychExperiments* may indeed make a difference in the general science education of psychology students. The students who use the site the most are at smaller schools where local science resources are most likely to be limited. The students find the site convenient to use and they report being able to complete more data collection activities than they otherwise would. Their instructors echo this view. In an instructor survey conducted in parallel with the student survey, 83% agreed with the statement that *PsychExperiments* offered an improvement to existing opportunities for students to conduct research.

Still, the evidence to date leaves open the question whether *PsychExperiments* will be a resource that helps fight scientific illiteracy. We need to first get a larger group of users and then be more analytical in our assessment of what benefits they have derived from their activities at the site. At that point we should be able to make a reasonable test of the hypothesis that students who have the opportunity to simulate being behavioral scientists benefit by understanding the nature of science better than those who do not and, further, that *PsychExperiments* increases the opportunities for meaningful simulation.

REFERENCES

McGraw, K. O., & Tew, M. D. (2003). *Creating experiments in Authorware: An interactive training manual* [on-line]. Available: http://psychexps.olemiss.edu/Developers/Documents/TrainManualOrder.htm.

NSF. (2002). Science and engineering indicators—2002. Available: http://www.nsf.gov/sbe/srs/seind02/start.htm

O'Neil, K. M., & Penrod, S. D. (2001). Methodological variables in Web-based research that may affect results: Sample type, monetary incentives, and personal information. *Behavior Research Methods, Instruments & Computers, 33*, 226–233.

Reips, U. D. (2000). The web experiment method: Advantages, disadvantages, and solutions. In M. H. Birnbaum (Ed.), *Psychological experiments on the internet* (pp. 89–118). San Diego, CA: Academic Press.

Rennie, J. (2002). 15 answers to creationist nonsense. *Scientific American, 287*(1), 78–85.

Teaching About Criminal Sentencing Decisions: The *Crime and Punishment* Simulations

Kent Portney
Tufts University

Steve Cohen
Tufts University

Jerry Goldman
Northwestern University

Sandy Simpson
Dorchester High School

"The house became smaller because the sun came out."

Chapter 1 introduced this seemingly incomprehensible sentence to provide an illustration of generative learning. Yet what does this sentence have to do with teaching college students about criminal sentencing? Helping students to learn and understand the complex story of sentencing in the criminal courts may be a much more challenging exercise than it at first appears to be. In a sense, teaching about criminal sentencing may be as challenging as making sense out of the opening sentence without hearing the word igloo (Auble, Franks, & Soraci, 1979). This one word provides the key that creates a context in which the previous sentence can easily be understood. Without this key, the sentence simply makes no sense. In many respects, the challenge in teaching much in political science, including issues in criminal sentencing, is like this problem. The fact is that information transfer found in traditional teaching methods (i.e., lecture and reading texts) is very often not suitable for the task of providing the context—the key—for students to make sense out of some aspects of criminal sentencing. Teaching about criminal sentencing is often a challenging task that has many of the characteristic impediments discussed earlier. The criminal sentencing process is fairly complex, involving many actors and a variety of constraints, including the statutes under which sentencing is carried out. However, there is more to the challenge than the complexity of the decisions and their contexts. So what makes this topic so challenging to teach? The answer is probably found in aspects of social cognition and attribution theory noted earlier.

In this chapter, we discuss the problem of teaching students about issues of variability in criminal sentences, and teaching about how one goes about explaining this variation. We report on analyses we conducted in order to assess the effectiveness of an instructional intervention using a technology-based multimedia simulation that we developed under a grant from the Fund for Improvement in Post-secondary Education (FIPSE) and have used in class. We rely on cognitive learning theory to help provide guidance into the ways that the instructional intervention can be said to produce superior learning outcomes.

ASSUMPTIONS AND FOUNDATIONS

The central problem in teaching about criminal sentencing is rooted in the fact that each student comes into class with preconceived ideas concerning how much variability there is, what causes this variability, and whether this variability is acceptable or not. Why is criminal sentencing, particularly the issue of explaining variation in criminal sentences, so difficult to teach? One of the primary reasons can be found in the works of Heider (1958; Ross & Fletcher, 1985) who hypothesized a fundamental drive in all people to reduce unpredictability. People, he suggested, are uncomfortable when faced with unpredictable outcomes. Rather than tolerate unpredictability, most people will attribute causes to events. There is comfort in having attributed causes to events, even if the causes are wrong (i.e., have no empirical validity), are appropriate only in certain idiosyncratic settings, tell only part of a story, or are ideologically driven.

What does this fundamental drive to reduce unpredictability matter for those trying to teach criminal justice sentencing? It matters because most students do not begin a class on criminal sentencing as the proverbial *tabula rasa*. Instead they typically begin a course having had at least some exposure to the basic problem of variability in sentencing decisions. Whether through the media, secondary education, or personal experiences and observations, most students will have some idea that fairness in sentencing is difficult to achieve. It is difficult to imagine a student with no concept of variability in sentencing. When asked to do so, most students can readily recite examples of criminal cases where they believe defendants were treated unfairly.

Inferring from the work on attribution, most students with exposure to sentencing issues will spontaneously attribute causes to the sentencing variability, in an effort to reduce the unpredictability. In most, if not all cases, these causes will have some legitimacy. However, the causes attributed are likely to include simple-minded reactions or incomplete explanations. Students often attribute virtually all variation in sentencing to a single cause, such as racism, gender bias, political corruption, judges who are too liberal or soft on crime, judges who are too conservative, inequality of wealth or income, incompetence, or other single factor. One reason why it is easy for students to quickly attribute these causes to sentencing variability is that the real agents of the causes, namely the judges and judicial system, are external to the student. According to the fundamental attribution error in social psychology, it would be more difficult to attribute and rely on causes like racism or incompetence if students themselves were the agents. It is clearly difficult to see yourself or your peers as racists or incompetents. Yet it is easy to see others this way.

As is abundantly demonstrated in the literature on criminal sentencing,[1] these causes do not tell the whole story. Factors like theories of criminal sanctions—deterrence, retribution, rehabilitation, and incapacitation—certainly play a complex role in decisions. However, faced with the need to attribute causes and reduce the unpredictabil-

---

[1]See Goldman and Portney, "The Role of Gender in Determining Criminal Sanctions: Results from Multimedia Experiments in Criminal Sentencing," paper prepared for delivery at the 1997 Meetings of the American Political Science Association, August 28–31, 1997, Washington, D.C.

ity, simple-minded attributions are very handy. These attributions play a vital role in helping students forge and maintain a tolerable cognitive balance. Without the attributions, students are faced with the difficult task of tolerating unpredictable behavior. Beliefs that play such an important role are tough to change through instruction. However, that is where teachers must start. Our way of thinking about teaching students criminal sentencing suggests that teachers need to consider the kinds of beliefs and ideas that occupy a students mind as they craft teaching methods and instructional designs.

TEACHING STUDENTS WHO HAVE PRECONCEIVED BELIEFS ABOUT SENTENCING

Taking into account the beliefs students bring to a course is not a new idea in education. Prior knowledge and beliefs, and the role they play in learning, has been recognized as a key issue in teaching difficult subjects, in particular Newtonian Mechanics (Carey, 1986; Smith, diSessa, & Roschelle, 1993) and probability. (Cohen, Smith, Chechile, Burns, & Tsai, 1996; Hammer, 1997; Konold, 1989; Pollatsek, Konold, Well, & Lima, 1984; Tversky & Kahneman, 1971, 1974). As noted in chapter 1, ideas that are inconsistent with the formal, theoretical foundations in these two fields are often called naïve (Carey, 1986). For example, many students develop what is termed a naïve physics that is useful for understanding observed physical behavior. Watching a Frisbee fly and then land does not suggest that a body in motion tends to stay in motion (Newton's 1st law). Yet, the naïve idea that physical objects in motion tend to come to a halt is a useful heuristic for everyday life, and its usefulness makes it resilient and even applicable in circumstances where it does not belong.

These naïve beliefs present challenges to teachers when they try to help students replace ideas inconsistent with formal, theoretical notions, or simply help them build on their prior understanding (instead of replacing it: Strike & Posner, 1992). This latter case is especially informative for teaching criminal sentencing. Based on our assumptions, the instructional goal is not to replace naïve beliefs like bias, incompetence, or both, for they certainly have a legitimate place in any network of understanding about sentencing. Incompetence, racial and gender bias, political corruption, etc., do exist.

Rather, the goal is to deeply extend and reconfigure each student's network of ideas and beliefs to included additional factors. This kind of shift may be nearly as profound as moving from a naïve physics to a Newtonian model (Strike & Posner, 1992).

Unfortunately, it is not easy to deeply extend and reconfigure belief networks. It often requires insight on the part of the student that their network is simply inadequate for explaining certain results. When it occurs, it is not unlike hearing the word igloo after reading the first sentence of this paper. The learner actually reintegrates and renders comprehensible a previously incomprehensible context. In our search for clues to making criminal sentencing understood more deeply, we look to cognitive learning theory for assistance. Because of the expectation that learning about sentencing resembles in important ways learning to decipher the opening sentence to this paper, we take as our learning model research on generative learning (Soraci et al., 1994).

The Generation Effect

Research on generative learning suggests a way to help students reconfigure their beliefs. At the heart of this effect is the result that students who generate their own responses to open-ended queries tend to have much better memory for responses than when the responses are provided to them (Soraci et al., 1994). This has been shown to be a robust empirical phenomenon that occurs across a wide range of learning contexts. In some sense this can simply be seen as support for active learning.

Related research suggests that the order of the information plays a key role. For instance, telling students the house became smaller because the sun came out followed by the word igloo results in much better memory than mentioning igloo prior to giving subjects the sentence. This result suggests an unusual instructional design. Start by creating ambiguity by providing a noncomprehended context, have the student actively engage in resolving the ambiguity, and superior learning occurs. While it may be best for students to resolve the confusion on their own, superior learning also occurs when the confusing sentence is proposed first and the key concept is subsequently revealed. This is important, since education often does not permit enough time for students to resolve as many puzzles as we would like them to.

We believe this kind of learning process is essential if students are really going to broaden their understanding of sentencing. Simply telling students that factors like deterrence or retribution influence sentencing decisions will not help most students appeal to these ideas when confronted with issues of criminal sentencing. Students may be able to recite these ideas on a test of recall, but they do not seem to avail themselves of these explanations when critically reviewing controversial decisions. Students must first appreciate the limited application of their preconceived ideas. Only then they will be in a position to extend their understanding.

The Design of the Instructional Intervention

In order to take advantage of the what we know about the generative learning effect, we devised an instructional intervention. This instructional intervention, suggested by the generation effect, has four steps:

Step 1. Introduce students to the topic of variation in sentencing. This can be done with traditional methods—lectures, readings from texts, or other written sources.

Step 2. Have students play the role of judge through sentencing simulations. This can be done through a variety of different techniques, although as we discuss later, the multimedia approach has distinct advantages over paper-and-pencil simulations or simple role-playing. This step is described in much more detail in the following. In order to facilitate Step 3, the simulation must not only establish the extent to which there is variability in the sentences students render, it must also yield compelling explanation for why these variations exist. Our approach is to conduct the simulation using an experimental design such that the characteristics of the cases that we would like to offer as explanations are systematically varied.

Step 3. Confront students with their own sentencing behavior and challenge the class to rationalize–explain the results with respect to variability. When the students render their sentences, these sentences must in some manner be recorded, and be tallied and summarized for presentation to the class as a whole. In other words, there must be a way to hold a mirror up to the students to show them what they produced. This process essentially causes the confusion that the generation effect requires.

Step 4. Teach theories of sentencing. Once students come to recognize the limits of their explanations, they are open to new and more complete or expanded explanations. Exposure to theories of sentencing and the literature positing alternative explanations offers students a mechanism to resolve the confusion they experienced as a result of seeing their own sentencing results.

A Rationale for a Possible Improvement

Our approach utilizes the instructive experience of simulation–role-play (Step 2 in the instructional intervention). It works as follows. Each student in a class plays the role of sentencing judge and renders her or his own sentences for the same set of cases. When all students have had a chance to play the role, the instructor tallies their sentences and confronts them with their results. When students see the enormous variability among sentences that they themselves—each student and his or her peers—we expect their naïve beliefs to weaken. These beliefs suddenly have a real limitation. To the extent that students collectively demonstrate sentencing variation, simulation results force students to either see themselves as biased, racist, or incompetent, etc., or to look for an expanded set of beliefs around which to structure their thinking about sentencing. This experience should force some students to challenge their (naïve) beliefs. Once these beliefs are challenged and naïve causes are seen as inadequate, students may be in a better position to develop a more complex appreciation of criminal justice sentencing.

The Use of Simulated Role-Playing

We prepared simulated role-playing in two different forms. In one form, we developed case files that contained written materials describing each of six different criminal felony cases. In the other form, we created a multimedia experience where students could feel like they are actually presiding over court proceedings.

The Multimedia Simulation

Our method for addressing these issues is to develop and use in class a technology-based multimedia simulation of the sentencing process. In this simulation, called *Crime and Punishment*, students sit at a computer and take on the role of a sentencing judge in sentencing some six cases that are composites of cases from Massachusetts and Cook County, Illinois. The simulation contains an array of documents typically available to sentencing judges, and allows students to take part in a sentencing hearing in which full-motion, CD-ROM-based, video presents the relevant actors—the prosecutor, defense lawyer, defendant, and the victim. The student gets the feeling of walking into the courthouse, via this visual context, passing through the metal detector, acknowledging the greeting of court personnel, and entering his or her chambers. Once in chambers, the student picks up a court docket and folder and walks into the courtroom. Upon hearing "all rise," the student proceeds to the judge's bench. The docket is placed on the desktop, depicted in Fig. 5.1, and the student can select a case by clicking on any of six items on the docket. At

FIG. 5.1.   Simulated judge's desktop showing the docket (right) and a case file.

this point, the previously unopened standard paper file opens up revealing two court documents describing the case at hand on one side, and a presentence investigation report on the other side. By clicking on either document, the student can read that document. When ready to do so, the student can view a sentencing hearing by clicking on the gavel sitting on the desktop. The sentencing hearing consists of full-motion video of the prosecutor explaining the case and making a sentence recommendation; the defense lawyer presenting mitigating circumstances; the defendant making a brief statement; and the victim delivering an impact statement. After all of the case materials are digested, the student proceeds to render a sentence. Within the constraints imposed by the governing criminal statutes in the case, students have full control over the severity and type of sentence to be imposed.

Crime and Punishment contains six different cases where the defendant in each case must be sentenced by each student. The first case encountered by the user, an armed robbery case, serves as an anchor and therefore was created with no variables (i.e., all students see the exact same case). The remaining five cases, possession of drugs with intent to distribute, armed robbery, grand larceny shoplifting, and sexual assault on a minor, are made accessible to the student through the court docket, as previously described. Thus, the multimedia application is, from the outset, considerably more interactive than is its paper-and-pencil counterpart.

The utility of the *Crime and Punishment* simulation is readily seen in the way characteristics of the cases are manipulated. Because the simulation is delivered to students over the Internet, we are able to vary characteristics of the cases in systematic ways. The simulation allows instructors to vary the race of the defendant (the defendant could be either African-American or white); the gender of the defendant (either male or female); the appearance of the defendant (either wearing street clothes or in a prison jump suit); the affect exhibited by the defendant (the defendant might not speak, or when the defendant speaks, he or she can be either animated or subdued); and whether or not the victim makes a statement. These particular case characteristics are allowed to vary because they represent the targets of the learning goals established prior to the simulation's creation. Other characteristics could be varied, and indeed, the digital technology makes it relatively easy to include additional characteristics in the future. For example, in the current simulation, all characteristics of the prosecutor are constant, that is, the prosecutor is always a white male. If a course wanted to investigate the role of the gender of the prosecutor in influencing sentencing severity, this characteristic could easily be added. Figure 5.2 provides screenshots of the video from the simulation, and gives a glimpse at how the race and gender of the defendant were digitally varied for one case. Of course, no one student would see more than one of these for a given case.

By allowing only one of these characteristics to vary and holding everything else constant, the effect of that variable on the sentences rendered by the students can be isolated. For example, an experiment can be conducted where the gender of the defendant is varied holding everything else constant. We do this by simply inserting a different video image into the courtroom scene while keeping the rest of the visual array constant. For classes that are sufficiently large, the simulation allows the instructor to vary more than one characteristic simultaneously, such as the race and the gender of the defendant. In the classroom experiments reported here, the simulations were implemented where only race and gender were varied, while all other characteristics were held constant. Again, because the simulation was delivered via the Internet, Step 3 in the instructional intervention—reporting the results to the class—was relatively easy since the aggregation of the data from all participating students was accomplished automatically.

After students read the documentation and participate in the video-based hearing, they must confront their decision—the type and severity of the sentence for that defendant. This decision is entered into the computer using a form similar to that used in actual courts, as depicted in Fig. 5.3.

Students are provided with the statutory language governing this case, which specifies the range of possible sentences that can be imposed. Students are asked to enter all relevant information about the sentence they wish to impose: number of months in prison, number of months on supervised probation, mandatory counseling, restitution, and fines. Additionally, students are asked to provide a written justification for the sentence imposed. The bottom portion of the sentencing form consists of a text box into which students type the reasons why they gave the sentence to that defendant. This written justification is important, as discussed in the following, because it provides a snapshot into the nature of the complexity of the decision reached by the student. It is the only place where information is

1. African-American female defendant

2. White female defendant

3. African-American male defendant

4. White male defendant

FIG. 5.2.   Four courtroom scenes from the *Crime and Punishment* sentencing simulation showing how the race and gender of the defendant were varied while holding everything else constant.

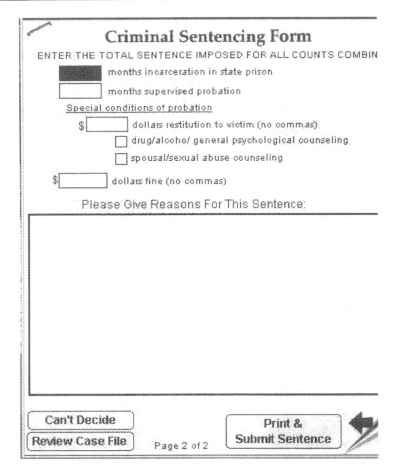

FIG. 5.3. Sentencing decision form, as found in the simulation.

gather about the reason why the students rendered the sentences they did. All of this information is communicated to the network server where it is stored and combined with the information from all the other students using the simulation. The results are instantly updated and made available to the instructor.

The Paper-Based Simulation

We also created paper versions of each of the cases found in the multimedia simulations. All of the information that was contained in the multimedia simulations, except the visual elements, was reduced to paper. The same experimental design was used, where the race and gender of the defendant was systematically varied. Preparation of four versions of each of the six cases was a considerably greater challenge than was the case with the multimedia simulation. The paper-based simulation was used in the context of the same instructional intervention as that used with the multimedia simulation. Logistically, aggregation and analysis of the resulting data for all students was much more labor-intensive than with the multimedia simulation because each student's sentences had to be hand-coded and keyed into the computer.

Assessing this Approach

We set out to try to determine whether students do, in fact, seem to learn more from using this instructional intervention approach. Thus we embarked on a learning assessment at Tufts and Northwestern Universities. Three Political Science classes were used in this assessment, as shown in Table 5.1.

Students in classes (2 and 3) were exposed to the same materials as those in class 1, plus the instructional intervention. As part of this intervention, students who used a simulation–role-play were confronted with the following results after they all had a chance to participate in the exercises:

TABLE 5.1
The Three Comparison Groups

Class 1	Class 2	Class 3
No Simulation[2]	CD-ROM Based Simulation[3]	Paper-Based Simulation[4]
Control class using traditional lectures and reading to teach variability in sentencing. This included extensive reference to empirical studies, and providing opportunities for students to analyze data from actual felony cases.	A class using a CD-ROM multimedia simulation that presented sentencing hearings and allowed students to play the role of judge and sentence convicted felons in six cases involving different kinds of crimes	A class using paper-based simulations where the cases were identical to those included in the multimedia counterpart

[2]Portney's "Judicial Politics" course, Spring semester 1995.
[3]Portney's "Judicial Politics" course, Spring semester 1996.
[4]Goldman's "The Politics of Local Justice" course, Winter term 1995–96.

1. Summary measures of their sentencing behavior (class means and standard deviations).
2. Histograms of sentencing distributions for the entire class.
3. Extreme sentences and the written justifications.

We hypothesized that if the instructional intervention (involving the four steps previously outlined) works, we would see particular patterns of differences among the three classes.

Hypothesis a. We would expect that students experiencing the instructional intervention would be better able to use theory to explain variation rather than point to naïve causes. In other words, we expected to see students rely more heavily on theoretical justifications, such as deterrence, rehabilitation, etc. Given the nature of the specific scenario students were asked to judge, we expected that the central difference would be between students who cited a deterrence rationale versus those who simply relied on attribution of naïve causes in rendering their decisions.

Hypothesis b. We would expect that students experiencing the instructional intervention to be more likely to accept variations as part of judicial process rather than ascribe variation to simple explanations. We expect that students not exposed to the intervention to be aware that there is substantial variability in sentences, and to attribute this perceived level of variability to simple causes that they see as bad or unacceptable. So, for example, a student might recognize that there are unequal sentences, and that this inequality is attributed to racism, incompetence, corruption, inequality in wealth, and access to resources, etc. Since the attributed cause is seen by the student is illegitimate and unacceptable, so too is the inequality of sentences. As students' understanding of the multiplicity of causes of sentence variability deepens, and as they come to recognize that much of the variability in sentences cannot be explained very satisfactorily by any hypothesized cause, we expect their acceptance of that variability will also increase.

Hypothesis c. We would expect students exposed to the instructional intervention to try to remedy variation by staying closer to what they would expect to be a middle range of sentences. Because students will not know with any certainty what other students will choose as sentences, it would be virtually impossible for them to know how they can contribute to reductions in sentencing variability. In the absence of information about what sentences others will render, they will opt to pay closer attention to the range of permissible sentences outlined in the language of the criminal statute(s), and will choose sentences that are closer to the mid-range of what is permissible. The result should be a reduction in variation.

After the course's sections on their respective treatment of issues of criminal sentencing were completed, students were administered a questionnaire, a copy of which is found in the Appendix, to develop specific information about what they may have learned. Three different measures were used to assess these hypotheses. To assess hypothesis a, we asked students to explain in what way it could be justified for a judge to sentence an African-American male to a longer prison term than a white male in order to stem the tide of drug crimes in a neighborhood (question 2). The problem is designed to evoke reference to racism as an explanation, or an answer of deterrence, or both. To assess hypothesis b we asked students, in question 6, to describe the actual level of intracourt variability in criminal sentencing, using a 5-point Likert scale, as being:

1. Far less than they would find acceptable.
2. Somewhat less than they would find acceptable.
3. Within the range of what they would find acceptable.
4. Somewhat greater than they would find acceptable.
5. Much greater than they would find acceptable.

To assess hypothesis c, we had students sentence two cases, one a case of sexual assault, the other a case of grand larceny. These cases, not found in the Appendix because of their length, were different from the cases incorporated into the role-play simulation.

In addition to addressing these three questions, we were interested in assessing how comparable the three classes were, and in learning how the CD-based simulation results would compare to the paper-based results. Students found the CD and paper simulations equally realistic, and typically took about 2 hours to complete the assignments. We had a clear a priori reason to believe the students in the three classes were comparable, but we opted to administer questions to provide specific evidence of this theory. These questions asked students to report on a variety of factors we thought might conceivably affect any intergroup differences in the assessment criteria, including differences in SAT scores, grade point averages, baseline knowledge of the judicial system, familial socio-economic status, and others, and no differences were discerned.

Results

The comparisons among the three classes show distinct patterns of difference. The results of the analysis are summarized in Table 5.2.

The data generally offer support for our hypotheses. In the first hypothesis, the issue is whether traditional teaching methods (compared to the instructional intervention) put students in a position to appeal to complex beliefs when thinking about controversial sentencing decisions. The data show that only 14% of students in the control group cited deterrence as a possible cause for the sentence disparity. In other words, for 86% of the students, deterrence was not an explanation that came readily to mind as an explanation for the sentencing scenario. However, when exposed to the instructional intervention, deterrence became a useful concept for 20% of the students participating in the paper-based simulation, and for 33% of the students using the CD-based simulation. We also see some support for hypothesis b. There was a similar effect in students' ability to appreciate what a difficult problem fairness in sentencing really is. Only 13% of the students reported that they considered the level of variability as "acceptable," while 23% of the CD-based simulation students and 43% of the paper-based simulation students reported the level of variability to be "acceptable." There appears to be some support for hypothesis c for the larceny case but not for the assault case. We expected to see the instructional intervention produce reduced variability compared to the control group. When we examine the standard deviations of the prison sentences, indeed, for the larceny case, both the CD-based simulation and the paper-based simulation interventions show lower standard deviations without affecting the mean sentence. Thus, the intervention seems to have influenced students who might have given sentences at either the high or low ends of the permissible range to opt for middle-range sentences. However, this pattern is not evident in the assault case.

TABLE 5.2

Learning Outcomes Among Three Groups of Students

Class	Percent of Students Using a Deterrence Rationale	Percent of Students Saying Variation is "Acceptable" (Responses 1, 2, or 3)	Prison Sentences in Months for the Larceny Case (Means and Standard Deviations)	Prison Sentences in Months for the Sexual Assault Case (Means and Standard Deviations)
Class 1: Control (n = 36)	14%	13%	88 (35)	173 (80)
Class 2: CD-based (n = 33)	33%	23%	92 (22)	185 (80)
Class 3: Paper (n = 51)	20%	43%	83 (29)	169 (89)

Those students in classes using the simulations (in the context of the prescribed instructional intervention) demonstrated an effect due to the intervention, regardless of the media used to deliver the simulation. There is more unacceptable variation and greater reliance on punishment theory when confronted with the most stimulating exercises. Yet the data also reveal striking similarities between paper and multimedia simulations. This suggests that any simulation has merit in relation to no simulation. The comparisons also suggest that variation in some kinds of cases (sexual assault) may be more difficult to reduce than in other cases.

We also expect that the learning effects from the instructional intervention, particularly using the multimedia approach, may well be greater for students who have lower verbal aptitude (i.e., students who are less likely to achieve high levels of comprehension from reading empirical and other works on sentencing variability). The more difficulty a student has in learning from more traditional sources, such as books, or research articles, the more likely that student will experience improvement in learning outcomes as a result of the instructional intervention. We also expect that the relative advantages of the multimedia-based simulation over the paper-and-pencil counterpart will be substantially greater for students whose reading comprehension is challenged. This expectation makes the results reported here all the more remarkable, since the assessment was conducted with the participation of students at two colleges where verbal aptitudes are likely to be higher than that found at many other institutions.

Although the multimedia role-playing simulation used in the context of the instructional intervention did not produce across-the-board learning improvements, it is clear that using such technology-based simulations is considerably easier than paper-and-pencil alternatives. Administering the simulation using an experimental design to an entire class of students, particularly a class with multiple sections, is a daunting task. Preparing four or more paper-based versions of each criminal case is a tedious task, one that most instructors would not have the time or resources to do. Furthermore, the collection, aggregation, and analysis of the results of the simulation—the sentences students render—adds considerable time to the process. The beauty of the multimedia-based simulation is that these administrative processes have been automated, and the time and energy that would have been devoted to more mundane tasks can be spent on preparing interpretations of the results. The practical fact is that the multimedia approach is much more likely to be used than its paper-and-pencil counterpart.

We also recognize that the design of the instructional intervention was heavily informed by a particular conception of belief networks and conceptual change. We are planning future research designed to assess a range of alternative instructional intervention designs based on other conceptions of belief networks, in order to examine the extent to which this approach holds more broad-based promise cannot be evaluated.

RACE AND JUSTICE IN AN URBAN CLASSROOM: A HIGH SCHOOL TEACHER'S PERSPECTIVE

Finally, in addition to the research and assessment challenge lays the promise of improving secondary education. As part of that goal, *Crime and Punishment* has been tested and integrated into several classrooms. The poignant and encouraging story of one high school reveals the potential.

Exploring issues of race and justice with high school students can be a very powerful experience for both teachers and students. Many teenagers still maintain lofty idealistic expectations of human behavior. Teenagers are acutely aware of their own definition of justice. Embarking on a discussion of race and justice in a dangerous urban high school can be down right inspiring, for reasons you would never expect.

Dorchester High School is in the Codman Square neighborhood of Boston, and enrolls about 1,000 students. Ninety-two percent of them qualify for free lunch. That means they live below the poverty level. Dorchester High is considered by some the worst school in the Boston public school system. Dorchester High is often described as a school out of control. At Dorchester there is always noise in the halls, intercom announcements during classes, lock downs, uninvited guests wandering into classrooms, fights, cops, false fire alarms, sometimes three a day. Many of the students have direct experience in the criminal courts. Most students do not pass state or city standardized test the first time. Most students have been touched by the increasing violence in the city. During the 2002–2003 year, two thirds of the student population consulted with the school's only student support clinician. These were students who were considering suicide, pregnant, or suffering from physical abuse, mental illness, or homelessness. All students see the realities of poverty, drugs, and violence every day.

Crime and Punishment was used in the curriculum of the school's Academy of Public Service. The Academy, established 10 years ago, is a 3-year program. Students take three classes a year together to prepare them for a career in federal, state, or local government or in community service. The Academy provides a curriculum infused with themes of public service, connecting activities, educational field trips, work experience, and college preparation. The Academy reaches out to the community to build bridges from the classroom to the world of work. Many students feel their schoolwork is disconnected from the world outside. In the Academy, an emphasis on the connections tends to entice students to be more willing to take risks and to push themselves a little harder. The Academy is built on the belief that in order for American democracy to work, everyone needs the opportunity to participate in it. The Academy explores the numerous ways students can participate and give back to their community now and in their future careers.

One of the classes in the Academy is an 11th grade class called Introduction to Public Service. This course offers students an introduction into public service careers and community service. The students engage in research, writing, and debate about the role of public service and public policy in contemporary American society. The course spends time focusing on the role of human relations in the world of work–service and the impact on policy. The class activities allow students to explore issues that affect society and gain an awareness of the public servants that develop solutions to these issues.

Teaching about race, especially internalized definitions of race in a classroom where the instructor is the only white person is often challenging. Teaching about public policy and race in a impoverished and violence stricken neighborhood can be a formidable task as well. This class looks at ideas and definitions of justice and just society as a theme throughout the school year. Race and class is a subplot to all conversations whether it is implicitly understood or explicitly addressed. In discussions about goal setting, study habits, dress codes, resume writing, federal budget analysis, public transportation, or the firefighter's test, there is always the extra dynamic of being black and poor. Getting the students to closely examine their own definition of other is just as extremely challenging, particularly in the context of the search for ways to introduce students to their own prejudices and assumptions. Scenarios, experiential activities, and simulations often have a profound impact on students' own perceptions.

During 2002–2003, after completing units on the prison industrial complex and the juvenile justice systems, students discussed issues of law, fairness, and the needs and responsibilities of society. The class was exposed to the complexities of judicial politics by exploring Supreme Court cases and current issues facing juvenile courts. Again, race and class were continually present in the conversations. These activities represented a continuous struggle to find ways of exploring these complexities of justice in a way that could continually push the students to examine their own understanding of justice and to try and refine their definitions. The students explored the role of a judge in the sentencing process. The class visited a computer lab at Tufts University, where they were able to participate in the simulation. There was no reference to race during the initial discussion. This simulation was presented to the students as a way for them to explore a process of the judicial system and to provide an understanding of the work a judge does. The simulation met these goals with far greater success than could have been achieved in class with textbooks, overheads, scenarios, or mock trials.

Each student worked at his or her own pace without distraction. Each student was completely engaged. Even the most unfocused students focused. Most students were more comfortable with a computer than they were with a textbook. Learning was brought into a realm that they owned. The class had a wide range of reading abilities and aptitudes. So each student went through the simulation and sentenced one of the six cases, and was then treated to a pizza picnic lunch. During this time, the students' conversations were telling. While much of the conversation was true to form for teenagers on a field trip, eating pizza outside on a beautiful day, each conversation turned at least once to the work they just accomplished. Students wondered if they could do the rest of the cases, they were asking questions about sentencing laws, they were asking each other about their decisions. A group of girls asked after lunch if they could do some mock trials in class the following week. As lessons go, this one was already a success and the best was yet to come. After lunch, the students returned to the classroom. Here the class was introduced to the idea of comparing data and showing the results of their own work. The first results showed the differences in sentencing between the girls and the boys in the class. These stark differences were interesting to the students, and the class spent some time interpreting the results. The results based on race were presented. The students sentenced black men to longer prison sentences than white men. There was a prolonged, embarrassed, silence, and then the room fell apart in nervous laughter. When the class regained its composure, a discussion ensued concerning how this could happen given the fact that the entire year had been spent exploring issues of race and justice. Students wondered aloud how they could have been racist in their sentencing with all their first-hand knowledge and expertise. They imagined the assumptions many judges base their sentencing decisions on.

When the class returned to the classroom at Dorchester High, another discussion took place on how much race and internalized definitions of race impact public policy in United States. The class reviewed many of the Supreme Court decisions that had been explored at the beginning of the unit. The discussion turned to solutions. The students really hoped they could organize a teach-in law day with judges, lawyers, and other students from the Academy to use the *Crime and Punishment* simulation to focus discussions and then develop an action plan. Then it was June 21st and they were gone. One student, as he was leaving, asked, "So what's with the blindfold any way miss? Do ya really think justice is blind to her own hatreds?" Next year this group of students will be in their senior Social Issues class. Maybe this will provide the opportunity to host a law day as a senior social action project. Either way, *Crime and Punishment* has become an important part of the curriculum. The impact on the students, their engagement in the simulations, and the sophistication of their conversations afterward has ensured that *Crime and Punishment* will continue to be a part of the curriculum.

APPENDIX
QUESTIONNAIRE USED IN THE ASSESSMENT
(FORMAT CHANGED FOR THIS APPENDIX)

1. Under which of the four theories of punishment would you expect greater variation in sentence severity across cases as a necessary

byproduct of its success? In other words, if each of the four theories were used to its most successful way, which one would likely produce the greatest variation? Why?

2. You live in a community that has had an alarming increase in the amount of drug-related crime. There is a widespread perception that this problem has its origins among the Black residents of your community. As a result of the police department's effort to get tough on crime, two people are arrested, charged, and convicted of the identical crime, possession of cocaine with the intent to distribute. Neither of these people has any prior record. Both are employed, and they are the same age. One defendant is Caucasian and the other is Black. Do you think that under these circumstances, the judge sentencing these two defendants would be justified in giving the Black defendant a more severe sentence than the Caucasian defendant. If so, explain why. If not, explain why not.

3. We have discussed a variety of factors that influence how severe a sentence a particular criminal defendant might receive. Aside from the purely legal factors, such as the severity of the crime and the prior record of the defendant, are there other "extra-legal" factors that play an important role in influencing sentence severity? Briefly explain which factors and why they have that influence.

4. The death penalty is least consistent with which theory of punishment?

a) incarceration
b) rehabilitation
c) retribution
d) deterrence

Please explain why you chose the previous answer.

5. Two judges, Judge Black and Judge White, each subscribes to one and only one theory of punishment. Each claims to subscribe to a different one. Yet, on two given cases that look very much the same, both judges handed out the same sentences. To which theories do you believe the judges subscribed? Please explain how you arrived at this conclusion.

6. Given everything you now know about the criminal courts in the United States, do you think the amount of intracourt variation in sentence severity for a given type of case is:

_____ Far less than I would find acceptable

_____ Somewhat less than I would find acceptable

_____ Within the range of what I would find acceptable

_____ Somewhat greater than I would find acceptable

_____ Far greater than I would find acceptable

Briefly explain why.

7. A judge who believes in the incapacitation model of punishment sentenced a white male to 12 years in prison for two counts of felony armed robbery. Is it possible for a judge who believes in rehabilitation to offer the same sentence? Why or why not?

REFERENCES

Auble, P. A., Franks, J., & Soraci, S. (1979). Effort toward comprehension: Elaboration or "aha!" *Memory and Cognition, 7*(6), 426–434.

Carey, S. (1986). Cognitive science and science education. *American Psychologist, 41*(10), 1123–1130.

Cohen, S., Smith, G., Chechile, R., Burns, G., & Tsai, F. (1996). Identifying impediments to learning probability and statistics from an assessment of instructional software. *Journal of Educational and Behavioral Statistics, 21*(1), 35–54.

Goldman, J., & Portney, K. (1997, August 28–31). *The role of gender in determining criminal sanctions: Results from multimedia experiments in criminal sentencing.* Paper prepared for delivery at the 1997 meeting of the American Political Science Association, Washington, DC.

Hammer, D. (1997). Misconceptions or p-prims: How might alternative perspectives of cognitive structure influence instructional perceptions and intentions? *Journal of the Learning Sciences, 5*(2), 97–127.

Heider, F. (1958). *The psychology of interpersonal relations.* New York: Wiley.

Konold, C. (1989). Informal conceptions of probability. *Cognition and Instruction, 6*(1), 59–98.

Pollatsek, A., Konold, C., Well, A. D., & Lima, S. D. (1984). Beliefs underlying random sampling. *Memory and Cognition, 12*, 395–401.

Ross, M., & Fletcher, G. (1985). Attribution and social perception. In G. Lindzey & E. Aronson (Eds.), *Handbook of social psychology* (Vol. II, 3rd ed., pp. 73–118). New York: Random House.

Smith, J., diSessa, A., & Roschelle, J. (1993). Misconceptions reconceived: A constructivist of knowledge in transition. *Journal of Learning Sciences, 3*, 115–163.

Soraci, S. A., Franks, J., Bransford, J., Chechile, R., Belli, R., Carr, M., & Carlin, M. (1994). Incongruous item generation effects: A multiple-cue perspective. *Journal of Experimental Psychology: Learning, Memory, and Cognition, 20*(1), 67–78.

Strike, K. A., & Posner, G. J. (1992). A revisionist theory of conceptual change. In R. A. Doschl & R. J. Hamilton (Eds.), *Philosophy of science, cognitive psychology, and educational theory and practice* (pp. 147–176). Albany, NY: SUNY Press.

Tversky, A., & Kahneman, D. (1971). Belief in the law of small numbers. *Psychological Bulletin, 76*(2), 105–110.

Tversky, A., & Kahneman, D. (1974). Judgment under uncertainty: Heuristics and biases. *Science, 185*(415), 1124–1131.

The Poetics of Simulation:
An Analysis of Programs in Ethics
and Conflict Resolution[1]

Robert Cavalier
Carnegie Mellon University

In this chapter, I discuss two CD-ROM applications in the areas of conflict resolution and dispute mediation. One is *Allwyn Hall*, a program designed to provide the user with an understanding of conflict resolution and the basic skills of dispute mediation. The other is *In All Respects*, a program designed to address that area of conflict resolution called Active Listening. Both programs are simulations: *Allwyn Hall* places the user in the role of a resident assistant in a college dormitory; *In All Respects* places the user in the role of a college TV producer. In the former program, users must successfully resolve several conflicts such as those involving roommates arguing over cleanliness and students arguing over noise in the study hall. In the latter program, users produce a documentary on "Racism on Campus" that must fairly represent the viewpoints of those in the community.

These programs were developed during the 1990s at Carnegie Mellon's Center for the Advancement of Applied Ethics (CAAE). The Center, situated within the Philosophy department, has a history of producing state-of-the-art interactive media applications. The Center itself evolved from a wing of the former Center for Design of Educational Computing (CDEC). Along with MIT's Project Athena and

[1]Sections of this chapter have appeared in different forms in previous articles and chapters where noted. I also want to thank Preston Covey and Andrew Thompson for their contributions to some of the ideas and sources contained herein.

Brown's Intermedia Project, Carnegie Mellon's CDEC in the late 1980s pioneered the design and development of what we today call interactive multimedia (Cavalier & Dexheimer, 1989). I mention this historical context because it sheds light on the unique background for these programs and helps the reader understand the emphasis on design that concludes this chapter.

PROJECT THEORIA

A guiding principle for CAAE's work is captured in the flagship title of its initiatives: Project THEORIA. The title is an acronym for "Testing Hypotheses in Ethics: Observation, Reality, Imagination, and Affect." The term plays off of the origins for both theory and theater in the ancient Greek verb *theorein*: to see, to view, to behold (Covey, 1993). We seek within Project THEORIA to provide a theater wherein to test various theories and hypotheses relating to concrete case studies, value inquires, and social controversies. The studies themselves incorporate narrative and thick description and place a high value on reflective engagement. Too often these aspects of moral reality are lacking in classroom discussions. As Danner Clouser wrote (1993):

> Trying out one's theory on real situations, thick with details, is very different from the philosopher's typical hypothetical case, which, if not simply invented, is so highly abstracted from real circumstances that only enough details remain to defend selectively the particular point the philosopher wants to make thereby. His or her use of cases is much more to *illustrate* theory than to test it. But when *solving* the moral problem is the main point, the relentlessness of the details becomes readily apparent. There is no refuge; there is one quagmire after another; retreating to the theory is not a viable option. (p. 11)

One of the first programs developed under Project THEORIA was an already a famous case in medical ethics. With this case we explored interactive multimedia as a pedagogical tool and also embarked upon a formal, quantitative assessment of the new media treatment of the case itself (Bynum & Moor, 1998).

A RIGHT TO DIE? THE DAX COWART CASE

A Right to Die? The Dax Cowart Case (Andersen et al., 1996) investigated a burn patient's request to be allowed to die. The case relates the story of a 25-year-old man who received second-degree and third-degree burns over two thirds of his body. At the time that we encounter Dax in treatment, his injuries have left him severely scarred, his hands are badly deformed, and the sight in his one remaining eye is at risk. As a patient, he undergoes daily treatments in an antiseptic tank—tankings that are so painful to him that he has persistently asked the doctors to stop his treatment. Dax feels that the length of his projected treatment and the quality of life that he can expect to regain do not warrant the torment he must suffer. The doctors know that if they continue his treatment, he will live; if they stop his treatment, he will surely die. A basic question posed at this point of impasse between Dax and his caregivers is: Does Dax have a right to die? And, if so, what does this mean?

Structurally, the simulation provides flexible navigation through the central, and often competing, issues of the case. In a Guided Inquiry section, as depicted in Fig. 6.1, users take a semi-Socratic tour of the case from the bare facts to a confrontation with doctors, pa-

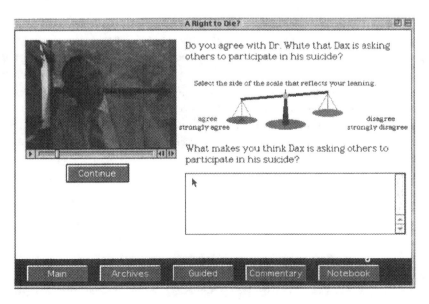

FIG. 6.1. A screen from the Dax Cowart Right to Die? simulation.

tient, and other principals over the issues of Medical Professionals' Obligations, Pain of Treatment, Quality of Life, and Patient's Rights and Capacities. At the end, a decision must be made as to whether Dax should have his request or not. Final sequences are determined on the basis of this recommendation. An Archive section contains video sections on the principals and main issues, as well as descriptions of other cases (e.g., Karen Quinlan). Recent state and federal court decisions on issues like physician-assisted suicide are also included.

In most instances, inside and outside the classroom, this case is analyzed via the philosophical and legal arguments for and against allowing Dax to have his request. Taking a model from the classic *Principles of Biomedical Ethics* by Beauchamp and Childress, the case can be cast as a conflict between the *prima facie* duties of beneficence, nonmaleficence, and respect for patient autonomy. Here the problem is to navigate between the doctors' duty to help and not harm their patients and the patient's right to refuse such help if he or she can demonstrate some rational consistency in requesting a denial of treatment.

In writing the *Teacher's Guide* for the simulation, we provide numerous suggestions for using the program. Just as one should never throw a disk at students and tell them to learn something from it, one should not throw disks at faculty and tell them to go forth and teach. Indeed, over and above the development of simulation software, one of the main impediments to the success of these programs is the thoughtful use of these programs in the classroom context. Among the suggestions offered in the Teacher's Guide is one that employs a constructivist learning model. The strategy uses the model of a hospital ethics committee (Minogue, 1996). Ethics committees often set hospital policy and such policy in turn is often driven by hard cases that come before it for prospective or retrospective review. Accordingly, I assign my class the Guided Inquiry section of the program and then have them role-play (in groups of five) an ethics committee discussion of Dax's Case and hospital policies issues arising out of this case. With one student as moderator, others discuss the case from the perspective of a patient advocate and a hospital administrator. This pedagogical approach places the reality of Dax's case within *a simulated model of real world decision making*.

From 1997–2000 we sought to discover if our interactive multimedia treatment of this case study did in fact improve learning outcomes for students who used this medium. We felt that the medium did have an advantage over text and film with regard to its representation of the complexity of these kinds of cases. We also felt that this kind of representation of the case would impact student appreciation for and recollection of the key people involved in the case, as well as a critical apprehension of the central issues relevant to the case.

For the purposes of this study we divided Introduction to Ethics and Introduction to Philosophy classes into three groups: text, film, and CD-ROM. A stratified and controlled sample for each group was achieved through the use of student scores on previous exams and student SAT (verbal) scores. Each group was given a functionally equivalent representation of the case and allowed 1.5 hours on the study task. Students in these groups would study the case individually under controlled circumstances (in classrooms or computer clusters) the evening before they were to take an essay exam. The text group used a narrative of the case and selected articles on the case; the film group viewed a 60-minute documentary on Dax's case; and the CD-ROM group was given selections from the Guided Inquiry and Archive sections of the program. The following day the students were given an in-class questionnaire dealing with the principals in the case and the issues in the case. The core questions, the answers to which were evaluated throughout the studies, involved three parts. The first part simply said: "Present the facts of the case." The second part asked the student to "describe the positions of each of the principals of the case" and then presented a list that included Dr. Robert White (Dax's psychiatrist), Dax Cowart (patient), Ada Cowart (Dax's mother), and Leslie Kerr (Dax's nurse). The third part asked each student how he or she would describe "the nature and relevance of the following issues in Dax's case" and then listed the following: Physician Obligations, Pain of Treatment, Quality of Life, Patient Rights and Capacities. The groups that worked with interactive multimedia performed significantly better on the tests. We identified the media element in this environment as reflective engagement, that ability of the medium to integrate the vivid representation of reality with demands of the critical thinking. "The hypothesis that students who participate in *reflective engagement* with real and compelling content (e.g., the Guided Inquires section) may have significant learning advantages over those who only read text or view videos seems to be supported by this study—at least in the realm of case analysis. In this regard, the study might place discipline-based, pedagogically sound interactive multimedia ahead of text and linear video in terms of student comprehension and retention" (Cavalier & Weber, 2002).

The assessment of the interactive CD-ROM validates Project THEORIA's assertion that this new media provides students with an element of practical wisdom that they would otherwise lack in discussing this case.[2] But if the conceptual framework for the discussion is limited to traditional categories of, for example, the types of ethical analysis found in most introductory textbooks, students might lack an important resource for approaching Dax's case. For while typical ethics books do well with theories such as Kant's deontological ethics and Bentham' utilitarian calculus, they do not to include sections on the field of conflict resolution and its relevance for ethical analysis.

Conflict Resolution

During the 1980s, books like *Getting to Yes: Negotiating Agreement Without Giving In* by Fisher and Ury and *Social Conflict: Escalation, Stalemate, and Settlement* by Rubin, Pruitt, and Kim created a curricular base for learning about conflict resolution and dispute mediation. The academic backdrop for these works goes back to initiatives such as the Harvard Negotiation Project and to academic disciplines such as social psychology and political science. A current taxonomy of this field shows that areas of interest to conflict resolution specialists include international, professional, and personal dispute mediation.[3]

A prototypical situation highlighting conflict resolution techniques is the following: Imagine two people arguing over an orange. They both say they want it and there is only one orange between them. Distributive justice might require an even divide (anything

---

[2]The use of the phrase practical wisdom refers to Aristotle's notion of *phroneisis* and refers, in this context, to the need to grasp the detailed complexity of particular circumstances in order to aim at the best human understanding of the issues at hand.

[3]For information about conflict resolution curricular and other resources, go to the Conflict Resolution Education Network at the National Institute for Dispute Resolution (www.crinfo.org/).

other than a 50/50 would be unfair). Now suppose that someone skilled in dispute mediation asks both parties to step down from their demands and state their interests in the orange. One party might say that he wishes to make orange juice; the other party, we discover, is only interested in the rind to make orange cake. Some simple brainstorming resolves the situation by allowing one party to use the juice and the other to use the rind. This is a win-win situation. No one feels slighted by the decision. Indeed, both parties are equally pleased by the outcome since both parties got what they wanted. Achieving this win-win situation in real life is usually not so easy, but there are techniques and concomitant skills that can be used to resolve apparently intractable conflicts.

The CAAE is unusual among areas in traditional philosophy for its interest in conflict resolution. Semester long courses offered within the Department of Philosophy deal specifically with conflict resolution and dispute mediation. If we now approach Dax's case through this curriculum, we can see a way out where there was not one before.

Consider the interests of the parties in this dispute. Dax describes his treatment in terms of being skinned alive (the daily removal of his bandages) and dipped in acid (his daily antiseptic baths). This painful treatment will go on for months (up to 270 days). In light of this, and with appeals to principles not unlike those found in Mill's *On Liberty*, he asked the doctors, not to actively kill him, but to allow him to die (a form of passive euthanasia). The doctors, especially his primary care physician and his burn specialist, appeal to principles that go back to the Hippocratic Oath: Doctors should help their patients and never harm them. The doctors felt that to acquiesce in Dax's request to refuse their help was tantamount to participating in Dax's suicide and they would not do this.

Viewing this situation as case in need of conflict resolution, it is possible to approach it in a manner similar to the prototypical case of dividing an orange. If we were to ask both parties to state their interests, we would find that Dax is mostly concerned with the pain that he experiences during his treatments and the doctors are mostly concerned with their ability to help this patient recover from his injuries. Some brainstorming might reveal that better pain management is called for: the doctors could increase the use of pain medication to a point where Dax could tolerate the treatments. Admittedly simplified, this analysis does show a role for conflict resolution in these kinds of ethics cases. In reality, many of the situations that come before hospital ethics committees could have been dealt with early on through dispute meditation techniques.

This recognition of the role that conflict resolution can play in addressing typical topics in ethics courses is explicitly employed in *The Issue of Abortion in America* (Cavalier et al., 1998). Extending Wertheimer's request to understand the argument of abortion from within the viewpoints held by the various interlocutors of the debate,[4] this program uses interactive multimedia to capture those thick descriptions that underscore the personal struggles behind the political rhetoric of the abortion controversy.[5]

Starting with a taxonomy of circumstances covering the possibility of terminating a pregnancy (such as rape, failed contraception, and fetal abnormality), the program enters the life histories of individuals and couples struggling with their decisions, as shown in Fig. 6.2. Through detailed analysis of the various positions that people hold, the user experiences the complex nature of the problem as part of the process of coming to a reasoned opinion about each of the general circumstances. The program also contains sections on the historical, legal, and medical dimensions of the issue, as well as overviews of religious and philosophical perspectives and positions in common ground movements. This latter section brings into focus the utility of conflict resolution methods. Through a series of questions, students are asked to state their particular perspective on the issue and list any pockets of uncertainty or mixed feelings that they may have. They are asked to consider what policies might lead to common agreement within certain areas of the abortion debate (e.g., sex education for early teens, broader support for adoption services). When students then discuss these kinds of cases in their simulated ethics committees, they can now bring common ground principles into the conversation.

---

[4]"By an argument I do not mean a concatenation of deathless propositions, but something with two sides that you have with someone, not present to him; not something with logical relations alone, but something encompassing human relations as well. We need to understand the argument in this fuller sense, for if we don't understand the human relations, we won't understand the logical ones either" (Wertheimer, 1974, p. 23).

[5]The source for this, and the following paragraph, comes from my chapter in Bynum and Moor (1998).

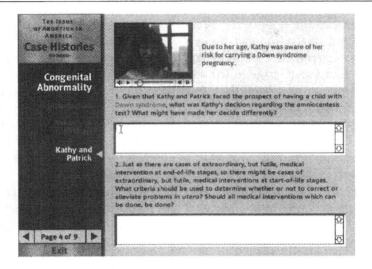

FIG. 6.2. A screen from *The Issue of Abortion in America*.

SIMULATION APPLICATIONS IN CONFLICT RESOLUTION

Allwyn Hall

In accord with our center's interest in advancing issues in applied ethics through the thoughtful use and development of educational technology, our work in conflict resolution naturally has an interactive media component. Beginning with a FIPSE grant in the early 1990s, Martha Harty embarked on the design and development of an interactive multimedia environment for developing skills in conflict resolution. The product of this effort is a CD-ROM entitled *Allwyn Hall*. The program addresses the social challenges that face students arriving on a college campus. Normal adjustment problems involving new friends and roommates, as well as typical situations involving the need to cooperate with others in a diverse setting often lead to conflicts that the students are ill-equipped to handle. These kinds of conflicts in turn can affect academic performance by consuming time and energy that could otherwise be devoted to study. The goal of *Allwyn Hall* is to help students gain the necessary skills to manage these conflicts better and in such a way that all parties involved can achieve a win-win situation (hence the terrible pun in "Allwyn" Hall).

To achieve the goal of the project, students are placed in the role of a resident assistant in a college dormitory called Allwyn Hall. Their task is to learn the basic elements of conflict resolution and then to employ that knowledge in the context of real, interactive situations. Depending on how well they deal with the conflicts they confront, the situations will either escalate or scale back (and become resolved to everyone's satisfaction). The student thereby becomes not only knowledgeable about the techniques involved in conflict resolution, but experienced in the use of those techniques. This is what makes the design of *Allwyn Hall* different from the previous works in Project THEORIA. In this program and the following (*In All Respects*), users are placed within a simulated environment that allows them to learn by doing. No only are they exposed to reality (as users in the Dax Cowart and the Issue of Abortion programs are), but they participate in the reality of real world scenarios.[6] Thus they not only *know that*, for example, conflict resolution techniques can involve three stages, but they also *know how*, for example, to employ those conflict resolution techniques in such a way as to get the desired result. This is the mark of Aristotle's practical wisdom that comes only from experience, and this is the kind of knowledge that a simulation is particularly good at achieving.

Once the CD-ROM is opened, the user is given the role of a resident assistant (RA) and the opportunity to learn about the basic methods for conflict resolution. The problem solving process employed in *Allwyn Hall* involves three stages. Put simply, Stage 1 (Air All Viewpoints) requires the user to find out the feelings of those involved in the conflict, their account of the conflict, what they want, what matters to them and what they need, and why this is important to them. Stage 2 (State the Problem) requires the RA to combine everyone's needs into a summary statement. Using neutral language, the RA tries to make the problem a joint concern that all parties can agree to ("how can we deal with our needs and still remain friends?"). Finally, this stage focuses on the future instead of the past.

---

[6]The programs on Dax and Abortion can be described as weak simulations while the programs on developing conflict resolution skills can be described as strong simulations. The former represent reality through the thick descriptions of real people in real situations, but the latter places the user in that reality through the adoption of a role to play. It is the aspect of role-play that connects the latter programs to the discussion of *poetics* at the end of this chapter.

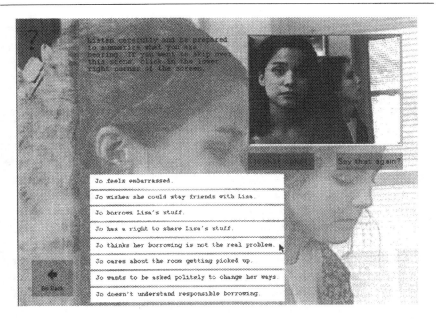

FIG. 6.3. A screen from the *Allwyn Hall* simulation.

Stage 3 (Create A Solution) tries to brainstorm on a solution based upon the problem statement identified in Stage 2. From a list that contains all the ideas proposed, the parties should choose those solutions that meet most of their needs.

After this orientation, the user (RA) enters a virtual hallway. By using the mouse to navigate down this hallway, the user can enter any of three rooms. In each room a conflict situation has or will arise.[7] An opening video sets up the conflict that the RA must resolve. All camera work is shot in the subjective, with actors addressing and looking at the user when appropriate. As the user interactively employs the three-stage strategy, the characters in the conflict situations respond directly to the user—and poorly managed situations will escalate. Figure 6.3 provides a sample screen from this simulation.

In one scenario, for example, Jo and Lisa are arguing over being roommates and Jo has asked the RA to come in to see what is going on. Jo angrily demands that she get a new roommate. If the RA can successfully mange the evolution of the situation by listening to Jo

---

[7]The three situations are: roommate conflict (Lisa and Jo); resource sharing conflict (group in the study hall); and a relationship conflict (involving Rico and Dave).

and Lisa and by brainstorming with them in order to find a solution, then, as in real life, there may be a reasonably good chance that the conflict may be resolved. After completing each encounter, the user receives feedback and may continue to another room or exit the program.

The assessment of *Allwyn Hall* used eight different groups of students (totaling approximately 180 students), ranging from no exposure to one class period of exposure to embedding the simulation in a semester-long course. The pretest and post-tests (pencil and paper surveys) looked for changes in attitudes toward conflict and inclinations to consider both sides and analyze conflicts in terms of parties' interests. The preliminary analysis showed shifts in both attitude and approaches to conflict, including use of specific conflict skills. Changes were correlated with levels of exposure to training using the CD-ROM. Another evaluation using a simulated negotiation situation was used to test long-term retention of the skills. Students who had received the full-semester training course 3–4 years prior outperformed controls in reaching fair outcomes in the negotiation. They did not show explicit skill use, but appeared to appreciate the perspective of the opposing party to a greater degree than controls.

In All Respects

In All Respects focuses on developing the skills of active listening. It places the user in the role of a campus documentary video producer. Recognizing that every point-of-view documentary involves editing choices that create a certain perspective on the subject matter, the challenge for the student is to create a video that listens to all sides and represents those views fairly. The program is at once an application dealing with the topic of racism on campus and an authoring system that can be customized to deliver content dealing with other social issues on campus (such as sexism). The latter involves producing different video segments and different text. These would then be formatted and inserted in the Director files to create an essentially different application.

The program simulates a campus media studio and, through the role of a producer, gives the user the opportunity to create a fully functional, stand-alone digital video. The program opens with a dramatic video on the issue of racism on campus and allows for up to three us-

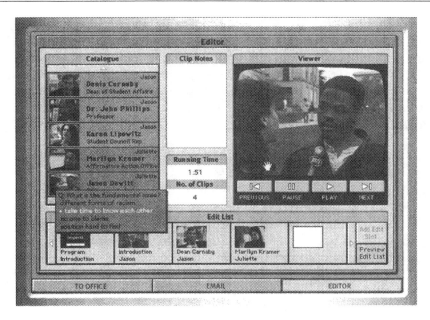

FIG. 6.4. A screen from the *In All Respects* simulation.

ers to insert their names and enter the program. Figure 6.4 shows a sample screen from this simulation. Using a 5-day timeline (located on top of the screen), the first day sets the stage. The dean of "Cole College" introduces the problem to be addressed and describes the task. There are three options on the bottom of the screen: mail, studio, and edit room. E-mail messages give the user context and directions, such as informing the user that he or she must go to the studio to assign various faculty and students to the reporters. Thus on Day 2 the user starts to make editorial decisions as he or she sees the list (and race) of potential interviewees. Users assign faculty, staff, and student interviewees to a male or female reporter. Choosing to omit potential interviewees or assigning them in an imbalanced way will give clues to the underlying algorithm of the program.

On Day 3 users are given a check list of questions for the reporters to ask their interviewees. Once again, editorial decisions are made as certain questions may be omitted from the list.

By Day 4 all of the interviews have been completed and the user goes to the studio to edit the documentary. A virtual video edit suite allows for realistic editing. The producer selects interviews to watch and then creates a linear video by dragging segments into a timeline.

Here the final sets of editorial decisions are made: which segments to use and what order to use them. Day 5 submits the edited video out for final production. A special feature saves the video as a separate run-time version. Prior to this stage, the user gets an e-mail message evaluating the fairness of the selection process and making suggestions, if necessary, on producing a more complete and balanced program.

NEW MEDIA, NEW OPPORTUNITIES

Recent work in New Media Studies suggests that we are beginning to understand interactive, digital media as a new medium for the first time. Roughly analogous to cinema's emerging self understanding through the employment of the cut, the mobile camera, lighting techniques, etc., in the first part of the 20th Century, we now see theories of human-computer interaction (HCI) articulate the unique contributions of interactive multimedia to the art forms of the 21st Century. Packer and Jordan's *Multimedia From Wagner to Virtual Reality* convincingly established a dialectic between artists and engineers ("Artboys and Geeks" as Gibson says in his forward to the book) that has driven digital media toward the establishment of its own unique categories. Manovich's *The Language of New Media* argued forcefully that the digitalization of all media forms creates new and fundamental principles of its own (its own grammar and logic).

In what way can these kinds of discussions shed light on the nature of the simulations discussed previously? In what way can we better understand the relation between the content of these programs and the media that delivers them? I use two authors whose books on digital media help us to understand how and why these programs work the way they do. The first is Murray's *Hamlet on the Holodeck: The Future of Narrative in Cyberspace* and the second is Laurel's *Computers as Theatre*.

The title of Murray's book suggests that advances in technology will bring with them new ways to raise age-old human questions such as those that Shakespeare addressed. As she investigates this possibility, she discusses the new aesthetics of the digital medium: immersion, agency, and transformation. The criteria one establishes for these new aesthetic pleasures may help us understand the nature of our simulations and why they work as they do.

Immersion is the "experience of being transported to an elaborately simulated place" and is "pleasurable in itself, regardless of the fantasy content" (Murray, 1998, p. 98). The aesthetic of immersion is most clearly seen in computer games and, as Turkle pointed out, on-line MUDs (or multi-user domains). It is also clearly present in *Allwyn Hall* and *In All Respects*. In the former program, the user is immersed in a dormitory setting; in the later, in a production studio.

"The more realized the immersive environment, the more active we want to be in it" and the sense of agency is achieved when our actions affect the simulated world in a realistic (causal) way (Murray, 1998, p. 127). Again, games are the most obvious example. When I am driving on a simulated racetrack, my movements should be modeled realistically. The more agency I experience, the more immersive the experience will be. In *Allwyn Hall* the sense of agency can be seen in, for example, the movement down the hall and into the various rooms. More importantly, this agency is invoked during the three-stage process of conflict resolution, where faulty or successful strategies are constantly reinforced by actor behaviors and screen options. During *In All Respects*, agency is achieved by the selection process (if the reporter is assigned a faculty member and given three questions to ask, the response to those questions is found in the video of that particular faculty member). In the video editing room, selections by the user are immediately modeled in the actual editing of the digital video clips.

Transformation refers, in a most general way, to the kinds of shape-shifting and mutability made possible in the digital medium. "The transformative power of the computer is particularly seductive in narrative environments. It makes us eager for masquerade, eager to pick up the joystick and become a cowboy or space fighter, eager to log on to the MUD and become ElfGirl or BackDagger" (Murray, 1998, p. 154). In both of our programs, this transformation is achieved through the function of role-playing. In *Allwyn* Hall, the user adopts the role of a Resident Assistant, and in *In All Respects*, the user adopts the role of documentary video producer. In a sense, role-playing ties everything together. If the quality of the design and interactivity of the program is good, then by adopting a role one is transformed into a participant in a highly immersive, agency rich simulated reality. This is the virtual world that one enters.

There is another aspect of transformation that may result from participating in these learning environments. Traditionally, story-telling itself has been seen to have transformative powers. Reading Tolstoy's *The Death of Ivan Illich* can change our view of ourselves and the world. A good story, well-told, can transform us. Tolstoy even saw this as the very function of Art. In this regard, Murray wrote that "[d]igital narratives add another powerful element to this potential by offering us the opportunity to enact stories rather than to merely witness them" (Murray, 1998, p. 170). It may be hoped that users of *Allwyn Hall* and *In All Respects* become more attuned to conflicts and more skillful in managing their own lives. They may transform themselves in people who seek win-win situations, who actively listen, and who ultimately get along better with those around them. Certainly this is one meaning of a successful life and no small outcome to be achieved.

Ancient Greek, the Urlanguage of philosophy, has much to offer in the way of understanding new media and its applications. As a director of a "Minor in Multimedia Production," I am constantly at pains to point out to my students that the origin of the word production goes back to the Greek word *poiesis* (creating, making). By locating this word within the tradition of the productive arts, I can locate the minor within the liberal arts tradition: it is not a vocation curriculum designed to get students into the job of webmaster. Such students may indeed become what Murray called interactive designers, but that will owe as much to an understanding of the meaning of the new media as it will to mastering the latest tools of the new media. Laurel also appreciated the rich tradition that lies behind the new media. Indeed, her book *Computers as Theatre* suggested that we go back to Aristotle's *Poetics* for a clearer grasp of what new media means and how it can accomplish the tasks that are most appropriate to it.

Aristotle's *Poetics* deals both with the problem of representation (*mimesis*) as such and with the principles and elements that underlie such representation on stage. In Laurel, these problems of representation are cast first through theories of Human Computer Interaction and then through an interpretation of the *Poetics* that leads to a practical guide for designing a computer-mediated representation.

One problem with traditional theories of HCI is their focus on the relation between user and computer as if the distance between the two is overcome through better icons and metaphors that enable the person to communicate with the 0s and 1s of the hardware. "In the theatrical view of human-computer activity, the stage is a virtual world. It is populated by agents, both human and computer-generated, and other elements of the representational context" (Laurel, 1993, p. 17). In the context of *Allwyn Hall*, the user, by adopting the role of Resident Assistant, enters (through immersion, agency, and transformation) the environment of the program. He or she is not an audience member watching a performance. He or she is part of the performance (the representation is all there is). This is what Laurel called an existential WYSIWYG. *Simulations*, in this sense, carry forth and transform traditions found in the history of theater.

Consider, for example, the notion of a dramatic *flying wedge*. This is the demand that a plot progresses from the possible (the butler was in the house) to the probable (as others are eliminated from suspicion) to the necessary (the butler, confronted by the inspector, confesses to the crime). We start out with many possibilities, but these are narrowed down to a single point as the play progresses.

In the new media, an interactive flying wedge emerges. "In human-computer activity, the shaping of potential is influenced by people's real-time choices and actions, pruning possibilities and creating lines of probability that differ from session to session and person to person" (Laurel, 1993, p. 72). In *Allwyn Hall*, different users will experience different paths and varying levels of success through the choices they make to manage the conflicts. Each iteration through the program will create its own flying wedge consistent with the whole action that unfolds in the completion of the task. Invariably the user will be brought closer to the end of his or her encounter with the three situations (Lisa and Jo, the group in the study hall, and Rico and Dave) and a debriefing by the person who provided the orientation will conclude the session.

The rise and completion of each conflict, as well as the experience of the program as a whole, has yet another connection to the tradition of theater. In 1863, Freytag used a triangular-shaped diagram to represent the shape of dramatic action (as a triangle, the action can be represented as rise and fall). "The 'complication axis' of a Frey triangle," wrote Laurel, "represents the *informational attributes* of each dramatic incident" (Laurel, 1993, p. 83). In *Allwyn Hall*'s roommate conflict, the opening video establishes the context for the unfolding action (Jo wants a new roommate because Lisa uses her things, doesn't return them, etc.). The opening video also demonstrates the inciting incidents as both Jo and Lisa argue over each other's actions. As the user begins to intervene and the three-stage process of conflict resolution unfolds, a crisis moment appears as the participants move toward resolution or destabilization. The climax is the moment at which one of the lines of probability becomes a necessity and the action falls as, in the best outcome, the roommates agree to work together on the solutions that everyone has suggested. The dénouement in this case is simply the exiting of the room on good or bad terms. So too, the dénouement of the entire program is the debriefing session in which the user is congratulated or advised on his or her performance.

Given that the traditions of theater can help us understand human-computer interaction in a way appropriate to the new media (and its capacity for simulation), what else might the tradition provide by way of insight? Laurel's answer is provocative and leads directly to an interpretation of Aristotle's *Poetics*.

The concept of *techne* provides a principled way to link the creative process of representation to human-computer interaction. For the poet does not simply pass into a state of divine madness as Plato would have us believe. There is a craft to multimedia production and if we are to follow Aristotle here, we need to attend to the categories he utilizes in his work in order to understand the nature of this craft.

In his *Physics* and *Metaphysics*, Aristotle describes the substance of things in terms of those causes or responsibilities that make something what it is and not something else. For example, a bronze vase can be known in terms of its four "causes." The *material* cause is the stuff that it is made of—the bronze metal. The *formal* cause is the general shape or pattern that it consists of—the shape of a vase rather than a plate or a sword. The *efficient* cause is that which is responsible for it coming into being—the artisan who hammered and shaped the material. The *final* cause is the purpose for which it is intended—to hold grain. Note that the final cause or *telos* has a certain priority in the causal nexus as it is that which is responsible for the selecting and shaping of material by the artisan.

Interpreting Aristotle, Laurel noted that "[t]he four causes are forces that operate concurrently and interactively during the process of creation" (Laurel, 1993, p. 41). She then did a causal analysis to describe the design process for the creation of an interactive multimedia simulation.[8]

---

[8]I am aware that the actual design and development of a complex simulation is often messy and chaotic. In our lab this usually means taking three to four talented people and putting them on a wild elephant for a year or so. Once they get off the ride,

In terms of the causes that make *Allwyn Hall* what it is, we can describe the production of this program as follows. Assuming that our goal (purpose) is to create an environment for the acquisition of some skills in conflict resolution, we might (our Muses willing) design a simulation for the development of these skills that fits the users' background (college students). This, in turn, might suggest a program that has the form of an RA confronting conflicts that need successful resolution. Once we have decided upon that form, we would need to fill it in with specific (material) content, for example, the three concrete conflicts and the characters and agents involved. The efficient cause of this production would be the programmers, video producers, project manager, and so forth along with the various tools that they use (Director, Photoshop, etc.).

In neo-Aristotlean terms, the description can be reduced to its formal and material causes. The formal cause shapes the material; the material cause fills in the shape of the experience. In this instance, the formal cause of the program is conflict resolution and the material cause of the program is a school dorm and various conflicts.

The analysis of *Allwyn Hall* is deepened by adding an HCI interpretation of Aristotle's six elements along with the causal relation among them. For Aristotle, a successful performance (which can be applied in this case to all computer-based simulations), requires the following: Action (plot-structure), Character, Thought, "Language" (Diction), Pattern (Melody), and Enactment (Spectacle).

Laurel reconfigured the HCI element of Action or plot-structure as the whole action as it is collaboratively shaped by the system and the user. In terms of *Allwyn Hall*, the plot-structure, the whole experience, is of this room and this dormitory and these conflicts in need of resolution—this is the action. The HCI element of Character is interpreted as the bundles of predispositions and traits, inferred from the agents' (human or computer origin) patterns of choice. In terms of *Allwyn Hall*, we can see this in the characters of Lisa and Joanne (who they are, how they manifest themselves in their gestures, attitudes, and choices).

---

we have a product. The literature on software engineering describes this as a spiral design process where iterative tweaking of the work in progress is a kind of dynamic formative evaluation. Yet it seems to me that both Laurel and Murray described the elements of multimedia design in a way that has explanatory power beyond the typical step-by-step procedures found in the literature.

The HCI element of Thought consists of the inferred internal processes leading to choice (cognition, emotion, and reason). This can be seen in the arguments and emotional appeals that Lisa and Joanne make. For example, Lisa says "Jo is selfish, she thinks she has a right to my things." In terms of *Allwyn Hall*, this element of thought can be elicited during active listening. The HCI element of "Language" (Diction) is found in the selection and arrangement of signs (verbal, visual, auditory, and iconic), the specific manner in which the thoughts are expressed (the script), and also the specific manner and consistency in which navigational buttons and boxes are placed on the screen (the specific manner in which one can move around the program).

The HCI element of Pattern (Melody) consists of the pleasurable perception of pattern in sensory phenomena. In terms of *Allwyn Hall*, this includes the meaningful arrangement of windows, layout of text, background pictures that refer to foreground scenes—design as well as audio–video quality. The HCI element of Enactment (Spectacle) relates to everything that is seen—the sensory dimensions of the action being represented. Determined ultimately by the plot-structure, this is the whole multimedia production as seen. It is the interactive stage with all its bells and whistles.

Today we can add another element to Aristotle's list. It is surely contained in Laurel's HCI reinterpretation, but we should be explicit about the added element of Interactivity as defined by Murray (with its aesthetic pleasures of immersion, agency, and transformation). Taken together, all these elements make *Allwyn Hall* a compelling application and one that seems to align itself with the possibilities of the digital medium per se.

With these new multimedia simulations, the story becomes *my* story—the human-computer interaction brings me *into* the representation of a reality. Multiple outcomes (interactive flying wedges) serve to create experiences of resolving a conflict or producing a documentary. And just as flight simulators provide pilots with the critical skills necessary to get into a real plane, so too we might envision simulations in the social sciences that enter into the practical wisdom of a person as he or she encounters the details of an interpersonal conflict or the subtleties of racial or sexual stereotyping. Done well, simulations are a kind of drama, and producers of such simulations would do well to attend to the traditions of theater that impact and are transformed by the emerging categories of the new media.

REFERENCES

Andersen, D., Cavalier, R., & Covey, P. (1996). *A right to die? The Dax Cowart case.* London: Routledge.

Bynum, T. W., & Moor, J. H. (1998). *The digital phoenix: How computers are changing philosophy.* Oxford, England: Blackwell Publishers.

Cavalier, R., Covey, P., Style, L., & Thompson, A. (1998). *The issue of abortion in America: An exploration of a social controversy on CD-ROM.* London: Routledge.

Cavalier, R., & Dexheimer, J. (1989). ICEC: A collaborative effort to advance educational computing, 1983–1989. *Academic Computing, 4*(3), 16–18, 58–60.

Cavalier, R., & Weber, K. (2002). Learning, media, and the case of Dax Cowart: A comparison of text, film, and interactive multimedia. *Interactive Learning Environments, 10*(3), 243–262.

Clouser, K. D. (1993). Hastings Center Report. *Special Supplement, 25*(6), S11.

Covey, P. (1993). The crucible of experience. In R. Heeger & T. Willigenburg (Eds.), *The turn to applied ethics* (pp. 55–72). The Netherlands: Kok Oharos.

Laurel, B. (1993). *Computers as theatre.* Reading, MA: Addison-Wesley.

Manovich, L. (2002). *The language of new media.* Cambridge, MA: MIT Press.

Minogue, B. (1996). *Bioethics: A committee approach.* Boston: Jones and Bartlett Publishers.

Murray, J. H. (1998). *Hamlet on the holodeck: The future of narrative in cyberspace.* Cambridge, MA: MIT Press.

Packer, R., & Jordan, K. (2001). *Multimedia: From Wagner to virtual reality.* New York: Norton.

Wertheimer, R. (1974). Understanding the abortion argument. *A Philosophy & Public Affairs Reader, 23.*

Virtual Sex: Creating Environments for Reducing Risky Sex

Lynn Carol Miller
Stephen John Read
University of Southern California

After more than 20 years (since 1980), there is still no cure for acquired immunodeficiency syndrome (AIDS). Many powerful drugs have been Food and Drug Administration (FDA) approved and prolong survival. Nevertheless, the realities of long-term and short-term drug side effects, as well as the increasing prevalence of multiple strains of human immunodeficiency virus (HIV) that are resistant to these drugs (Chesney, Morin, & Sherr, 2000; Siegel, Schrimshaw, & Raveis, 2000) underscore the importance of HIV prevention. Behavioral interventions to prevent HIV infection are essential, particularly among high-risk groups such as MSM (men who have sex with men). Making this even more critical is a new generation of MSM who are now in danger of exposure in a second wave of HIV infection (CDC, 1998, 1999a, 1999b; Hogg et al., 2001; Mutchler, 2000).

CAN INTERACTIVE TECHNOLOGIES CHANGE RISKY BEHAVIOR?

Wolitski, Valdiserri, Denning, and Levine (2001) argued that one of the reasons for this new wave of HIV infection is that "outdated or overly simplistic safer sex messages for MSM (a common criticism in recent years) have led to a backlash against existing prevention efforts" (pp. 883–884). It is crucial, therefore, that HIV prevention interventions keep pace with changes in HIV-related trends and successfully compete for the attention of MSM using technological advances that can enhance message delivery. Attention grabbing and engaging, interactive video (IAV) may be better able to compete with and counter messages that might deter men, especially younger men—the MTV generation—from engaging in safer sexual practices. Our goal was to develop a virtual interactive environment that would enhance men's use of safer sexual practices in risky situations. Our central question was: Could learning in virtual environments reduce risky practices in actual sexual encounters?

At a theoretical level, IAV with virtual sexual encounters not only can integrate many theoretical concepts thought to be important for changing risky sexual practices, it also can create realistic, emotionally textured scenarios. These may enhance information processing and increase retrieval of the messages relevant to safer sex specifically and health promotion more broadly.

However, is there evidence that IAV can enhance such learning? In the educational domain, IAV and its interactivity have been found to enhance transfer of learning in new contexts compared to other noninteractive media (Moreno, Mayer, Spires, & Lester, 2001). Yet, the literature on the use of IAV to produce health behavior is more limited. Nevertheless, it is quite promising. IAV has been shown to be effective in asthma education (Bartholemew et al., 2000; Lieberman, 1995), smoking prevention (Tingen, 1997), alcohol education (Reis, Riley, & Baer, 2000), diabetes management (Brown et al., 1997), and healthful diet change (Brug et al., 1999; Campbell, DeVellis, Strecher, & Ammerman, 1994; Kreuter & Strecher, 1996; Winett et al., 1991).

In the current work, we have developed and tested an intervention that helps to fill the intervention-innovation gap in safer sex education. While relying on the components of interventions that past research suggests are critical to HIV prevention change, it utilizes CD ROM interactive video (IAV) technology—an attention-grabbing medium—to reengage MSM on a virtual date. In doing so, it readily provides practical experience and training in vital cognitive and behavioral skills (in a realistic, mildly sexually arousing narrative) for recognizing and negotiating potentially risky sexual situations.

To proceed through the sexual scenario the user must actively make dating choices and see the behavioral consequences of these choices. As he makes choices that impact the unfolding sexual sequence, he interacts with peer counselors who serve as guides. These guides make the risks in sexual decisions more salient and they provide advice and modeling for how to deal with risky situations. Because the emotions evoked on the virtual date, including sexual arousal, are apt to be similar to those in a real sexual scenario, this intervention may also enhance the encoding of HIV prevention messages and their subsequent retrieval and use in emotionally similar real-life risky encounters (Bower & Forgas, 2000).

If IAV—as a medium—can enhance, or be as effective as one-on-one counseling alone, this could provide a remarkable tool in the fight against the spread of HIV and other sexually transmitted diseases (STDs). Interactive media have the major advantage that once interventions have been developed they can be delivered to a wide range of individuals with a relatively small investment per individual. Moreover, the initial development costs can be amortized over a large number of different individuals. Further, in contrast to traditional methods that require one-on-one instructors, the IAV can be used without instructor assistance, helping to alleviate man-power shortages at delivery sites. Therefore, IAV could be extremely cost-effective and make interventions—previously not feasible—doable.

In addition, although safer sex educators often alter the original message over time, IAV products do not suffer from such slippage or change in the message. As previously mentioned, this technology may be much more attention getting and motivating for MSM, and especially for growing numbers of young people—those most at risk for contracting the virus. Interventions can be targeted to particular audiences: That is, the user's characteristics, such as ethnicity, could trigger the particular IAV shown on the DVD. IAV interventions can also be response tailored: That is the user could receive messages that are framed and designed, based on research, to reduce risk taking given the participant's specific pattern of decision making in the IAV. We turn now to a more detailed description of the theoretical approaches that guided the development of the IAV before describing the IAV and the intervention in more detail.

THEORY THAT GUIDED CONTENT INCLUSION DECISIONS IN IAV

In developing the IAV for MSM, we examined the existing literature regarding what theoretical elements appeared to be effective for changing HIV risk behaviors and tried to build these into the IAV. In addition, we considered literatures concerned with virtual environments, the rich situational features that might be better captured via IAV (and their relevance to behavior change), and the emotional facets of safer sex negotiation that might be better captured via IAV than through traditional one-on-one interventions. We review some of this literature below.

Social-Cognitive Theory-Based Components Designed into the IAV

Guided by a variety of theoretical approaches such as Bandura's (1994) cognitive social learning theory, cognitive behavior therapy (Beck, 1970), and the theory of planned behavior (Ajzen, 1985, 1987, 1991; Ajzen & Fishbein, 1980), various researchers (for reviews see DiClemente & Peterson, 1994 and Fisher & Fisher, 1992) have demonstrated that extensive training in cognitive and behavioral skills can significantly reduce high risk sexual practices (e.g., anal sex without a condom) and increase the level of perceived self-efficacy and behavioral intentions to practice safer sex. Based on this work, Kelly (1995) identified a number of theory-based components that should be included in a behavioral intervention for changing risky sexual behavior for men who have sex with men. These include increasing perceived self-efficacy for making behavior change and a belief that those changes will reduce risk (Ajzen, 1991; Bandura, 1994) and forming a strong behavioral intention to use safer sex behaviors when appropriate (Ajzen, 1985). They also include teaching behavioral skills (such as condom use and assertiveness skills), and self-management skills for managing cognitions and behaviors relevant to risky situations (Beck, 1970). Additional components include teaching problem-solving skills for dealing with obstacles and problems, and reinforcing successful behavior change efforts.

Kelly, St. Lawrence, Hood, and Brasfield (1989) embedded training that included these components in 12 weekly, 75-minute group sessions. Kelly, St. Lawrence, Betts, Brasfield, and Hood (1990) used an abbreviated seven-session version. Individuals were trained in cognitive and behavioral strategies designed to manage potential risk triggers and to guide self-change efforts. Instruction included how to make practical life changes, such as avoiding sex when drinking, avoiding risky settings, and keeping condoms handy. Individuals also practiced cognitive self-statements to guide and reinforce their own change efforts. In role-play rehearsal they practiced sexual assertiveness and communications skills in response to confederates who simulated coercive partners. Finally, most sessions used modeling, behavioral rehearsal, feedback, and assignments to practice risk-reduction skills in real life. This program resulted in substantial reductions in risky sexual activities, such as unprotected anal intercourse. Furthermore, these risk reductions were maintained over an 8-month follow up.

Others (Jemmott & Jemmott, 1994, 1999; Jemmott, Jemmott, & Fong, 1998) also presented several successful interventions based on these principles, targeted at heterosexual African-American adolescents. Recently, our team used a modified version of the Jemmott and Jemmott (1999) intervention for women at risk and our initial analyses showed that this intervention was also very effective in changing risk behavior of the Los Angeles sample of women over time. These and other programs (e.g., Fisher, Fisher, Williams, & Malloy, 1994) have been quite effective in changing risky sexual behavior, but they are quite labor intensive and expensive to deliver, as well as requiring a considerable time commitment from participants.

Situational Cues and Implementation Intentions: Theory and Simulation Application

Situational cues captured in virtual environments might also enhance learning and subsequent successful reduction of risky sexual practices in similar real-life situations. As McConnell, Leibold, and Sherman (1997) noted, individuals often have stable internalized propensities and attitudes that are inconsistent with one another. Nevertheless, some attitudes (e.g., favoring using condoms) might be linked to some specific situational features; other attitudes (e.g., inhibiting condom use) might be linked to other contextual features. Insuring that the situational and affective features that men are likely to encounter are, in fact, more tied to safer choices might reduce HIV risk taking and result in greater generalization to similar contexts (Van der Plight, Zeelenberg, Van Dijk, De Vries, & Richard, 1998).

Gollwitzer's work (1990, 1996; Gollwitzer & Moskowitz, 1996) on what he terms implementation intentions and behavioral mind-sets suggests that going through our realistic, concrete simulation should greatly enhance the likelihood that the skills learned in simulated situations should transfer to real-life situations. Gollwitzer (1990, 1996) defined an implementation intention as a specific intention about when, where, and how to approach and achieve a goal, that is the individual essentially says, "When these situational conditions are met, I will initiate behavior x." As Gollwitzer (1990, 1996) noted, such intentions form linkages between specific situations and the appropriate behavior, and pass control of the behavior to relevant situational cues. In a series of studies, Gollwitzer (1990, 1996) demonstrated that when individuals have formed a specific implementation intention, they are much more likely to actually achieve the goal when faced with the appropriate situation. In addition, individuals better recall the environmental features that cue the plan and the relevant features seem to demand peoples' attention, even when they are under high cognitive load. Furthermore, individuals respond to the relevant features much more quickly and automatically, they are quicker to initiate the linked plan or action, and the linked plan is activated automatically, with little need for conscious intention.

Getting individuals to the point where the initiation of the appropriate strategy is almost automatically initiated by the appropriate environmental cues would be particularly advantageous in situations, such as sexual encounters, where anxiety, sexual arousal, and drug and alcohol use may inhibit the formation of conscious intentions. Because virtual environments (IAVs) could provide a rich array of realistic situational cues, such environments might increase the likelihood that subsequently encountering similar real life situations will automatically activate learned behavioral responses (e.g., safer practices).

Virtual Worlds: Role of Emotional Engagement and Congruence on Learning and Real-Life Situations

In addition to providing practical experience and education for men at significant risk, other aspects of this IAV make it a potentially valuable tool. For instance, this method of instruction is apt to be far more engaging and involving than such traditional passive instruction, as lectures or films (Moreno et al., 2001). Furthermore, in contrast to role playing, this method is more realistic and can be utilized privately and anonymously without the user's fear of being judged for the choices he makes. Since the user is in control, we expect this approach will foster a sense of self-efficacy and will empower gay men in future sexual negotiations.

Another strength of the video is that it can be sexually arousing, increasing the similarity between the intervention and a typical sexual encounter. Instruction that occurs under psychological and emotional states similar to those under which the behavior will be enacted should improve transfer to the subsequent situation (Bower & Forgas, 2000). Since our IAV incorporates safer sex education into a semi-realistic context (including sexual arousal), this should greatly enhance the recall and application of critical cognitive and behavioral skills, such as self-control strategies and sexual negotiation techniques.

Multiple Conflicting Messages and Subtle Message Tailoring

As mentioned earlier, there is a growing body of messages that MSM are exposed to that conflict with traditional use a condom and safer sex messages. In the face of multiple conflicting messages and attitudes (some of which men might concurrently have activated), how might researchers best reduce risk? Persuasion and attitude researchers have identified a variety of subtle message effects that might effectively reduce risk (Wood, 2000), but these often need to be tailored for specific situational factors. For example, as previously discussed, ensuring that in the presence of particular situational features, that a pro-condom set of motivations and implementations are activated might significantly reduce risk in that context in the future.

Framing effects can exert a profound impact on health behavior (Rothman & Salovey, 1997) such that some frames (e.g., gain frames) work best for prevention while other frames (e.g., loss frames) work better for detection or when individuals confront more risky situations. In our IAV, we built in framing elements that mapped onto prior research. That is, generally, messages—provided by guides—were framed as gains (e.g., use condoms to stay safe, avoid HIV). But, when the individual was about to take a risk (e.g., have unprotected anal sex), the guides automatically popped up providing a loss-framed message (e.g., "Are you kidding? Anal sex without a condom. Don't you know how dangerous that is? Even if you are HIV positive you can still get other strains of the disease and get AIDS faster. Don't fool yourself into thinking being on top is safe. If you still want to have anal sex (and I know you do), you can still change your mind and put one on right now."). Individuals in the IAV who take greater risks might benefit from such differently framed messages. Some individuals (e.g., sexual sensation seekers) have been found to take bigger sexual risks (Kalichman & Rompa, 1995). MSM who score higher on this reliable individual difference measure have significantly higher levels of unprotected anal sex (Chng & Geliga-Vargas, 2000).

Tailoring different messages to different responses is quite possible with IAV. In many respects, many successful one-on-one interventions are tailored to the specific circumstances of the participant within the structure of the intervention elements. Yet, tailoring some messages in one-on-one counseling sessions (e.g., differential framing) could be extremely difficult. Even if the training needed to produce such nuanced tailored messages could be achieved and sustained in clinic settings, there is a more practical problem. Loss frames, for example, might work in HIV prevention only when participants are caught up in the sexual sequence and have—in fact—decided to take the risk anyway.

Perhaps because it is used privately, making such risky decisions happens fairly frequently in our interactive video. In contrast, in our experience, rarely, if ever, does the participant in a role-playing interpersonal intervention act out a scenario where they choose to engage in risky behavior regardless of the counselor suggestions. Thus, IAV may offer greater flexibility in tailoring messages relevant to real-life sexual sequences, as well as greater reliability and technology transfer. Thus, there are a number of reasons why IAV could potentially be quite effective, including message tailoring.

ENGAGING MEN WHO HAVE SEX WITH MEN: THE TARGET AUDIENCE

In the following, we describe the content of the IAV, as well as the study evaluating the IAV's efficacy. In this research we designed and assessed the effectiveness of the IAV as an intervention by comparing it with a more traditional method of intervention: counseling alone.

Description of the Gay Men's IAV

Our IAV places gay men in an interactive, virtual environment that portrays a realistic sexual interaction similar to ones men might encounter in their own lives, a first date. It has been explicitly designed to include those features that have been identified as central to changing risky sexual behavior. It provides both modeling and directed practice of the cognitive and behavioral skills needed to successfully negotiate safer sex. Participants, in the guise of their video character, negotiate safer sex with the other character in the video. As part of this, they are given advice and possible scripts and tactics to use in negotiating. Participants are also given instruction in self-management skills and given self-instructions for such things as recognizing risky situations, such as the use of drugs and alcohol, or going into the bedroom without previously reaching an agreement to engage in safer sex. Further, as they go through the IAV, participants are rewarded for making good choices, in the form of praise from two guides, and punished for making risky choices, in the form of criticism or gentle rebuffs from the guides.

In addition to providing participants with cognitive and behavioral skills, this IAV does several other things. First, providing explicit negotiation skills and tactics, and the experience of successfully negotiating safer sex with their partner, should increase perceived self-efficacy by providing a concrete instance of successful negotiation. Second, the IAV explicitly encourages individuals to form behavioral intentions to have safer sex. Third, work in cognitive therapy on imaginal and observational rehearsal (e.g., Davison & Wilson, 1973; Kazdin, 1986) suggests that the opportunity to rehearse safer sex behaviors provided by the IAV should increase the likelihood of engaging in safer sex. Fourth, work by Gollwitzer (1990, 1996) and Gollwitzer and Moskowitz (1996) suggested that more realistic situational cues in the IAV may increase the likelihood that in subsequent encounters safer sex behaviors will be automatically activated. Fifth, work on state congruent learning (Bower & Forgas, 2000) suggests that the emotions (e.g., sexual arousal) that can be activated in such virtual worlds may enhance activation of the desired behaviors in similar emotional contexts.

Initial Research and Focus Groups

Before we began constructing the IAV we first performed extensive research and focus groups to identify the steps and choice points in a typical gay male sexual encounter and the obstacles that may prevent gay men from engaging in safer sex. This research was used as a foundation for the sexual sequence we used in the video, a first date. Moreover, during the writing of the script for the IAV we continually consulted with counseling staff from the Gay and Lesbian Community Services Center (GLCSC) in Hollywood, California. We did so both to determine the educational content of the video and to ensure that the video would be viewed as realistic and sensitive to gay men's experience. In addition, our two main production personnel, who wrote the script, filmed the video, edited it, and programmed the IAV were both MSM, as was our primary research assistant during the construction of the video.

Description of the IAV

Because of constraints in our production resources, the video was targeted at white gay men around 18 to 35 years in age, which is currently one of the largest risk groups in the United States. The highly realistic and visually rich video has high production values. It is introduced by two guide characters who explain the objectives of the video and set up the story for the user. The guides are attractive young gay men intended to appeal to the target audience. Men who use the video are asked to identify with the main character and are given the opportunity to make choices, ask questions, and guide their character's actions. Throughout the encounter, the user is in control and is able to govern the behaviors of his character.

The user is put in the shoes of "Dave," a gay male character who has just gone out on a first date with "Mike." The story begins as Dave comes over to Mike's house after the date. The two sit on the couch and begin to talk. Mike is an attractive, sexually aggressive character whose objective is to have sex with Dave as soon as possible. The user's objective is to help Dave negotiate safer sex with Mike. As Mike makes sexual advances (e.g., offers wine, kisses and touches Dave, etc.), the user faces choice points at which he makes decisions regarding how the action will progress. An advice option is always available; advice is given by the guide characters. If the user is unsure of how to bring up the topic of safer sex, for example, the guides are there to offer possible strategies and lines that Dave could utilize to ensure safer sex with Mike. In addition, if the user chooses one of several risky options, such as drinking alcohol or having unprotected anal sex, the user will receive unsolicited advice from the guides (i.e., a mandatory intervention). For example, the guides would warn of the dangers of unprotected anal sex. Positive feedback is also given when the user makes good decisions, such as choosing to use condoms.

The action in the video unfolds in one of two general ways. During the couch scene between Mike and Dave, the user is presented with options that include negotiating safer sex, advice about how to bring up the topic of safer sex, and immediately going to the bedroom to have sex with Mike. If the user chooses for Dave and Mike to have sex right away, before negotiation has occurred, the guides appear and warn the user to negotiate safer sex on the couch. The guides also point out how to carefully listen to what the partner is saying and not saying, and how to effectively communicate and insist on safer sex, but still not offend their partner and have a good time. Although the user can progress to the bedroom for sex without having actively negotiated an agreement to use safer sex with Mike, he can do so only by deliberately ignoring very strong warnings. Once the user decides to move to the bedroom, he may then choose from a menu of sex acts ranging from mutual masturbation to anal sex. The acts are portrayed in an explicit but nonpornographic way (the actors simulate sex, but no buttocks or genitals are shown). Each sex act can be either with or without a condom. If the user chooses a risky action without a condom, they will receive a warning from the guides.

During the couch scene, the user can choose for Mike and Dave to not have sex that night but to meet again for a future date. If the user chooses this option, he can then flash forward to a future date by which time Dave and Mike have gotten to know each other better, well enough for the user to feel comfortable for a sexual encounter to occur. This option is included to make it clear to the user that sex need not occur on the first date; waiting is an option. The scene opens with Dave and Mike kissing on the couch, and the remaining options are the same as in action sequence 1. At any point during the date, the user can also choose to exit from the date, by pressing an EXIT button, (and exiting skills are shown).

At the end of the sexual scenario, the guides provide feedback. They guide the participant through a review of his behaviors—where his choices were safer ones, and where they were potentially risky. As they do so, the guides also take the participant back to earlier choice points where risks were taken and with video play-backs offer alternative safer narratives for negotiating the sequence between Dave and Mike. Thus, each participant is provided with modeling of safer sex negotiation.

SCRIPT DEVELOPMENT AND PRODUCTION PROCESS

Script Development

Initial drafts of the script were written by our two directors, based on the focus group results and a detailed map of the kinds of behaviors we wished to address and the kinds of changes we wished to create. These drafts were then discussed and worked on at a series of 2–3 hour weekly script meetings. We paid particular attention to such things as the realism of the actions and dialogue and whether the actions and dialogue would be interpreted as we intended and would have the impact we intended. This process continued on a weekly basis for several months until we had the final shooting script.

Personnel at the script meetings typically involved the two directors, a faculty member from the Cinema School, two professors from the Annenberg School for Communication, one Psychology professor, a graduate student research assistant, and a representative from the GLCSC, where the video was ultimately evaluated. Four members of this team were themselves gay, so they could bring their personal experience to bear. The three professors were experts in AIDS and behavior change and three members of the team were experts in Cinema production.

As noted earlier, the sexual scenario that formed the center of the script was based on extensive focus group testing of typical sexual scenarios for gay men. In addition, the various pathways in the scenario and the actions were based on the focus groups and the kinds of behaviors we were interested in targeting. For example, since we wanted to model the central character dealing with his partner's refusal to use a condom, we created pathways in which the partner refused to use a condom and we could then show different responses to that refusal.

EQUIPMENT AND SOFTWARE

For editing we used a PowerMacintosh 9500, with a Targa video board, which digitized a standard analog video input. Digitized video was captured on a 6 gigabyte RAID array and backed up on a

TABLE 7.1

Equipment and Software Used in the Production of the Interactive Video

Equipment	Software
Sony DV camera	Macromedia Director
PowerMacintosh 9500 computer	Adobe Premiere
Targa Video digitizing board	Adobe After Effects
6 GB external RAID drive	Media Cleaner Pro
1.3 GB magneto-optical drive	Photoshop
CD burner	SoundEdit 16
	Microsoft Word

magneto-optical drive. A PowerMacintosh 8100 was also used for a variety of tasks (see Table 7.1).

At the time we created our IAV, Sony and several other manufacturers had just released the first generation of digital video (DV) cameras. However, at that point there was neither the software nor the hardware available to allow us to directly transfer and edit the DV (this is obviously no longer the case). So rather than using the Firewire output on the Sony camera, we had to use the analog output and use the Targa board to digitize the video for editing. The video was completely edited in Adobe Premiere. The guides were shot against a blue screen background and then various backgrounds were composited using Adobe After Effects.

The resulting video was then compressed with Media Cleaner Pro into a series of Quicktime movies, using the Cinepak codec. Because of the amount of time needed for compression with the technology available at that time, compression was typically done in batches over night. Current technology now allows one to create MPEG video, which is much higher quality, in close to real time. That is, 30 seconds of video would take 30–60 seconds to compress.

The interactive structure for the IAV was programmed in Macromedia Director. The video was presented at quarter screen size (320 × 240) in a frame, with a series of clickable buttons that could be used to make choices. Clicking on a selection would jump to a new video clip and a new set of selection buttons. The static graphics for the entry screen and other framing graphics were created in Photoshop. Background music and speech were edited with Soundedit 16.

To represent the various pathways in the video date and the various interventions by the guides we had 98 individual video clips, resulting in a total of 521 MB of video. The different clips were relatively evenly distributed between the sexual scenario itself and the interventions from the guides. We also had about 10 MB of Director files. Thus, we almost completely filled a standard CD-ROM disk.

Because of the large amount of video and the relatively small hard disk sizes (compared to today), only limited amounts of video could be edited at a time. Thus, much of the video had to be stored off-line, using magneto-optical drives.

Also, because the only reasonable target platform at that time was relatively low speed CD-ROM drives, with capacities of around 640 MB, we had to heavily compress our video and present it in a quarter screen window. The need to heavily compress our video led to much lower quality than would be currently possible. With current technology, we could present full screen video of much higher quality, which should greatly increase user involvement in the IAV.

We are currently working on a new version of a safer sex IAV for MSM of three different ethnicities and taking advantage of several major new developments since we produced our first IAV. The most important overall trend in this area is that the video and computer hardware, as well as the available software, have advanced so dramatically, that it is now possible for groups with the necessary technical skills to develop near professional quality projects on affordable equipment.

First, we now directly transfer the DV from a near professional level DV camera to our computer (a dual processor Macintosh G5) using a Firewire connection, which allows us to obtain near professional quality video. Second, we are using Apple's Final Cut Pro to edit the DV, rather than having to use analog video. Final Cut Pro allows one to develop a professional quality product on relatively affordable standard hardware and is being widely used in professional settings. Third, we will now deliver the final IAV on DVD rather than CD-ROM. Using DVD allows us to present full-screen video of much higher quality, allows us to present much more footage, and thus more choices, and will allow us to take advantage of the ability to play the resulting DVD on any standard DVD player or DVD equipped computer. Programs such as Apple's iDVD and DVD Studio Pro, as well as Macromedia's Director, allow one to create interactive DVDs that can be played on standard DVD players.

For our previous IAV we produced a single version in the Macintosh version of Director, which restricted the final video to the Mac platform. We could have produced a Windows version, if we had wanted to buy a Windows version of Director. However, the resulting version would still have been restricted to playback on a computer. In contrast, an interactive DVD can be played on the increasingly prevalent standard DVD players, as well as on computers.

Personnel

Our primary production personnel were two MFA students from USC School of Cinema, Television, and Film: Kirk Marcolina and Derth Adams. Kirk was trained as a director and Derth as a cinematographer. When they initially started on the project they were Masters students, but they continued on the project after graduation until production was complete. They were largely responsible for script writing, casting, shooting of the video, editing it, and programming the interactivity using Macromedia Director. Production of this project was greatly facilitated by the availability of such top notch students at USC.

Although Kirk and Derth did essentially all of the day-to-day work on the project, the on location shooting involved an additional small crew drawn from the USC Cinema school. The crew included a sound person, a lighting person, and a set dresser, in addition to Kirk as director and Derth as cinematographer. Several of our graduate students acted as gofers on the set. Although we purchased the video camera, we rented the lights and sound equipment for the on location shooting. The video itself included two young adult male actors, who played the individuals on the date, and two young adult males who played the roles of the guides.

Production

The actual video shoot took place in three main locations. The initial part of the video was shot in the living room of one of the two directors and the sex scenes were shot in the bedroom of one of the PIs of the grant that provided funding for the video. Scenes with the guides were shot in front of a blue screen at the Annenberg Center and later composited with appropriate backgrounds. Most of the editing and programming of the video, as well as the script development, took place largely in the Annenberg Center at USC.

Casting

All the roles in the video were cast by placing an ad in the classifieds section of *Variety*, which is a movie industry magazine in which movie and TV projects are typically advertised. Actors submitted head shots and resumes and were then called in by Kirk and Derth for an audition. Actors were paid the standard daily wage for such projects, but undoubtedly worked on the project primarily for the experience and the additional line on their resume. In general, our ability to do this project was greatly facilitated by the presence of the USC Cinema School and by our location in Los Angeles.

Production Costs

Production of the IAV probably cost around $90,000 to $100,000. About $15,000 of that was for the purchase of hardware, software, a kiosk for use of the IAV at the GLCSC during the evaluation phase of the project, and media (such as CDs and magneto-optical cartridges). Probably another $8,000 or so was used for various production costs, such as the hiring of actors, additional crew for the actual shooting, rental of lights and sound equipment, food for the cast and crew, and other miscellaneous costs. By far the bulk of the cost was for the salary of the two directors, who worked between 20 and 30 hours a week on the project for about a year and a half.

Evaluation Costs

Evaluation of the IAV was funded by a 2-year grant from the Universitywide AIDS Research Program of the State of California. The grant was for a total of about $150,000 in direct costs and was used to pay research personnel and participants in the study.

LONGITUDINAL STUDY TO ASSESS IAV PROTOTYPE'S EFFECTIVENESS

One goal of our longitudinal study was to assess if the IAV actually provided any learning beyond that which might occur with standard HIV counseling alone. The learning context for this IAV was the

GLCSC in Hollywood, California. We had worked closely with staff at the center over the course of development of the IAV to insure that our IAV was compatible with the messages that men who had sex with men were receiving at the clinic and received in post-HIV negative test counseling. One of their staff members worked with us not only in script development, but also in developing a knowledge base, part of the IAV that men could use: This too was compatible with the center's approved messages for MSM.

To examine whether the IAV would be effective beyond standard counseling, we randomly assigned MSM who had just had an HIV negative test to one of two conditions: To receive the GLCSC's standard required post-HIV negative counseling alone, or to receive such counseling in conjunction with use of the Gay Men's IAV. We followed these men up for 3 months, with 8 weeks of call-in behavioral data following the first session to assess whether the IAV exposure significantly affected their risk-taking behavior.

Method

Eligible participants were MSM, 18 years or older, who were clients of the GLCSC in Hollywood, CA who had just received a negative AIDS test. Participants in all conditions received the center's required one-on-one safer sex counseling in session 1, during which they were given relevant information and behavioral techniques concerning safer sexual practices and received imagery instructions (to imagine safer sex negotiation with a partner who seems unwilling). In addition, MSM who wished to participate in this study were randomly assigned to receive IAV or not. At the end of session 1, we collected demographic information, and self-reports of HIV-related beliefs, attitudes, behavioral intentions, and perceived self-efficacy for performing safer sex behaviors in sexual situations. Also measured were perceived skills for initiating safer sex, and history of condom-negotiation experiences and skills. Measures of these potential mediators were also collected again 3 months later. Between these sessions, there were eight weekly phone-in behavioral assessments starting immediately after the first session. For these phone-in assessments, participants were carefully instructed to phone-in their responses to a 21-item questionnaire every week on scheduled days. Each week, participants reported how frequently they had engaged in specific sexual behaviors during the previous week and indicated whether or not they were currently in a serious–committed relationship. The assessment measured receiving and giving anal, oral, and rimming behavior; each was measured separately for behaviors both with or without a condom and for those performed with a male or female partner. Each participant chose a unique code name that was used to identify their responses and was given a phone number to a voicemail service where they would give their code name and report their responses to the weekly behavior assessment.

Retention of men in the study was good. Of 136 interested and eligible men who completed the first session, 110 (81%) completed the set of eight phone-in weekly behavioral assessments and 104 (76%) completed the intervention through session 2. No significant differences in baseline measures were found for men who completed the study and those that did not.

RESULTS

In analyzing the phone-in data, we focused on the questions about frequency of protected and unprotected anal sex. We created a single variable of frequency of protected anal sex, summing giving and receiving anal sex with a condom, across the eight phone-ins. We also created a single variable of frequency of unprotected anal sex, summing giving and receiving anal sex without a condom, across the eight phone-ins. As is typically true of measures of sexual behavior, these variables were highly skewed. Thus, we used a square root transformation (Tabachnick & Fidell, 1996) and deleted two outliers on the protected anal sex measure (66 times and 55 times over the 8 weeks).

Because the main actors were white MSM, participants were divided into the audience that matched the actors on ethnicity (white MSM) and the audience that did not (non-white men—African American and Latino MSM). Our analyses showed that, regardless of ethnicity, participants who received the IAV engaged in higher levels of protected anal sex and lower levels of unprotected anal sex, compared to those in the control group (see Table 7.2). A covariance analysis controlling for possible preintervention differences in sexual behavior still showed a pattern in which those who watched the

TABLE 7.2
Unadjusted and Adjusted Means of Pre and Post test
Protected and Unprotected Anal Sex Behaviors

	Type of Behavior		Control		Experimental (IAV)	
			Non-EA	EA	Non-EA	EA
Nonadjusted post test	Protected	M	1.50	.98	2.31	1.35
	Unprotected	M	1.46	2.18	1.68	1.17
Adjusted post test	Protected	M	1.55	.91	2.31	1.38
	Unprotected	M	1.48	1.91	1.78	1.33

Note. Scores are the square root transformation of the original values. EA—European-American.

IAV showed higher levels of protected sex and lower levels of unprotected sex, compared to the control group (see Table 7.2).

Interestingly, there were no significant effects of experimental condition (IAV or not) on cognitive variables typically associated with behavior change, such as beliefs about self-efficacy, attitudes, and behavioral intentions of performing HIV prevention behavior. In addition, there was no change in these variables from session 1 to session 2. These findings are not necessarily inconsistent with traditional models of behavior change (Ajzen, 1991; Bandura, 1986; Beck, 1970; Becker, 1974; Fishbein & Ajzen, 1975; Kasprzyk, Montano, & Fishbein, 1998). That is, the potential cognitive mediators—self-efficacy, attitudes, and intentions of performing HIV prevention behavior—were all relatively high in all conditions. Although there were no significant differences among the experimental groups (IAV or not) on these variables, this may be due to a ceiling effect. All participants in this study received imagery instructions, as well as a one-on-one HIV prevention counseling session designed to manipulate beliefs, attitudes, and intentions.

Due to the GLCSC's constraints on us, participants were assessed on these measures only after the respective intervention sessions. Therefore, we could not ascertain whether the intervention caused an immediate impact on these potential mediators. Nevertheless, despite similarly high levels of these mediators for those who received IAV and those who did not, statistically significant differences in protected anal sex behavior occurred among men who viewed the IAV versus those who did not.

Finding that risk behavior differed by experimental treatment, despite no differences in psychological mediators, is quite consistent with models of behavior change such as those of Gollwitzer (1996), and Mischel and Shoda (1995). These models suggest that although beliefs, attitudes, and intentions are necessary elements of successful long-term behavior change, changes in these variables, alone, are not sufficient to produce behavior change. Findings of this study are consistent with Gollwitzer's claim that traditional paradigms may often fail to elicit actual behavior change (Gollwitzer, 1996) because they manipulate beliefs, attitudes, and intentions regarding a particular behavior without committing the individual to the mechanics of its implementation. These models suggest that self-regulatory plans and behavioral mindsets are necessary to ensure the successful execution of a desired behavior. In the IAV, observational rehearsal was built into the IAV. Such rehearsal has been shown to play a role in behavior change. The findings indicated that behavioral rehearsal via IAV—which provided an environment where an individual can observe and practice a desired behavior within a hypothetical situation—might have significantly affected behavior.

CONCLUSION

The need for improved HIV intervention programs is critical. Many commentators have suggested that interactive media could have a major impact in changing a variety of risky behaviors, such as risky sex. Unfortunately, the claims for the efficacy of interactive media often far outstrip any empirical validation of their effectiveness. Our research on the Gay Men's IAV provides one of the very first attempts to empirically examine the effectiveness of interactive media in changing risky sexual behavior and to demonstrate that IAV can be effective. Thus, IAV can provide an innovative tool to foster active learning of safer sex behaviors in simulated sexual interactions.

REFERENCES

Ajzen, I. (1985). From intentions to actions: A theory of planned behavior. In J. Kuhl & J. Beckmann (Eds.), *Action-control: From cognition to behavior* (pp. 11–39). Heidelberg, Germany: Springer.

Ajzen, I. (1987). Attitudes, traits, and actions: Dispositional prediction of behavior in personality and social psychology. In L. Berkowitz (Ed.), *Advances in experimental psychology* (vol. 20, pp. 1–63). San Diego, CA: Academic Press.

Ajzen, I. (1991). The theory of planned behavior. [Special Issue: Theories of cognitive self-regulation]. *Organizational Behavior and Human Decision Processes, 50*, 179–211.

Ajzen, I., & Fishbein, M. (1980). *Understanding attitudes and predicting social behavior*. Englewood Cliffs, NJ: Prentice-Hall.

Bandura, A. (1986). *Social foundations of thought and action: A social cognitive theory*. Englewood Cliffs, NJ: Prentice Hall.

Bandura, A. (1994). Social cognitive theory and the exercise of control over HIV infection. In R. J. DiClemente & J. L. Peterson (Eds.), *Preventing AIDS: Theories and methods of behavioral interventions* (pp. 25–59). New York: Plenum.

Bartholomew, L. K., Gold, R. S., Parcel, G. S., Czyzewski, D. I., Sockrider, M. M., Fernandez, M., Shegog, R., & Swank, P. (2000). Watch, discover, think, act: Evaluation of computer-assisted instruction to improve asthma self-management in inner-city children. *Patient Education and Counseling, 39*, 269–280.

Beck, A. T. (1970). Cognitive therapy: Nature and relation to behavior therapy. *Behavior Therapy, 1*(2), 184–200.

Becker, M. H. (1974). The health belief model and personal health behavior. *Health Education Monographs, 2*, 324–473.

Bower, G. H., & Forgas, J. P. (2000). *Affect, memory, and social cognition*. New York: Oxford University Press.

Brown, S. J., Lieberman, D. A., Gemeny, B. A., Fan, Y. C., Wilson, D. M., & Pasta, D. J. (1997). Educational video game for juvenile diabetes: Results of a controlled trial. *Medical Information, 22*(1), 77–89.

Brug, J., Campbell, M., & van Assema, P. (1999). The application and impact of computer-generated personalized nutrition education: A review of the literature. *Patient Education and Counseling, 36*, 145–156.

Campbell, M. K., DeVellis, B. M., Strecher, V. I., & Ammerman, A. S. (1994). Improving dietary behavior: The effectiveness of tailored messages in primary care settings. *American Journal of Public Health, 84*(5), 783–787.

Centers for Disease Control and Prevention. (1998, February). HIV/AIDS surveillance report. Atlanta, GA: Department of Health and Human Services.

Centers for Disease Control and Prevention. (1999a). Increases in unsafe sex and rectal gonorrhea among men who have sex with men—San Francisco, California, 1994–97. *MMWR, 48*, 45–48.

Centers for Disease Control and Prevention. (1999b). Resurgent bacterial sexually transmitted disease among men who have sex with men—King County, Washington, 1997–1999. *MMWR, 48*, 773–777.

Chesney, M. A., Morin, M., & Sherr, L. (2000). Adherence to HIV combination therapy. *Social Science and Medicine, 50*(11), 1599–1605.

Chng, C. L., & Geliga-Vargas, J. (2000). Ethnic identity, gay identity, sexual sensation seeking and HIV risk taking among multiethnic men who have sex with men. *AIDS Education and Prevention, 12*, 326–339.

Davison, G. C., & Wilson, G. T. (1973). Processes of fear-reduction in systematic desensitization: Cognitive and social reinforcement factors in humans. *Behavior Therapy, 4*, 1–21.

DiClemente, R. J., & Peterson, J. L. (1994). *Preventing AIDS: Theories and methods of behavioral interventions*. New York: Plenum.

Fishbein, M., & Ajzen, I. (1975). *Belief, attitude, intention and behavior: An intro-duction to theory and research*. Reading, MA: Addison-Wesley.

Fisher, J. D., & Fisher, W. A. (1992). Changing AIDS-risk behavior. *Psychological Bulletin, 111*(3), 455–474.

Fisher, J. D., Fisher, W. A., Williams, S. S., & Malloy, T. E. (1994). Empirical tests of an information-motivation-behavioral skills model of AIDS-preventive behavior with gay men and heterosexual university students. *Health Psychology, 13*(3), 238–250.

Gollwitzer, P. M. (1990). Action phases and mind-sets. In E. T. Higgins & R. M. Sorrentino (Eds.), *Handbook of motivation and cognition* (vol. 2, pp. 53–92). New York: Guilford.

Gollwitzer, P. M. (1996). The volitional benefits of planning. In P. M. Gollwitzer & J. A. Bargh (Eds.), *The psychology of action: Linking cognition and motivation to behavior* (pp. 287–312). New York: Guilford.

Gollwitzer, P. M., & Moskowitz, G. B. (1996). Goal effects on action and cognition. In E. T. Higgins & A. W. Kruglanski (Eds.), *Social psychology: Handbook of basic principles* (pp. 361–399). New York: Guilford.

Hogg, R. S., Weber, A. E., Chan, K., Martindale, S., Cook, D., Miller, M. L., & Craib, K. J. P. (2001). Increasing incidence of HIV infections among young gay and bisexual men in Vancouver. *AIDS, 15*(10), 1321–1322.

Jemmott, J. B., & Jemmott, L. S. (1994). Interventions for adolescents in community settings. In R. J. DiClemente & J. L. Peterson (Eds.), *Preventing AIDS: Theories and methods of behavioral interventions* (pp. 141–174). New York: Plenum.

Jemmott, J. B., & Jemmott, L. S. (1999). Reducing HIV risk-associated sexual behavior among African American adolescents: Testing the generality of intervention effects. *American Journal of Community Psychology, 27*(2), 161–187.

Jemmott, J. B., Jemmott, L. S., & Fong, G. (1998). Abstinence and safer sex HIV risk-reduction interventions for African American adolescents. *Journal of the American Medical Association, 279*(19), 1529–1536.

Kalichman, S. C., & Rompa, D. (1995). Sexual sensation seeking and sexual compulsivity scales: Reliability, validity, and predicting HIV risk behavior. *Journal of Personality Assessment, 65*(3), 586–601.

Kasprzyk, D., Montano, D. E., & Fishbein, M. (1998). Application of an integrated behavioral model to predict condom use: A prospective study among high HIV risk groups. *Journal of Applied Social Psychology, 28*(17), 1557–1583.

Kazdin, A. E. (1986). Covert modeling: Imagery-based rehearsal for therapeutic change. In L. Krueger, J. E. Shorr, & M. Wolpin (Eds.), *Imagery: Recent practice and theory* (vol. 4, pp. 131–153). New York: Plenum.

Kelly, J. A. (1995). *Changing HIV risk behavior: Practical strategies*. New York: Guilford.

Kelly, J. A., St. Lawrence, J. S., Hood, H. V., & Brasfield, T. L. (1989). Behavioral intervention to reduce AIDS risk activities. *Journal of Consulting and Clinical Psychology, 57*, 60–67.

Kelly, J. A., St. Lawrence, J. S., Betts, R., Brasfield, T. L., & Hood, H. V. (1990). A skills training group intervention to assist persons in reducing risk behaviors for HIV infection. *AIDS Education & Prevention, 2*, 24–35.

Kreuter, M. W., & Strecher, V. J. (1996). Do tailored behavior change messages enhance the effectiveness of health risk appraisal? Results from a randomized trial. *Health Education Research, 11*(1), 97–105.

Lieberman, D. A. (1995). Three studies of an asthma education video game: Executive summary. Report to the NIH: *National Institute of Allergy and Infectious Diseases*, Grant #R43 AI34821, 1–17.

McConnell, A. R., Leibold, J. M., & Sherman, S. J. (1997). Within-target illusory correlations and the formation of context-dependent attitudes. *Journal of Personality and Social Psychology, 73*, 675–686.

Mischel, W., & Shoda, Y. (1995). A cognitive-affective system theory of personality: Reconceptualizing situations, dispositions, dynamics, and invariance in personality structure. *Psychological Review, 102*, 246–268.

Moreno, R., Mayer, R. E., Spires, H. A., & Lester, J. C. (2001). The case for social agency in computer-based teaching: Do students learn more deeply when they interact with animated pedagogical agents? *Cognition & Instruction, 19*, 177–213.

Mutchler, M. G. (2000). Making space for safer sex. *AIDS Education and Prevention, 12*(1), 1–14.

Reis, J., Riley, W., & Baer, J. (2000). Interactive multimedia preventive alcohol education: An evaluation of effectiveness with college students. *Journal of Education Computing Research, 23*(1), 41–65.

Rothman, A. J., & Salovey, P. (1997). Shaping perceptions to motivate healthy behavior: The role of message framing. *Psychological Bulletin, 121*, 3–19.

Siegel, K., Schrimshaw, E. W., & Raveis, V. H. (2000). Accounts for non-adherence to antiviral combination therapies among older HIV-infected adults. *Psychology, Health, and Medicine, 5*(1), 29–42.

Tabachnick, B. G., & Fidell, L. S. (1996). *Using multivariate statistics* (3rd ed.). New York: HarperCollins.

Tingen, M. S., Grimling, L. F., Bennett, G., Gibson, E. M., & Renew, M. M. (1997). A pilot study of preadolescents to evaluate a video game-based smoking prevention strategy. *Journal of Addictions Nursing, 9*(3), 118–124.

Van der Plight, J., Zeelenberg, M., Van Dijk, W. W., De Vries, N. K., Richard, R. (1998). Affect, attitudes, and decisions: let's be more specific. *European Review of Social Psychology, 8*, 33–66.

Winett, R. A., Moore, J. F., Wagner, J. L., & Hite, L. A. (1991). Altering shoppers' supermarket purchases to fit nutritional guidelines: An interactive information system. *Journal of Applied Behavior Analysis, 24*(1), 95–105.

Wolitski, R. J., Valdiserri, R. O., Denning, P. H., & Levine, W. C. (2001). Are we headed for a resurgence of the HIV epidemic among men who have sex with men? *American Journal of Public Health, 91*, 883–888.

Wood, W. (2000). Attitude change; persuasion and social influence. *Annual Review of Psychology, 51*, 539–570.

8

The ICONS Suite
of Negotiation Simulations

Victor Asal[1]
State University of New York at Albany

The International Communications and Negotiation Simulations (ICONS) Project has developed a suite of World Wide Web–based, text-centered simulations that serve as a tool to teach aspects of international and domestic politics for social science classes at both the university and high school levels. Simulations provide a kind of counterpoint to the theoretical learning in a politics or negotiation course. "The ICONS Project aims to capture the complexity and subtlety of international political issues through detailed scenarios focusing on real or plausible policy" (Ip & Linser, 2001). A typical ICONS simulation puts students into the position of world leaders and asks them to navigate the often thorny world of international diplomacy. Simulations can be developed around routine diplomatic tasks, such as negotiating trade agreements or human rights accords, or they can focus on the dangerous decisions involved in managing humanitarian interventions or preventing full-scale war. ICONS provides for both synchronous and asynchronous communications among participants and supports an educator's use of online simulation by providing a simulation controller (SIMCON), who monitors the exercise and carries out a host of administrative and educational activities in relation to the simulation. ICONS' premise is that simulations offer the social science students an opportunity to learn from first-hand experience in much the same way that laboratory experi-

[1]I would like to thank Elizabeth Blake, Farah Chery, Alex Jonas, Elizabeth Kielman, Brigid Starkey, Tim Wedig, Kathie Young, and Jonathan Wilkenfeld for all their help.

ments allow students of the physical sciences to observe actual physical processes. Each year, ICONS runs approximately seven university-level and five high school–level simulations, with an average of 15 teams per simulation. Since 1990, 162 universities and 129 secondary schools from 37 countries have participated in ICONS simulations.

The first ICONS simulations were developed at the University of Maryland in the early 1980s by Jonathan Wilkenfeld. The goal was to immerse students in the complexities of international relations negotiations. The ICONS simulation model is based on work originally done at the University of California at Santa Barbara in the early 1970s by Robert C. Noel, who pioneered the use of computers as communications tools for interpersonal simulations with his POLIS simulation. The earliest ICONS simulations focused primarily on conflict. However, in the early 1990s—with the end of the Cold War and a new set of complexities arising in international politics—the ICONS team worked to diversify the types of scenarios and simulations offered, focusing more on day-to-day international relations, where cooperation among states is as much a feature of relations as conflict (Starkey & Blake, 2001).

In early ICONS efforts, the rudimentary electronic communication tools were UNIX based and required quite an investment in time and effort by students and teachers and instructors alike. The most significant technological advance of the mid-1990s was ICONS' move to a World Wide Web–based software package that drastically reduced the amount of effort students and teachers needed to expend to use the software (Starkey & Blake, 2001). The current ICONSnet software "utilizes Oracle database and web server products, and is written as a series of PL/SQL database packages" (Starkey & Blake, 2001, p. 546). The flexibility of the database approach makes it possible to modify the system to fit various pedagogic needs, and has allowed the ICONS team to support increasingly complex simulation scenarios.

Participants in ICONS simulations develop an appreciation for the complexities of politics by assuming the roles of decision makers for the state, group, or organization they will represent in the simulation. This sometimes means assuming the identity of a group with views very different from their own. ICONS thrusts students into the heart of a negotiation problem, allowing them to step inside and see how difficult it can be to reach an agreement with a diverse set of actors with different goals and ambitions. They come to understand how political solutions that initially seemed obvious can, in fact, require much delicate negotiation to achieve. Students are then asked to compare their simulation experiences with their theoretical learning as a means of enhancing the curriculum and enriching their view of the world. The following comment sums up one student's assessment of his participation in a recent ICONS simulation on the war on terrorism:

> The simulation provided a better perspective of what each country would stand for in the war of terrorism. It allows one to see war from the other countries' side and understand their beliefs concerning war. It also gave a clearer perspective of the negotiations that must take place to keep peace. (http://www.icons.umd.edu/iconsqst/plsql/ questionnaire.intweek2001_responses)

ICONS uses the mechanism of simulations (including research, participation, and reflection) to teach students about both the content and process of political negotiations and other international interactions. ICONS simulations can be structured to focus on either the process or the content of a negotiation, depending on the needs of the students and interests of the instructor. The following sections of this chapter illustrate how different simulation setups can be used to teach a variety of lessons. The following specific topics are addressed in this chapter:

- Components of an ICONS simulation
- The ICONS methodology
- Learning assessments of ICONS
- ICONS simulation scenarios
- Advantages and disadvantages of ICONS
- Sample ICONS simulation

In addition, readers are invited to explore a beta version of the ICONS online simulation builder software that will allow anyone to create a completely customized simulation that can be offered online. Please note that all the links in this chapter can be found as well at: http://www.icons.umd.edu/serg.

COMPONENTS OF AN ICONS SIMULATION

ICONS simulations can be categorized on the basis of both their substantive and technical components. Long known for its 5-week simulation of the international system (including emphasis on economic, security, human rights issues), ICONS has in the past several years begun to diversify the content of its simulations, as well as the structures that can support them. ICONS now offers simulations in regional politics (Africa, Americas, New Europe); international political economy (Nigerian oil issues); American politics (the U.S. Senate simulation); and the environment (International Whaling Commission). Outlines of these various simulation scenarios are provided in Scenarios.

From a technological standpoint, the suite of ICONS simulations comprises the following components: a communications package allowing for synchronous and asynchronous communication; a proposal center that helps participants organize their proposals and permits voting; an action center that allows participants to take actions that affect the success or failure of strategic goals set by the various players; consensus-building functions that facilitate group brainstorming and prioritizing sessions; an online research library to launch student research, including a database of statistical data on a number of countries that allows students to compare relevant data for parties to the negotiation; and an optional translator function that allows a group to participate as an online translator service for specific foreign language teams. In addition, ICONS provides documentation to simulation participants, including role sheets that outline goals and provide information developed specifically for each team in the simulation activity; scenarios that lay out the issues; game mechanics, or the rules governing the interactions among participants. While not every simulation uses all of these components, each is evaluated by ICONS staff members in the assembly of simulations that support an instructor's particular educational goals. In addition to these technological components, ICONS simulations all share one key human element: the SIMCON. Whether they are run by ICONS staff or by the individual instructor, every ICONS simulation assumes the involvement of a controller, who monitors the interactions of students and the development of the negotiations. This human element is essential to keeping the simulations productive and facilitating effective use of the negotiation tools that ICONS makes available.

Communications Package

The communications package, called ICONSnet, is the basic software structure on which all of ICONS simulations are built. ICONSnet is accessible via the World Wide Web, requiring only a web browser, and is designed to be intuitive, allowing both teachers and students to reduce the time and effort needed to participate in the online exercises. In response to questions about the user-friendliness of the software, participating faculty members recently commented that "they often do not even need to conduct formal training sessions with their students" (http://www.icons.umd.edu/about/inetfeat.htm) because students pick it up so quickly. ICONSnet runs on top of Oracle's relational database and application server products (http://www.icons.umd.edu/about/iconsnet.htm).

ICONSnet is designed to allow various members of a single team to log on from multiple computers and jointly represent a particular team, to allow for user anonymity (which can be educationally very important given different simulation requirements), to support foreign language translation, to facilitate archiving of all messages for later reference during and after the simulation, and to support the participation of anyone who can connect to the World Wide Web (http://www.icons.umd.edu/about/inetfeat.htm).

ICONSnet supports both synchronous and asynchronous communications. Given that a typical ICONS simulation can include teams from a number of time zones, asynchronous communication is essential. Many ICONS simulations are conducted over a period of three to five weeks with several hour-long real-time (synchronous) conferences during that period. Figure 8.1 shows a typical ICONSnet new message (asynchronous) screen. As can be seen, the user can choose to view all new messages, to view those related to specific issues, or to view only selected messages. As message numbers are assigned sequentially, they not only serve to uniquely identify each message, they also indirectly provide users with a sense of overall message volume in the simulation. Students can choose to send messages to one other team, to themselves (useful if a team is in more than one location using different computers), to a group of other teams, or to all the teams in the simulation (see Fig. 8.2 for a screen shot of an ICONSnet send message form). Using this form of communication, students can stay in contact on a daily basis—sending messages back and forth and negotiating over the issues of the simulation without having to be present online at the same time. The key difference between the ICONS

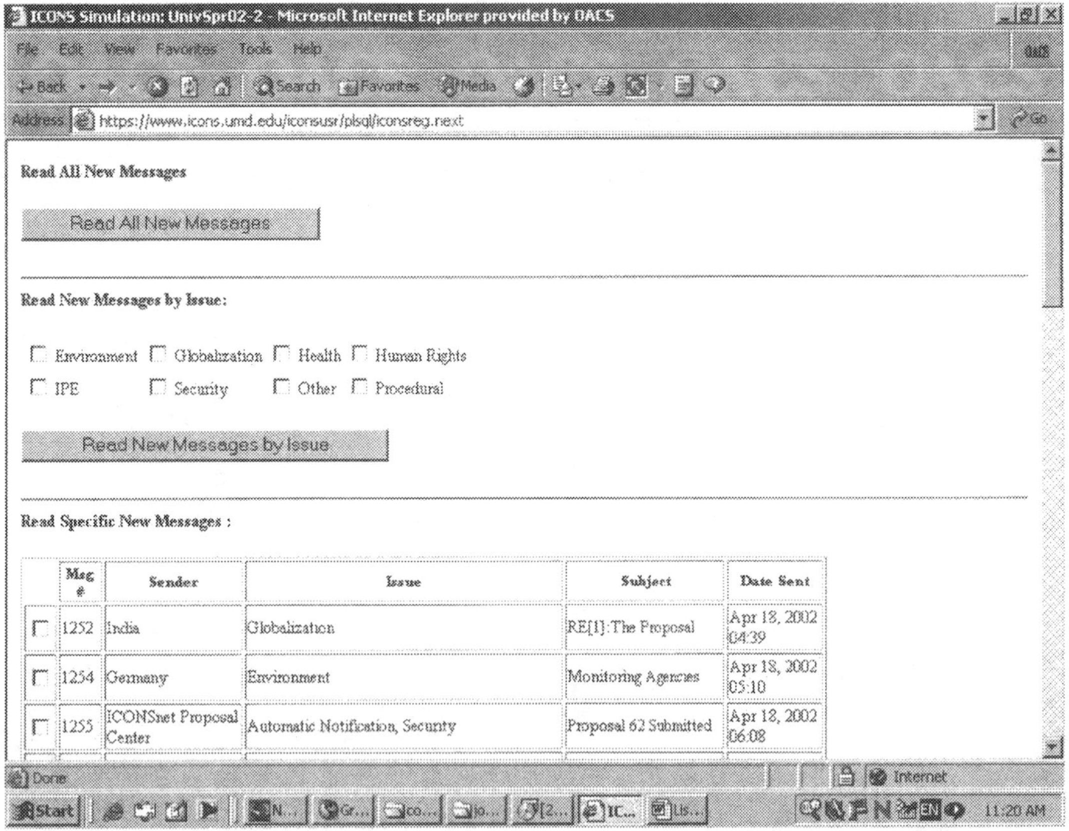

FIG. 8.1. New message screen—asynchronous.

ICONS Simulation: UnivSpr02-2 - Microsoft Internet Explorer provided by OACS

File Edit View Favorites Tools Help

Address https://www.icons.umd.edu/jconsusr/plsql/iconsreq.next

Read All New Messages

[Read All New Messages]

Read New Messages by Issue:

☐ Environment ☐ Globalization ☐ Health ☐ Human Rights
☐ IPE ☐ Security ☐ Other ☐ Procedural

[Read New Messages by Issue]

Read Specific New Messages :

Msg #	Sender	Issue	Subject	Date Sent
☐ 1252	India	Globalization	RE[1]: The Proposal	Apr 18, 2002 04:39
☐ 1254	Germany	Environment	Monitoring Agencies	Apr 18, 2002 05:10
☐ 1255	ICONSnet Proposal Center	Automatic Notification, Security	Proposal 62 Submitted	Apr 18, 2002 06:08

166

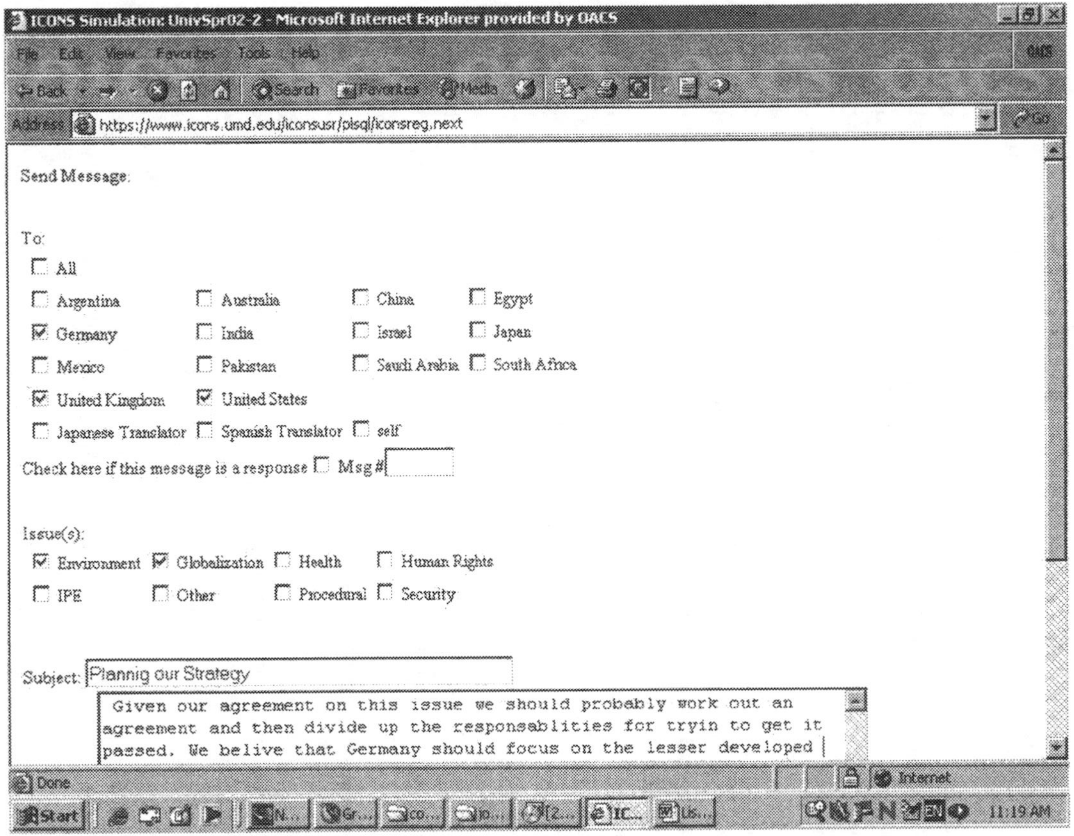

FIG. 8.2. ICONSnet send message form.

approach and e-mail is that participants are known to each other only by their simulation roles, which is crucial for helping participants remain in character, and that the system specifically supports interactions among teams of students.[2]

The synchronous communication, that is, conferencing, is structured to be different from Internet chats. First, the user has control over retrieving new messages, instead of having them interrupt the flow of the negotiation by popping up on the screen. This allows the student to stop and process the message without being overwhelmed by the continuing flow of messages. This ability to choose when to view additional information is important, because the synchronous conferences can sometimes involve more than a dozen teams online at the same time. Users view new messages when they have sent out responses to earlier messages and are ready to absorb additional incoming information. Second, ICONS conferences are typically monitored by SIMCONs who monitor the debate and hold the users to an educationally appropriate standard of discourse. Third, besides allowing for public exchanges, conference communications can be sent to another individual team or to any subset of teams participating in the conference. Finally, all conference communications are archived so that they can be consulted later. This is accomplished by accessing the synchronous communication screen, as shown in Fig. 8.3.

The Proposal Center

The proposal center is a recent innovation developed to help focus the communication and move the negotiations toward productive outcomes. It provides a central location where simulation participants can post, modify, and vote on proposals[3] developed through the course of the simulation exercise. It was developed to provide more structure for the proposals advanced by simulation participants and for concrete statements of approval or disapproval by the parties

---

[2]Since ICONS has traditionally been a team activity, it is important that a group of students playing a particular simulation participant speak with one voice. For that reason, ICONSnet was designed to facilitate message management by a team of students sharing one login account.

[3]To avoid constraints on the negotiation strategies used by participants, we refer to proposals rather than treaties or other terms that have a clearly defined meaning in international law.

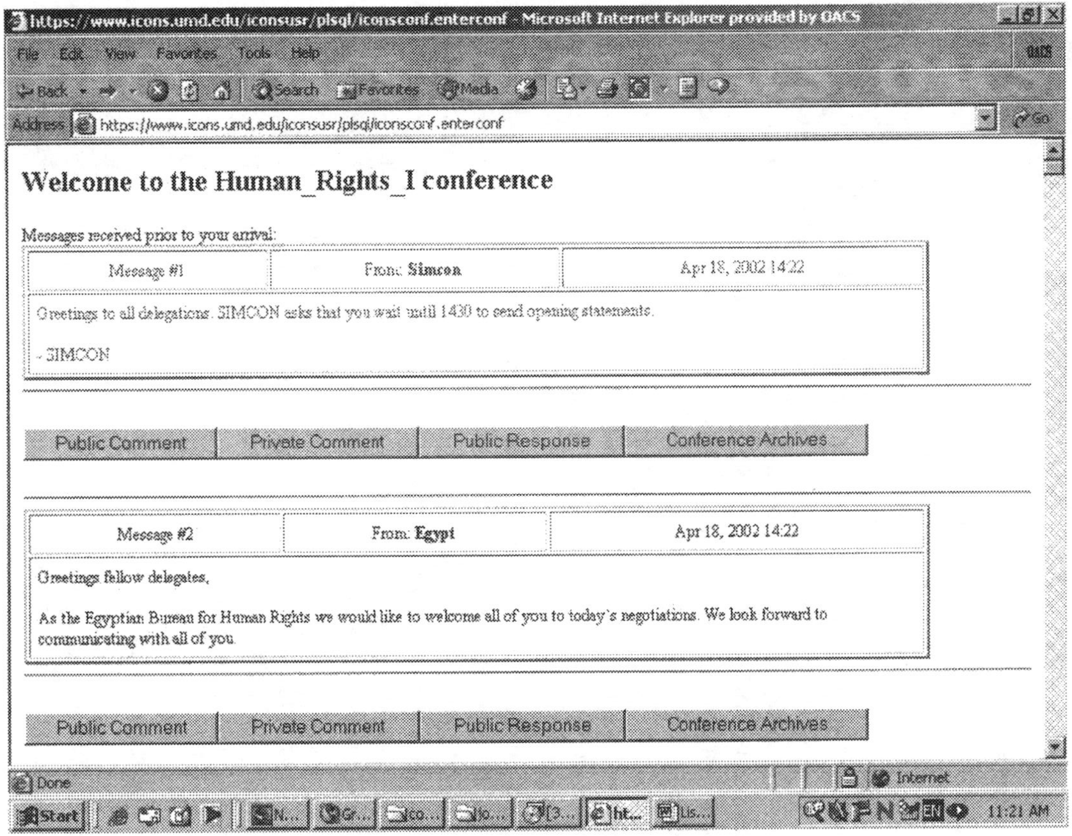

FIG. 8.3. Synchronous communication screen.

169

to the negotiation.[4] In certain simulations, the proposal center has been structured to support the recording of various actions. If, for example, the parties to the negotiation choose to impose sanctions on each other, make military incursions, or provide foreign aid, they use this feature to record these actions. There is also a proposal center variant developed to support a simulation of U.S. Senate committee activity.

The proposal center provides a very useful distinction for the participants between preliminary negotiations and actually following through with those threats–actions–offers. In addition, the proposal center provides a structure for the development and evaluation of concrete proposals—with participants coming to a central location to make or amend their proposals, and cast their votes (see Fig. 8.4). For a more detailed overview of how the proposal center can be used see: http://www.icons.umd.edu/help/net7.html.

For a given simulation, the proposal center can be designated to have open-ended choices, closed-ended choices, or some combination of the two. In other words, the options for action, voting, or proposing can either be generated totally by students in open text format or be preset (closed option–radio button) selections from which the students cannot deviate. This flexibility in setting up the proposal center allows the instructor to choose the kind of interaction that is appropriate for her or his pedagogic goals or the time constraints in using the simulation. Closed options, for example, work particularly well in simulations with limited time because they focus the discussion quickly, forcing participants to make hard choices quickly. Open-ended structures allow for a good deal more creativity, but also require more time for participants to create, explain, and understand their own and others' proposals.

The Research Library

The online research library provides a very useful starting point to support the participants' understanding of the countries they are

---

[4]"Since the international system does not operate by majority rule, ICONS does not have any set rules concerning whether a proposal 'passes' or 'fails.' After viewing the level of support for each proposal, each country will have to make its own decisions about whether the negotiations were successful and whether they themselves succeeded in achieving their negotiation goals" (http://www.icons.umd.edu/resource/proparea.htm).

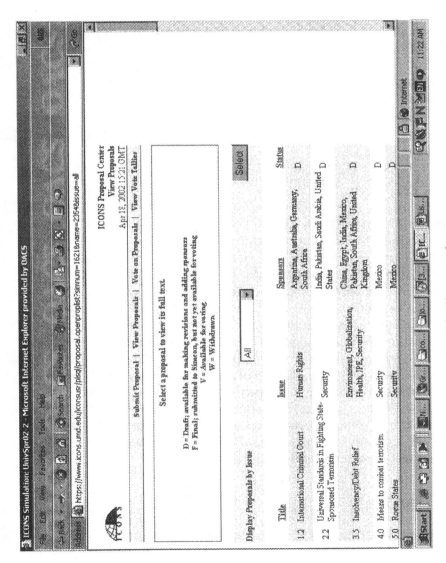

FIG. 8.4. The proposal center.

representing in the simulation. A new feature provides basic and *comparable* statistical data and basic information on each of the countries in a simulation. Often students consult sources that offer drastically different information. While a certain level of controversy regarding the facts of a political situation is often appropriate, ICONS now provides certain baselines of data upon which all simulation participants can rely. Students can now compare a series of statistics from GNP per capita to life expectancy rates to carbon dioxide emissions (per capita), as shown in Fig. 8.5. To use the comparison function, go to http://www.icons.umd.edu/reslib/plsql/country.compare_stats.

Scenarios

Every simulation needs a shared context—a common starting point that defines the issues under contention, any previous relationships, and the ground rules for interactions among the participants. All ICONS simulations start with a scenario that spells out this basic information for participants. The range of content covered by ICONS simulation activities is most clearly illustrated by the number and types of scenarios presently offered. ICONS scenarios cover five basic areas of political negotiation: regular diplomacy, international crisis, historical simulations, and process-oriented simulations. To a greater or lesser extent, the aim of all simulation scenarios is to teach both negotiation content and process. That said, several of the simulations detailed in the following section were specifically constructed to highlight certain procedural aspects of negotiations and include role sheets for participants, so that students can immediately begin to construct negotiation strategies.

Role Sheets

Because ICONS simulations are built around the process of negotiations, the task of identifying key interests is a major part of any team's preparation for the negotiations, and will determine to a great extent how the negotiation process will proceed. Where ICONS uses role sheets to help participants to identify their interests in simulations, the focus is on the negotiation process itself. It is true that for some simulations, the time students spend on performing research to

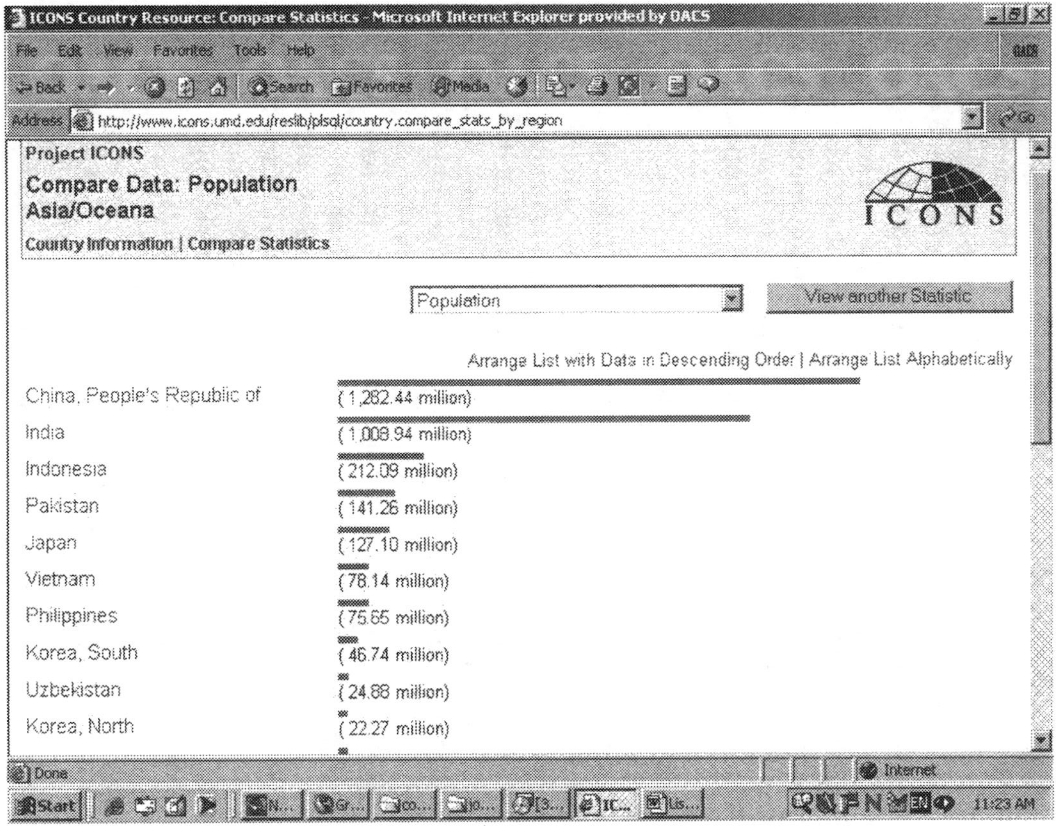

FIG. 8.5. A comparison of populations.

identify their national interests is a major part of the learning process. Indeed, much of the benefit in this mode comes from the students' learning about the countries, groups, or organizations they will represent before they ever interact in the simulation.

However, for certain learning situations ICONS provides the students with role sheets that lay out basic interests of their teams, so they can focus immediately on the tactics and strategies that they will use to try and achieve their goals. While providing role sheets sacrifices some learning opportunities by forgoing the research phase, it maximizes the time available for the simulation itself. As previously noted, this arrangement works particularly well for simulations with serious time constraints. Examples of role sheets in a mini-simulation on global warming are included as part of an Appendix.

Translator Function

One of the components that distinguish ICONS from other simulations is its truly global reach. ICONS simulations currently include teams in North and South America, the Middle East, Europe, and Asia. The majority of simulation communications are conducted in English, but ICONSnet allows for translators to support teams that cannot communicate in alternative languages used by some teams in the simulation. (For example, a team in Argentina may prefer to send messages in Spanish. Teams in the United States that do not have Spanish-language capability can request translations of these messages into English.) The translator team automatically receives messages for translation according to predetermined translator paths and then can work at translating messages over time, saving drafts as they work, or translate messages immediately (for a detailed description of this process see http://www.icons.umd.edu/help/net10.html).[5]

THE ICONS METHODOLOGY

ICONS simulations give students the opportunity to build knowledge in a collaborative fashion through four distinct stages: prepara-

---

[5]For the most part, translators are students in foreign language translation courses whose instructors choose to use ICONS as a part of the course curriculum. Whether translation is available during a given simulation depends on whether such a class is available.

tion, participation, debriefing, and evaluation. This discussion focuses primarily on the first two stages, for they most strongly contrast with typical learning and assessment approaches. What happens during each of these stages varies, depending on the simulation selected and the goals of the educator. For example, a process-oriented simulation using extensive role sheets will probably require less time for research during the preparation phase. The teaching goals of the educator also come into play. The debriefing and evaluation will be structured differently depending on the pedagogical goals of the educator.

Stage 1: Preparation

Educators with different educational goals, time constraints, and topical interests participate in the simulation from across the United States and the world.[6] Thus, student participants bring vastly different amounts of prior knowledge to their participation. The preparation stage allows students to establish a common foundation of knowledge and skill before the simulation begins. The process starts with the scenario and role sheets, if provided. If acquisition of content knowledge is a goal, students need to conduct extensive research to familiarize themselves with the simulation issues and determine their basic interests. They must also become familiar with the priorities and interests of the countries and organizations with whom they will negotiate. Torney-Purta (1996) referred to these preliminary policy papers as "scaffolding for negotiation," that helps the students organize their thinking and move down the road to appreciating the complexity of the international system (p. 208). (If role sheets are provided, then additional research may not be necessary.) The team then must agree on decision-making procedures and set their goals and strategies for the negotiation. The internal negotiations over positions, goals, and strategies, marks the beginning of

---

[6]For different perspectives on how ICONS is built into course syllabi and the different kinds of courses ICONS is used for at the university level, go to http://www.icons.umd.edu/gvpt450/course.htm, http://csf.colorado.edu/isafp/syllabi/hansons.htm, http://www.lib.uconn.edu/~mboyer/syl220f.htm, http://www.cooper.edu/engineering/projects/gateway/eid/global/resources/gloutlne.html, http://faculty.smu.edu/mlusztig/PLSC%203390%20Syllabus.doc, and http://homepage.mac.com/vicfalls/africanpolitics.html.

collaborative learning and can be very intense, as the students wrestle with questions about what goals are appropriate, achievable, ethical, and effective.

If the pedagogical goal of the simulation is primarily to have students learn and retain information, then the preparation stage can be the most important of the four stages. In any event, careful work done at this point can be a powerful motivator, setting the stage for a successful simulation experience.

A position paper, a team-written statement of goals and strategies, is a useful tool for assessment of student performance in the preparation stage. At the University of Maryland, all students get a grade for the section they worked on (usually with one or two other students), as well as a grade for the policy paper as a whole. This is often the students' first experience with group work, and the exercise reinforces the notion that their success in the simulation is dependent upon the efforts of the entire group. Another assessment technique is to require students to evaluate each other as collaborators in producing the policy paper. The insights that students provide on their peers is a useful tool for the instructor to use in evaluating each student's contribution to the finished products.

Stage 2: Simulation

The simulation stage comprises three interrelated activities: asynchronous, synchronous, and intrateam communications. Conducting negotiations asynchronously gives students time to reflect on the messages that they send and receive and allows them to work at times that are most convenient for them, while synchronous conferences provide more immediate feedback. In addition, students must continuously negotiate within their groups, planning strategies and responding to challenges and opportunities created by other teams. During this time, students' thinking is constantly challenged by the opposing views of other teams and policy or strategy disagreements within the teams. The simulations thus encourage students to examine real-world problems from a variety of viewpoints.

Some time during this process, students develop a sense of real ownership of their positions and goals. In conducting ICONS simulations, I often observe what I would call productive stress infect the students and last until the end of the simulation. Students care about how their country negotiates and most work diligently—and in many cases passionately—to help their country succeed.

Besides the complete learning experience that the simulation provides, educators can focus on teaching moments in the simulation. As the simulation proceeds asynchronously, a teacher can identify interesting interactions or messages that illustrate certain points. By bringing them up for discussion in class, instructors can focus students on the educational purpose of the simulation and raise interesting questions of motivations and perspectives.

Educators using ICONS can evaluate the performance of their students in several ways. ICONS staff members at the University of Maryland do not use success in passing resolutions or getting agreements as a measurement because none of the simulations takes place on a completely level playing field. Consequently, a more appropriate assessment is of the quality and amount of effort the students put into their roles as negotiators of the simulations. The archiving feature of the software, which allows teachers to tailor their search for messages by a number of different criteria, provides a useful tool for reviewing and assessing simulation performance. It is thus possible to zero in on what each particular group of students is doing, and examine the level and quality of their participation. In addition to this qualitative check, ICONSnet can generate a quantitative report to be generated for each country, detailing the number from the team on each issue in the simulation. While quantity of communication is not synonymous with good or effective communication, it can provide a quick way to spot problems.

Finally, each student can be asked to evaluate the quality and effort of their peers. Given the complex nature of interactions in the simulation, with group learning taking place both face-to-face and online, these peer evaluations can be an invaluable asset in determining the nature of each student's participation.

Stage 3: Oral Debriefing

ICONS staff members encourage participating instructors to offer both oral and written debriefings for their students. While both forms of debriefing get at similar questions, the collaborative nature of the oral debriefing and the individual work of the written assessment complement each other and succeed in bringing out very different realizations from the students. In the oral debriefing, the students get an opportunity to proclaim their victories, vent their frustrations, and begin to process the meaning of the simulation. Oral debriefings done at the close of a simulation are quite cathartic, as participants justify their actions, thank their allies and ask pointed questions of their negotiation adversaries. This is also a good time to ask the students to relate their simulation experience to the real world in general or to specific cases they have studied.

Thus, debriefing provides a starting point for the students to process the simulation in a context larger than that provided by their roles. During this initial sharing of information students often react with genuine surprise as the assumptions others made about their motives in the simulation prove to be untrue or overly simple. Equally revelatory is hearing about various negotiations that took place beyond their involvement or knowledge. Suddenly, other teams' actions that once seemed inexplicable begin to make sense as the students gain a more complete picture of the simulation.

Oral debriefing can also be used as an opportunity for the participants to work as a group to apply theory to what happened in the simulation. At the start, most oral debriefings are anecdotal and the facilitator, whether focusing on theory or not, should help get the students to think analytically about their experience. Helping students to focus on how and why their countries succeeded or failed in achieving their goals can be helpful in this process. One useful question is to ask the students to discuss the realism of the simulation. The analysis that follows often sheds light on the forces of history and politics that the simulation captures. More importantly, it can encourage the students to focus on the causal forces that the simulation does not capture. (For a list of useful debriefing questions, see http://www.icons.umd.edu/resource/debrief.htm.) The collaborative analysis that oral debriefing allows often results in insights that many students working alone would not realize. A brainstorming exercise about the causes and outcomes of various actions in the simulation can provide a very useful starting point for the students as they embark on a written debriefing of the simulation experience.

Stage 4: Written Evaluation

After an oral debriefing, a written evaluation is important because it allows the students to be reflective about their experience and carefully organize their thoughts (Petranek, 1992). For example, students can be asked to rigorously apply a theory or set of theories to the simulation, or make an in-depth comparison between the simulation and historical cases. To help students in their written evaluation, ICONS makes the messages of all teams available to all participants through the archive, which is open to all after the simulation. Students can examine the development of agreements as they moved from initial proposals and were debated and changed through negotiation. They can trace different threads of negotiation, some of which they may not have been aware of during the simulation. ICONS also encourages open-ended (concept maps, interviews, open-ended questions) and close-ended (multiple-choice knowledge items, attitude and other rating scales) evaluations of the simulation as ways of assessing the extent of learning. These are discussed in more detail in the following section.

LEARNING ASSESSMENTS OF ICONS

The ICONS simulations were not developed to support any theoretical pedagogy. Rather the creators of ICONS felt that participation in online role-play exercises could give students an authentic experience through which to learn about and examine the content and process of international interactions. One of the key aims of the simulation was to convey the complex nature of international relations, and, through role play, help students feel what it was like to construct and implement foreign policy. The distributed, online nature of the simulation exercises forged virtual negotiation communities where input and perspectives were far more broad than those that could be achieved in a single classroom.

Since this intuitive beginning, ICONS made efforts to become more sophisticated in its approach to pedagogic structure and theory. In the mid-1980s, ICONS began working with Torney-Purta to develop an approach to assessing its pedagogic efforts. ICONS uses the mechanism of the simulation to help students construct more complex schemata to use in comprehending the political world around them (Torney-Purta, 1990). Specifically, ICONS adopts a constructivist problem-based approach to learning. ICONS simulations create opportunities for students to "build their own knowledge in response to sensory inputs from authentic experiences" (Brown & King, 2000, p. 245). Brown and King (2000) argued that ICONS simulations:

... (1) Anchor all learning activities to a larger task or problem; (2) support the learner in developing ownership and control of the problem . . . ; (3) design an authentic task/problem; (4) design the task and environment to reflect the complexity of the environment . . . ; (5) give ownership of the solution process to the learner; (6) design the learning to challenge, as well as support, the learner's thinking; (7) encourage testing alternative views; and (8) ensure reflection on both the content and the learning process. (p. 247)

ICONS challenges students to work collaboratively to deal effectively with "ill-structured real-world problems" (Brown & King, 2000, p. 247), and a multiplicity of actors with competing goals and interests. This challenging environment helps the students to increase their understanding of concepts and content, as well as improve their skills and strategies (Torney-Purta, 1998). The joint nature of this process is crucial: "simulations can . . . allow students to work in teams constructing knowledge together, providing insight and motivation to each other" (Torney-Purta, 1998, pp. 207–210). This problem-solving approach also serves one of ICONS key educational goals—that of increasing the student's appreciation for the complexity and interconnectedness of the international system.

This problem-based learning also works at increasing the participant's motivation by creating expectations of knowledge and performance because ". . . the participants are working towards a superordinate goal and responding to the opinions of their peers and seeking status from them, not primarily from an adult leader or teacher" (Torney-Purta, 1995, p. 357). The anecdotal evidence for the motivating impact of this approach is strong. Rottier (1995) recounted her students'enthusiastic preparation:

> I knew my students were definitely into their work when I received a phone call from a group one evening, on the second day of our spring vacation. My students were at the Library of Congress, about 20 miles from their homes, on their own, doing more research and had a question regarding their work. (p. 2)

Rottier (1995) also reported that students often told her that ICONS was the best class they had in high school, a comment the author has often heard from his university students. Rottier also reported a spillover effect in terms of how the students viewed the world outside of the United States. Before the simulation her students rarely read the newspaper, and when they did it was not likely to be the international news. By the end of the simulation, students were reporting that they were reading the newspaper almost every day and spending a great deal of time reading articles about foreign affairs (Rottier, 1995).

More structured assessments of ICONS simulations support the anecdotal evidence that ICONS' mix of online simulations and a problem-based learning approach result in a powerful teaching tool. In various studies, participation in ICONS has been shown to result in increased content knowledge and a more complex view of the world (Torney-Purta, 1996, 1998). Torney-Purta used presimulation and postsimulation concept maps, answers to factual questions, and answers to open-ended questions to measure the impact of ICONS on participating students. Torney-Purta found a positive relation between the experience in the simulation and knowledge gained, as well as increased levels of complexity in students thinking about the international system (Torney-Purta, 1996). One of the most intriguing results—given ICONS' interest in imparting more complex thinking—lies in comparing before and after concept maps about global problems generated by high school participants (see Fig. 8.6).

Student A's presession schemata of actors, action, and constraints in international debt crisis.

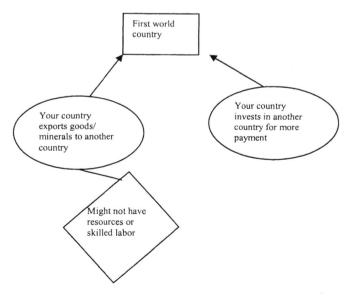

FIG. 8.6. *(Continued)*

Student A's postsession schemata of actors, action, and constraints in international debt crisis.

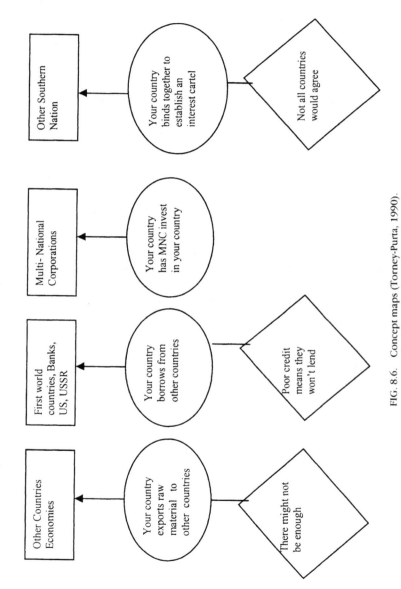

FIG. 8.6. Concept maps (Torney-Purta, 1990).

Students were also asked to elaborate on questions about economic strength, European Union expansion, and environmental standards. . . . Late responses tended toward greater sophistication and revealed awareness of the interrelatedness of problems and issues. On certain factual questions, such as "Is your country a member of the EU?" correct responses went from 25.3 percent early in the semester to 88.5 percent late in the semester.

Students generally said that their knowledge of economics, politics, and the environment had increased during the semester. Regarding students' reactions to the course as a whole, on a 7-point scale the mean for "interested" ranged from 5.5 in the lowest semester to 5.8 in the highest. The mean for "challenged" ranged from 5.2 to 5.3. The mean for "identified with country" ranged from 5.1 to 5.6.

A 1996 evaluation of courses meeting the Distributive Studies Requirement in Behavioral and Social Sciences included a question about the course's ability to elicit active involvement in learning. On this item, International Negotiation Seminars received an average rating of 4.26 on a five-point scale, as compared to a mean of 3.37 for the other courses surveyed. (http://www.ed.gov/offices/OPE/FIPSE/LessonsIV/umd.html)

In another, more recent, study both students and teachers reported statistically significant gains in understanding, skills, and motivations (Brown & King, 2000). Students had significant gains in "knowledge of the country assigned, interest in the country and knowledge of U.S. foreign policy" (Brown, Mayall, Toman, & Schrader, 2000, p. 13). As an added benefit, "teachers also reported an increase in knowledge and use of educational technology . . ." (Brown et al., 2000, p. 15).

Anecdotal, qualitative, and quantitative research all support the conclusion that the problem-based approach to learning that ICONS uses is an effective teaching tool, and one that motivates students and helps them deepen their understanding of the subject, as well as gives them an opportunity to develop a wide range of skills.

ICONS SIMULATION SCENARIOS

This section gives a sense of the breadth of types and topics of the simulations ICONS currently makes available to instructors for incorporation into their curriculum as an experiential component, or

TABLE 8.1
Elements That Characterize ICONS Scenarios

Scenarios	Content vs. Process Emphasis	Short vs. Long Duration	Current vs. Historical
Regular diplomacy simulations (e.g., New Europe)	Content	Long	Current
International crisis simulations (e.g., India–Pakistan)	Process	Short	Current
Historical simulations (e.g., War Crimes)	Both	Long	Historical
Process-oriented simulations (e.g., IWC)	Process	Short	Current
Domestic political simulations (e.g., The Senate)	Process	Long	Both
Consensus-building simulations (e.g., Aceh–Indonesia)	Both	Long	Current

counterpoint, to the theoretical learning in a given politics or negotiation course. Table 8.1 characterizes the various ICONS simulations, based on their structure and focus. Traditionally the regular diplomacy simulations are run for a large number of classes at remote locations (with ICONS supplying the simulation control), while the more-focused simulations have often run for a single class or small set of classes at one location, with the instructor functioning as the simulation control.

Regular Diplomacy Simulations

The focus of the regular diplomacy simulations is routine day-to-day multilateral diplomatic exchanges on a whole host of important international issues. Teams of students represent the senior foreign policymakers of a country and are responsible both for determining the nation's foreign policy goals and for developing the diplomatic strategies used to achieve those goals. Each country team is further divided, with various subsets of students taking primary responsibility for a specific set of issues outlined in the scenario. In a recent international system simulation these issues have included the following: international security, global environment, human rights, international political economy, globalization, and world health. The work of these subgroups and overarching policy goals and strategies are laid out in a policy paper that the students write before the simulation.

The actual simulation usually lasts between 3 and 5 weeks, with most of the communication being asynchronous. In addition, the negotiators from each country responsible for a particular issue area come together two or more times for a real-time negotiation. Using both modes of communication, synchronous and asynchronous, the students try to come to agreement on joint policy initiatives. Currently ICONS offers the following regular diplomacy simulations: international system, the international relations of Africa, New Europe, Middle East, and the Americas. As currently written, the scenarios for these simulations stress the achievement of multilateral solutions to pressing international issues, exploring the non-zero-sum negotiations. An archive of the scenarios for these simulations at both the high school and university levels is available at http://www.icons.umd.edu/archive/index.html.

International Crisis Simulations

The focus of this set of simulations is decision making in times of crisis. They are constructed to highlight time constraints, threats to a country's basic values, and the threat of military violence. In many ways, these are unique simulations in the ICONS suite of simulations. Both of the crisis simulations currently offered use software in addition to that which supports the traditional simulations. Crisis simulations are also structured somewhat differently, given their pedagogic goals.

The India–Pakistan Nuclear Crisis is a multiteam simulation examining the possibilities of nuclear confrontation on the Indian subcontinent. India, China, Pakistan, two different Kashmiri rebel groups, and the United States are drawn into a military or security crisis they must manage the best they can. The simulation is given further complexity through the addition of intranation conflict. Participants are provided with role sheets that spell out very serious policy differences among members of the same team. In addition to the two-level nature of this simulation, it is further differentiated from other ICONS simulations in that it uses an action map (see Fig. 8.7 for a screen shot). The action map is additional web-based software that allows the participants to move troops and deploy both conventional and nuclear weapons against each other, providing a visual context for the decisions made throughout the exercise.

The Peru–Ecuador Border Crisis is a two-person simulation (unique among all ICONS simulations) that puts the participants

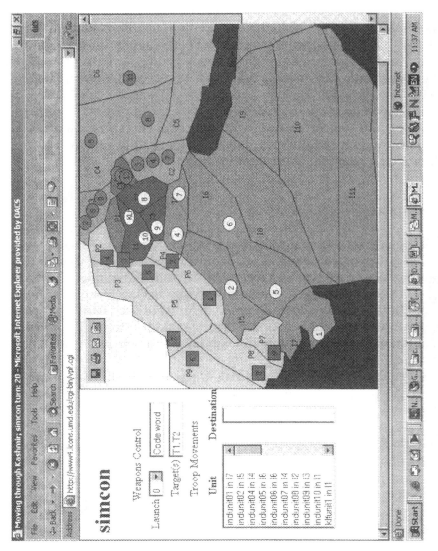

FIG. 8.7. The action map.

into the roles of the leaders of two countries involved in serious border skirmishes that threaten to explode into all-out war. In addition to a typical ICONS scenario and role sheets, the participants in this exercise have access to an additional online decision support system to help students evaluate the value of the various possible outcomes. This system assigns point values to the options for action open to the negotiators, and allows them to numerically compare all the possible outcomes—from a mixed-sum multi-issue agreement through arbitration all the way to a declaration of war. For each of these possible outcomes, participants can also see how the values of these possible outcomes are affected by the passage of time (see Fig. 8.8 to see a screen shot of the generalized decision support system). This feature allows the students to be very specific about their goals and intentions and allows the instructor and students to compare actions and outcomes across simulations to see how personalities and choices impact crisis decision making.

Historical Simulations

The ICONS historical simulations allow students to examine historic outcomes as events that were not inevitable. By becoming participants, students can use their own experiences to shed light on the interactions, decisions, and constraints that shaped the historical events they are studying. ICONS currently offers two historical simulations:

Patriots to Tea (1765–1775) helps students to understand the dramatic political transition that took place in the American colonies when, during the space of 10 years, a crucial number of people renounced their loyalty to the crown of England. Participants take part as members of different factions in the city of Boston. Various parties, including the royal Governor, push for different outcomes, with each group having the ability to inflict economic or political harm on others.

The London War Crimes Conference: Determining the Fate of Germany's Leadership (1945) places participants in the position of the representatives of the Four Powers that met in the summer of 1945 to determine what various crimes were committed by German forces during World War II. This exercise places students in a situation and time where the definitions and justifications for prosecut-

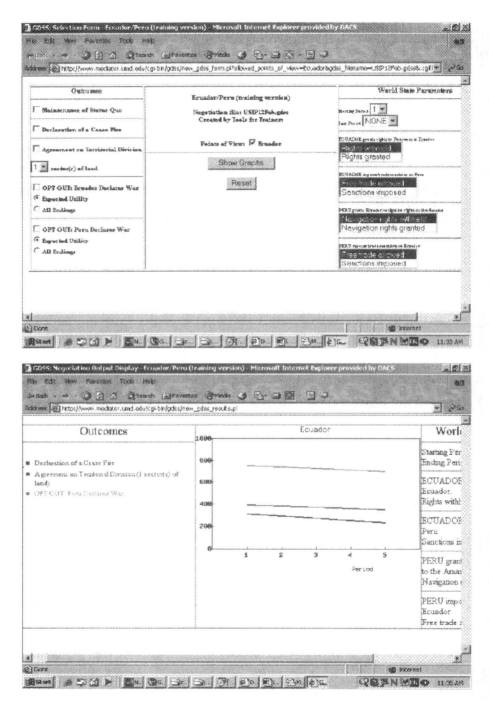

FIG. 8.8. The generalized decision support system.

ing war crimes and crimes against humanity were just being devised. With the outcome at the start of the conference far from clear, the parties have to weigh ethical and political considerations, both domestic and international in determining the fate of the German leadership and reaching a consensus position.

Process-Oriented Simulations

Process-oriented simulations focus primarily on the negotiation process, emphasizing various strategies and tactics that parties to a negotiation can use to affect the outcome they desire. These simulations outline roles for participants, and they tend to be less concerned with the content of the case.

The International Whaling Commission (IWC) has participants play the roles of 10 member states that are negotiating over the future of the current ban on whaling. Everything needed in terms of content is provided to the participants, and the possible outcomes presented to them are highly structured. The simulation is built to illustrate the dynamics and strategies inherent in multilateral negotiations and to allow participants to make key negotiation decisions within a relatively short period of time.

The Global Warming Mini Simulation is similar in its goals to the IWC. The purpose of the simulation (whose role sheets and scenario are included in the Appendix) is to serve as a vehicle to introduce participants to the ICONS software and to familiarize them with some very basic multilateral negotiation skills. Because of its brevity and focus, ICONS has used it for teacher training purposes.

Domestic Politics Simulations

For the last several years, ICONS has been asked to create domestic political negotiations related specifically to some aspect of American politics. Hence, a simulation based on the mark-up activities of the United States Senate is currently being beta tested.

The Senate Simulation has participants take the roles of 15 senators and their staffs, each holding seats on two of five committees modeled in the simulation. Each committee comes with a list of bills preassigned, as well as generalized committee rules to guide member actions. The Senators are given biographies and interests and are asked to decide how they value each of the bills under consideration. Using the tactics and strategies typical of parliamentary politics the world over—from logrolling to pork barreling—the senators negotiate both in committee and on the Senate floor to pass the bills they favor. Although this simulation is currently at beta-test stage, early evidence suggests that ICONS' experience in international negotiation modeling is proving useful in designing comparable simulation situations in the area of American politics.

Track II Consensus-Building Negotiations

In addition to its educational simulations, the ICONS Project has begun, with the help a grant from the U.S. Institute of Peace, to adapt its simulation software for use as a conflict resolution tool. With the goal of supporting negotiation training for practitioners, ICONS has created tools to support second track diplomacy, which will be used by groups outside the education community that are interested in conflict consensus-building tools.

The Aceh–Indonesia Simulation facilitates the training of practitioners and participants in second track diplomacy. The scenario presents an intractable conflict, which provides the basis for teaching participants about the role that consensus-building measures can take in addressing stubborn problems that have long resisted the diplomatic solutions. Specifically, the ICONSnet software has been adapted to include brainstorming and consensus-building features.

ADVANTAGES AND DISADVANTAGES

Any instructor who is considering the use of simulations as a tool for teaching and learning should be aware of the advantages and disadvantages of online simulations. Some students learn best through interactive, peer-driven experiences, and ICONS simulations serve such students very well. The simulation exercise often represents the first opportunity students have to shine and see themselves as academic leaders. On the other hand, some students prefer traditional teaching methods, such as lecture and individually graded work (Torney-Purta, 1998). The emphasis on group work differentiates ICONS from other approaches. Group work allows the students to act collaboratively, place their work in a wider context, and deal with contextual and procedural complexity (Brown & King, 2000). Nevertheless, the group work approach can come with some costs. Some students do not enjoy depending on fellow students, and the possibility of conflict should be considered. While this conflict is usually productive, it is imperative that the instructor be aware of this issue, should it threaten to derail a team's simulation experience.

Simulations also challenge students in new and sometimes uncomfortable ways. Often there is no absolute right answer to the choices that must be made during a simulation. Student-led political negotiations, like real-world politics, often are not fair. Frequently, the good and hard-working do not accomplish their goals. Ambiguity is part of any negotiation, and it can be a new and perplexing phenomenon for participating students. These factors need to be made explicit and discussed with students.

Despite some of the frustration this complexity can create, it is this richness of experience that makes simulations worthwhile. Simulation as an educational tool, it should also be recognized, takes a great deal of effort from both educators and students. Although ICONS structures its simulations to reduce the time and effort instructors must expend in order to integrate the activity into their curricula, that is, by providing role sheets, scenarios, structure, and a facilitator (SIMCON), it should be recognized that running simulations is still hard work.

Besides the motivational benefits of ICONS' approach to learning, many of its advantages stem from its technological framework. Obviously, educators need access to computers and the Internet in order to use ICONS. While the learning curve for ICONSnet is not steep, the use of ICONS still demands an investment in time on the part of the instructor and the students. All of the communication between groups is text based, and this can prove frustrating for students who would prefer face-to-face interactions. At the same time, these technology constraints force the students to focus on their written communication skills in order to negotiate successfully. Constructing a message in order to negotiate well is a useful challenge of a whole different order than simply writing an assignment for the teacher. Involvement in online exercises also brings other clear benefits. It often allows students to participate in simulations with people from around the world, exposing them to perspectives and dealing with issues they might not otherwise encounter. Finally, it provides the teacher with a mechanism for adding meaningful complexity to student interaction in a manageable and appealing way.

A NOTE ABOUT THE APPENDIX: EXPLORING ICONS

An Appendix to this chapter contains the ICONS Global Warming Mini Simulation. This simulation has been used in two contexts: (a) to teach some basic aspects of negotiation in a very limited time frame; and (b) to facilitate teacher training in both ICONSnet usage and simulation pedagogy. The Global Warming Mini Simulation[7] is an example of an ICONS closed-option simulation, where the proposal center offers fixed choices from which to choose when negotiating an agreement. As noted earlier in the chapter, this feature focuses the simulation on the negotiation process and creates a very different experience from an open-option simulation, where proposals, actions, and choices are developed entirely by the participants. The role sheets and the scenario give a sense of the structure and support materials ICONS provides to launch this kind of simulation.

Interested readers can access this simulation as one of the countries for which a role sheet is included, using the password "123" at http://www.icons.umd.edu/serg. This site is a demonstration community and the messages will be cleared out periodically. Readers who would like to explore the structure of an ICONS open-option simulation should go to http://www.icons.umd.edu/demo.html. The demonstration community located at this site allows participants to create their own password, log in, and examine how this set of ICONSnet components works. Samples of open-ended scenarios ICONS has used are available online at http://www.icons.umd.edu/archive/index.html.

APPENDIX: GLOBAL WARMING MINI-SIMULATION

Created by Beth Blake and Tim Wedig

By signing the Kyoto Protocol to the 1992 U.N. Framework Convention on Climate Control in December 1997, 38 industrialized coun-

---

[7]Please note that this simulation was developed in summer 2001 and that the international situation has now changed. The simulation is still useful though as an illustration of how multilateral negotiations are conducted online.

tries agreed to adopt binding targets for reducing emissions of greenhouse gases (carbon dioxide, etc.) believed to be responsible for global warming. The United States committed to a 7-percent reduction from the base year 1990, while Japan committed to a 6-percent reduction. The largest percentage reduction by signatories is that of several European countries that committed to an 8-percent reduction. Developing countries, including India and China, make up the rest of the 160 parties to the protocol and are under no obligation to begin reductions because of the potentially negative effects on economic growth.

Although the results of Kyoto are consistent with a 1995 agreement that rich countries should act to cut emissions before discussing what poorer countries should do, critics in industrialized countries claim that not requiring developing countries to reduce is unfair, and prevents real progress from being made. (Emission levels in developing countries are expected to overtake those of the developed world in about 15 years.) Developing countries, though, claim that, historically, the industrialized countries are responsible for global warming, and that they themselves need the time that the industrialized countries had to concentrate on economic development.

The sixth session of the conference of the parties is to be held in Bonn, Germany. One of the original purposes of this meeting was to work out the details of an emissions credit trading system, which is an attempt to provide free-market incentives to cut pollution and encourage technological innovation. Each participating country would receive an emissions limit; if they are able to cut their emissions below the limit, they can then sell their excess right to pollute to countries that cannot meet their own limits. Two issues that must be worked out are whether countries should get additional credit for maintaining undeveloped land to serve as carbon sinks and whether industrialized countries should get credit for transferring technology to developing countries.

Following the Bush administration's statement that the United States would not be a part of the Kyoto framework, the conference is likely to also focus on more fundamental discussions of participation in a global warming regime. Specifically, can the treaty be amended (in its present form) to allay the concerns of developed countries about the exemption of developing nations?

Proposal Options

Each country can build its own proposal by selecting one of the choices under each of the following headings. If a country chooses to submit a proposal, it is not required to make a selection for each category.

Emissions limits for industrialized countries:

1. Binding limits
2. Voluntary limits
3. No limits

Emissions limits for developing countries:

1. Binding limits
2. Voluntary limits
3. No limits

Emissions credit trading system:

1. System that favors additional credits for undeveloped land
2. System that favors additional credits for technology transfers
3. System that allows credits for undeveloped land and technology transfers
4. No emissions credit trading system

Brazil

Brazil has the strongest industrial base in South America, as well as the largest (although rapidly shrinking) rainforest in the world. Brazil is aggressively pursuing an economic development strategy that relies on manufacturing, and is opposed to an agreement that would limit this development in any way. However, Brazil is interested in emissions trading plans that would allow the rainforest to be applied against industrial emissions. In addition, Brazil has taken the position that developed nations should undertake the bulk of reductions in greenhouse gases since they have created the global warming problem to this point.

1. Developed nations: favors binding limits, opposed to voluntary and no limits
2. Developing nations: favors no limits, opposes binding limits but could accept voluntary limits
3. Emission credits: favors credits for undeveloped land, could accept credits for technology transfer

Canada

Canada is no stranger to the effects of industrial emissions, having faced an acid rain crisis in the 1980s due to emissions from U.S. factories blowing over the border and affecting fisheries and forests. Canada has been actively working on meeting their Kyoto goals since 1995. In late 2000, the Canadian government unveiled its plan to reduce greenhouse gas emissions, which would cost $550 million and would take Canada one-third of the way toward meeting their Kyoto target. The Canadian government has stressed greenhouse gas reduction, efficiency, and technological improvements to address the issue of global warming.

Positions:

1. Developed nations: favors binding limits, does not favor voluntary or no limits
2. Developing nations: favors voluntary limits at present, moving toward binding limits as nations become more developed and technology is more available
3. Emission credits: favors credits for undeveloped land and technology transfers, as part of a binding agreement

China

The recent acceptance into the World Trade Organization (WTO) of China has created opportunities for attracting investment previously unavailable to China. The need to increase foreign investment and trade has led China to become a destination for polluting industries in Asia that are fleeing strict environmental laws in their own countries. Therefore, China is reluctant to reach an agreement that would hamper this economic development plan. In addition, despite being the largest market in the world, and a major regional economic power, China is insistent on being considered a developing country for the purposes of these negotiations.

1. Developed nations: favors binding limits, opposes voluntary and no limits
2. Developing nations: favors no limits, opposes binding limits, would accept voluntary limits
3. Emission credits: favors credits for technology transfer, opposes credits for undeveloped land

Denmark

Denmark is strongly supportive of the Kyoto treaty, as much of the country is threatened by sea level increases from global warming. Large sections of the country have traditionally flooded roughly every decade, which increases the stakes for global warming in Denmark. Denmark has been active in environmental legislation since the 1960s, and has undertaken a vigorous program of restoration and regulation since that time. They are strongly in favor of reaching an agreement as soon as possible.

1. Developed nations: favors binding limits, does not favor voluntary limits, opposed to no limits
2. Developing nations: favors binding limits, does not favor voluntary limits, opposed to no limits
3. Emission credits: does not favor credits of any type at the present

France

France has been active in pursuing ratification of the Kyoto treaty, both domestically and internationally. Much of this emphasis has been on energy policy issues, particularly nuclear power on which France has staked much of their effort. France has been quite critical of the U.S. retreat from the Kyoto agreement, and has been seeking to strengthen European opposition to the U.S. stance. France's goal is to have the Kyoto agreement fully ratified and in effect before the 2002 Johannesburg Summit.

Positions:

1. Developed nations: favors binding limits, does not favor voluntary or no limits
2. Developing nations: favors binding limits, although lower than for developed nations, does not favor voluntary or no limits
3. Emission credits: favors credits for undeveloped land and technology transfers, as part of a binding agreement

Germany

Germany has been active in pursuing ratification of the Kyoto treaty, both domestically and internationally. As the home of the largest and most electorally successful Green Party in the world, environmental issues have been high on the German agenda. In particular, Germany has a competitive edge in Green technology, and is supportive of efforts to increase reliance on technology as part of an agreement. However, Germany has been less critical of the U.S. position on Kyoto than other European nations, and seeks to find a compromise that will appeal to all developed nations.

Positions:

1. Developed nations: favors binding limits, does not favor voluntary or no limits
2. Developing nations: favors binding limits, does not favor voluntary or no limits
3. Emission credits: favors technology transfer credits, does not favor credits for undeveloped land

India

India has become a major regional economic power in south Asia, due in large part to industrial production. This has created serious environmental problems, including air and water pollution especially in urban areas. With the world's second largest population, which is concentrated in these urban areas, environmental concerns are rapidly rising as a priority. Since 1990, however, India's economy has grown rapidly due to a strong computer software and technology sector. As India moves more toward technology and becomes less reliant on heavy industry, the structure of the economy will resemble the developed nations more than developing ones.

1. Developed nations: favors binding limits, would accept voluntary limits, opposed to no limits
2. Developing nations: favors voluntary limits, would accept binding limits, opposed to no limits
3. Emission credits: favors credits for technology transfer and undeveloped land

Japan

While Japan is a global economic power, it is still a relatively small island nation with a rapidly decreasing amount of land available for practical usage (much of the land is mountainous and not useful for farming, etc.). Because of this, Japan is sensitive to the issue of sea level increases from global warming. However, Japan is also hesitant to create further burdens on Japanese industries already suffering from an economic downturn. Japan favors technological solutions that create the least amount of disruption for their industries, many of which have already relocated production to nations in the Pacific Rim.

1. Developed nations: favors voluntary limits, opposes binding and no limits
2. Developing nations: favors voluntary limits, opposes binding and no limits
3. Emission credits: favors credits for technology transfers, opposes credits for undeveloped land

Kiribati

Kiribati is a small island nation in the South Pacific that is very sensitive to the possibility of sea level increases from global warming. Due to the low elevation of much of Kiribati, even a slight increase in sea levels would prove to be disastrous for the island. Kiribati does not have domestic industry, and relies on tourism for the bulk of its foreign trade. Therefore, reaching a strong agreement as quickly as possible is the highest priority for Kiribati. Even though opposed to credits for technology transfers and undeveloped land, because it would still allow larger amounts of greenhouse gases to be emitted, Kiribati would support them if it means reaching an agreement more quickly.

1. Developed nations: favors binding limits, opposes voluntary or no limits
2. Developing nations: favors binding limits, opposes voluntary or no limits
3. Emission credits: opposes credits of all types, but would concede credits if it brings a quicker and stricter agreement

Mexico

As part of the North American Free Trade Agreement (NAFTA), Mexico has benefited from the relocation of many industries fleeing strict environmental regulations in the United States and Canada. As such, Mexico is reluctant to embrace any agreement that would create pressure on these newly arrived industries. However, the northern border region of Mexico has also become heavily polluted and the toll on people and the environment has been severe. Therefore, Mexico would prefer to find a solution that leads to improvement, but still preserves their competitive edge in attracting industry.

1. Developed nations: favors binding limits, opposes voluntary or no limits
2. Developing nations: favors no limits, opposes binding limits or voluntary limits
3. Emission credits: favors credits for technology transfer, opposes credits for undeveloped land

Nigeria

While a developing country, Nigeria does have large petroleum reserves that provide substantial foreign trade income. In addition, Nigeria has an industrial base involved in oil refining and other production. However, recent political and ethnic instability created a situation in which the government ceded much of the control over the oil industry to foreign multinational corporations. Therefore, the government of Nigeria does not have much regulatory oversight over the environmental standards of this industry. With its recent democratic transition, Nigeria is beginning to stabilize its economy, but is still heavily dependent on the oil industry for its economy.

1. Developed nations: favors no limits, opposes binding limits, could support voluntary limits
2. Developing nations: favors no limits, opposes binding and voluntary limits
3. Emission credits: favors credits for technology transfers and undeveloped land

Russia

Due to the difficult transition from Soviet-era economics to a more capitalist mode of production, Russia is hesitant to participate too strongly in an agreement. This is in large part due to their outmoded and highly polluting industry, which can not be easily replaced with, or even retrofitted to, greener technology due to financial limitations. Due to the economic problems Russia has experienced, they are also hesitant to accept being categorized as a developed nation for purposes of emissions quotas. However, Russia is receptive to technology transfer, either to Russia from abroad or as an export from Russia once the technology is developed.

1. Developed nations: favors no limits, does not favor binding limits, would accept voluntary limits
2. Developing nations: favors no limits, does not favor binding limits, would agree to reduced voluntary limits
3. Emission credits: favors credits for technology transfer and undeveloped land

South Africa

South Africa is the regional economic power in sub-Saharan Africa, but is still a developing nation. The post-Apartheid transition is still underway, which includes economic restructuring, as well as political and social changes. South Africa is, however, committed to environmental issues, and therefore would like to see an agreement be reached that addresses the problem of global warming while still providing opportunities for developing nations to build their economies quickly.

1. Developed nations: favors binding limits, opposes no limits, would accept voluntary limits
2. Developing nations: favors voluntary limits, opposes binding limits and no limits
3. Emission credits: favors credits for technology transfers, opposes credits for undeveloped land

Trinidad and Tobago

As an island nation, Trinidad and Tobago is particularly concerned about the threat of global warming and the resulting rise in sea levels. With an economy largely based on tourism (with some industry), any loss of coastal lands would be devastating to the economy. Therefore, Trinidad and Tobago favors a strong agreement and a fast resolution to the debate. In order to accomplish this, they are willing to make some compromises in terms of credits for other nations.

1. Developed nations: favors binding limits, opposes voluntary and no limits
2. Developing nations: favors binding limits, opposes voluntary and no limits
3. Emission credits: favors no credits, but is willing to accept credits for technology transfers and undeveloped land to reach an agreement

United States of America

The United States has been very reluctant to reach a substantive agreement on global warming due to two main factors: active opposition by powerful corporations, and the reluctance of officials to challenge the resource-intensive lifestyle of its citizens. Due to these factors, the Kyoto agreement stalled in Congress after 1997, and has since been repudiated by the current administration. Currently, the United States favors more study about the validity of global warming theories, leading to voluntary market-based solutions.

Positions:

1. Developed nations: favors no limits at present, may support voluntary limits in the future, opposed to binding limits
2. Developing nations: wants all countries to be subject to the same limits, no difference between developed and developing nations
3. Emission credits: as part of a market-based solution, would favor credit-trading systems for both land and technology

REFERENCES

Brown, S. W., & King, F. B. (2000). Constructivist pedagogy and how we learn: Educational psychology meets international studies. *International Studies Perspectives, 1*(3), 245–254.

Brown, S. W., Mayall, H. J., Toman, J. J., & Schrader, P. G. (2000, April). *The importance of subject-matter knowledge, situated learning, and communities of practice when instructing with technology*. Paper presented at the meetings of the American Educational Research Association, New Orleans, LA.

Ip, A., & Linser, R. (2001, January/February). Evaluation of a role-play simulation in political science. *Assessment*. Available: http://horizon.unc.edu/TS/assessment/2001-01.asp.

Petranek, C. F. (2000). Written debriefing: The next vital step in learning with simulations. *Simulation and Gaming, 31*(1), 108–119.

Rottier, K. (1995). Project ICONS is powerful. In C. Lucas & L. Lucas (Eds.), *Practitioners write the book: What works in educational technology*. Available: http://www.tcet.unt.edu/pubs/whatwork.htm.

Starkey, B. A., & Blake, E. (2001). Simulation in international relations education. *Simulation and Gaming, 32*(4), 537–551.

Torney-Purta, J. (1990). From attitudes and knowledge to schemata: Expanding the outcomes of political socialization research. In O. Ichilov (Ed.), *Political socialization, citizenship education and democracy* (pp. 98–115). New York: Teachers College Press.

Torney-Purta, J. (1995). Education in multicultural settings: Perspectives from global and international education programs. In W. D. Hawley & A. W. Jackson (Eds.), *Toward a common destiny: Improving race and ethnic relations in America* (pp. 341–370). San Francisco: Jossey-Bass.

Torney-Purta, J. (1996). Conceptual changes among adolescents using computer networks in group-mediated international role playing. In S. Vosniadou, E. DeCorte, R. Glaser, & H. Mandl (Eds.), *International perspectives on the design of technol-*

ogy supported learning environments (pp. 203–219). Mahwah, NJ: Lawrence Erlbaum Associates.

Torney-Purta, J. (1998). Evaluating programs designed to teach international content and negotiation skills. *International Negotiations, 3*, 77–97.

RELEVANT WEB SITES

All of these links can be accessed at http://www.icons.umd.edu/serg.

http://csf.colorado.edu/isafp/syllabi/hansons.htm (Accessed March 25, 2002)

http://faculty.smu.edu/mlusztig/PLSC%203390%20Syllabus.doc (Accessed March 25, 2002)

http://homepage.mac.com/vicfalls/africanpolitics.html (Accessed March 25, 2002)

http://www.icons.umd.edu (Accessed March 25, 2002)

http://www.icons.umd.edu/about/iconsnet.htm (Accessed March 25, 2002)

http://www.icons.umd.edu/about/inetfeat.htm (Accessed March 25, 2002)

http://www.icons.umd.edu/gvpt450/course.htm (Accessed March 25, 2002)

http://www.icons.umd.edu/help/net10.html (Accessed March 25, 2002)

http://www.icons.umd.edu/help/net7.html (Accessed March 25, 2002)

http://www.icons.umd.edu/resource/debrief.htm (Accessed March 25, 2002)

http://www.icons.umd.edu/resource/pospaper.htm (Accessed March 25, 2002)

http://www.lib.uconn.edu/~mboyer/syl220f.htm (Accessed March 25, 2002)

http://www.ed.gov/offices/OPE/FIPSE/LessonsIV/umd.html (Accessed March 25, 2002)

http://www.icons.umd.edu/demo.html (Accessed March 25, 2002)

9

Disaster Control: A Simulation for Learning the Skills of Emergency Management

John O'Looney
University of Georgia

Melissa P. Dodd
Boston Public Schools

The *Disaster Control* digital simulation situates students into a simulated real-world disaster in which they make key decisions that impact the outcome of an emergency situation to help them learn the skills and process of decision making in emergency management (EM). The simulation was designed by the Carl Vinson Institute of Government at the University of Georgia in conjunction with a technical assistance contract with the Georgia Emergency Management Agency to help improve the reaction of emergency managers to potential natural and human-made disasters. Though designed as a training program, our purpose is to describe how to use it so students learn to appreciate the complexities of decisions within the field of EM. Students outside the field of EM may have difficulty understanding the challenges from the point of view of those responsible for making decisions due to their complex and dynamic nature. The simulation overcomes this challenge by throwing students into a structured real-world disaster in which they are responsible for making critical decisions that will have a lasting impact on the outcome of the emergency situation. By using *Disaster Control* as part of a social science curriculum, students learn to understand the complex nature of decisions within EM by confronting decisions that real emergency managers experience out in the field. We see this educational application as a key extension of training simulations.

In this chapter, we first address the need for the *Disaster Control* simulation and its purpose. Digital simulations provide active environments for learning about decision making in EM. We then describe the simulation environment, outlining its main components and features and how they connect to the learning objectives of the simulation. Third, we provide the theoretical and pedagogical frameworks that support *Disaster Control* as a learning tool. Fourth, we discuss the learning goals of the simulation. By scripting in implicit learning goals, the digital simulation challenges participants to enhance discipline-specific skills, as well as higher-order thinking skills and understanding germane to decision-making processes. Finally, we discuss how the EM simulation can be integrated into college-level social science courses to help students understand the multifaceted complexity of decision-making processes.

NEED AND PURPOSE

The field of EM is filled with instances where decisions during a disaster response plan severely influence the impact of a threatening event. Hurricane Andrew, which wreaked havoc on southern Florida, south-central Louisiana, and the northwestern Bahamas in 1992, provides a salient example of how decision making on the part of emergency managers impacts the outcome of a natural disaster. Hurricane Andrew was reclassified in 2002 from a category 4 to a category 5 hurricane, the highest rating on the Saffir/Simpson Hurricane Scale. Andrew was the costliest hurricane in U.S. history, resulting in an estimated $25 billion in economic loss (Jarrell, Landsea, Mayfield, & Rappaport, 2001). Despite its magnitude and cost, few people died as a direct result of Hurricane Andrew, which was attributed to emergency preparedness and evacuation programs (Rappaport, 1993). The outcomes of decisions made during emergency events have a ripple effect in society, affecting political, social, and economic spheres at the local, state, federal, and even international levels. As a result, the complexity of EM issues is difficult to convey. How do students interpret the quality and challenges of EM, and thus the decision-making process, in light of complex outcomes like those reported for Hurricane Andrew? How can students learn to interpret and analyze these decisions after the fact?

We suggest it is not possible for students to fully appreciate the work done during an emergency if they do not have personal experience with the challenges of EM. Analyses of the Hurricane Andrew disaster exemplify the importance of understanding effective decision making on the part of emergency managers. Disaster management involves complex decision-making skills that necessitate knowing when to search for information, and how to integrate that new knowledge within the context of hundreds of other pieces of existing data, to make the most appropriate decision to respond to the disaster. Decision making in this situation is one where rationality is bounded by the inability to actually process all information sources within strict time considerations. Disaster managers have to learn how to make near-optimal decisions without the benefit of being able to completely analyze a problem. How can students, with hindsight, possibly appreciate and accommodate these barriers to sound decisions? We suggest students required to understand EM decisions should experience the challenge for themselves. This approach to learning finds its foundation in the theoretical frameworks of constructivism, situated learning, cognitive apprenticeship, and generative learning.

For these reasons, learning how emergency managers make decisions needs to be situated within the context of a simulated disaster that provides students with realistic and authentic opportunities to understand the complexity of the decision-making process. Williams (1996) identified computer simulations as a way to provide a rich and responsive context that mirrors the real workload of emergency managers to help students effectively learn EM skills. Written accounts and case studies of natural disasters, such as those of Hurricane Andrew, offer us only a glimpse of what happens when a major natural disaster occurs, how people are affected by it, how difficult it is to deal with, and what implications its outcomes have on future emergency response plans and legislation. In contrast, digital simulations eliminate the real-world consequences of error, providing a safe context for students to experience the process and challenges of a domain, such as EM (Naidu, Ip, & Linser, 2000). By using a digital simulation, students begin to understand decision-making strategies based on limited information. The overload of information in EM often inhibits the ability to make optimal decisions, which result from thorough and rational analysis of the data. Furthermore, when used in a classroom setting, students can see how their colleagues, when presented with the same data, might make different decisions that lead to alternative outcomes. Given the range and speed at which emergency managers make decisions, and the constraints that they are typically under while making these decisions, a digital simulation offers the best means of representing the myriad factors at play during EM interventions. This baptism by fire help students see how even the best trained emergency manager might fall victim to the complex circumstances under which they make decisions. The following two sections outline the environment of the simulation, which offers students their first exposure to the complexity of decision making in EM.

THE SIMULATION ENVIRONMENT

Disaster Control was initially designed to allow a single player to use the simulation in a self-instructional manner or in conjunction with a facilitator. The facilitator sets up a scenario to address particular roadblocks in a student's skill set or to teach the decisions associated with a given phase of EM. At the beginning of the simulation, the participant reads a prescenario that sets the context (i.e., "You are the disaster manager for a coastal area that is known to experience hurricanes.") and reviews the learning objectives for each phase. The simulation utilizes costs, time, user settings, quizzes, customized threat scenarios, and scouting components to further construct the context for a simulated emergency (Fig. 9.1). As participants move through the simulation, they accrue costs resulting from expenditures and disaster-related damages. Not only does an emergency manager need to make fast decisions, often with limited time and information, but also consider the financial costs of decisions. Expenditures in the simulation relate to the costs that ensue due to a participant's decisions (i.e., for deciding to continue the training of personnel or to open up additional slots at an emergency shelter for evacuated residents). Disaster-related damages include the direct cost and estimated loss of economic product due to evacuation-related decisions. Property damage, deaths, and injuries also increase the cost of a disaster.

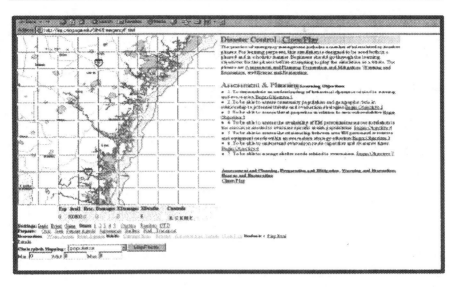

FIG. 9.1. *Disaster Control* environment.

Throughout the simulation participants receive damage reports that provide information on the damages for the current period, for the total simulation run, and for each area impacted. The reports also provide breakdowns of the damages that are attributed to particular threats. Finally, the reports record the number of deaths and injuries that were avoided due to the evacuation procedures put in place by the player prior to the impact of the threat. Students use the reports during the simulation to evaluate the impact of their strategies and to help them determine their next course of action. Students can also use the reports after they complete a simulation to assess the effectives of their response plan. The damage reports provide instructors with an assessment tool to evaluate their students' learning of the complexity of EM decision making. The most important feedback built into the *Disaster Control* simulation is the calculation of simulated human and economic losses that result from the decisions made by the player through the threat scenario. In this respect, feedback is both immediate and concrete. Participants can assess their progress during the simulation based on the human and economic losses that transpire through the simulation.

Within a simulation, time occurs in 8-hour periods. Each period represents one of three phases of day: daytime, evening, and night. These phases are indicated both by labels in the damage reports and by color codes of the sun icon located below the map (see Fig. 9.1). When a participant calls for an evacuation during a given time period, it will not actually occur until the next daytime period to reflect the length of time an evacuation takes in real-time. The actual number of seconds that will elapse before the next period occurs can be set by the player, using the "Length of Day" constant, and can be rapidly changed during the course of the simulation by clicking the S(low), M(edium) or F(ast) links. Since *Disaster Control* models the time pressures of EM situations, the impact of a player's decisions, both in human and economic terms, becomes increasingly time sensitive. For example, if a player calls for an evacuation too soon, substantial economic damage can occur even if the player has correctly identified the place and approximate time of the disaster.

The instructor, and even the participant, can devise any number of more or less challenging disaster management scenarios through the *user settings* component. Making changes to the simulation settings alter the level and type of challenge. The simulation includes four types of settings:

1. Settings to specify the degree to which a random event will occur during the simulation;
2. Settings to specify the probability of occurrence and location of nonrandom events;
3. Settings to specify the cost factors and other key assumptions under which the participant will act;
4. Settings to specify the particular characteristics of the threats that the participant will face.

Although self-directed participants could specify any of these settings prior to their simulation, to create a truly unexpected disaster situation, certain settings should be set by the instructor without the participant's knowledge.

The two types of events, agent–threat events and flow events, whether random or planned, that occur during the simulation can be turned on or off through the user settings. Each type of event can greatly impact the decisions of the emergency manager and must be considered when building a response system to a particular disaster scenario. Furthermore, events unfold in the simulation based on decisions made at the outset. Agent–threat events include a threat location, agent location, agent communication loss, threat direction, and rain, among others. Flow events include changing the evacuation flow at a particular location or changing the evacuation flow by direction among others. Random events are unknown (to the player), and include agent position changes, threat position changes, occurrence of rainfall, the development of a new threat, and an agent contactability change, among others.

Using the customizing options, the simulation facilitator specifies any number of threats and their corresponding characteristics, including when, where, type, duration, and the probability that they will occur. The *customizing threat scenario* component enables the facilitator to develop a scenario to demonstrate a particular learning objective or to draw attention to certain decisions within the EM process. The quiz component enables participants to test their burgeoning conceptualization of EM by answering questions throughout the simulation. Participants earn extra resources to assist them during the simulation by answering the questions correctly.

The simulation offers two *scouting* functions to scaffold learning of EM decision making by providing just-in-time support to help players make informed decisions. Just-in-time learning support involves using players' mistakes and successes as key opportunities to direct them to materials, activities, and feedback that reinforce the key learning objectives of the simulation or allow them to move to the next level of challenge or learning task (O'Looney, 2003). The find function raises the contactability rating of all the agents so that the player can respond to a threat faster. The damage evaluation calculates the number of rescue and restoration workers needed to address the consequences of a particular threat (Fig. 9.2). The simulation charges players every time they use one of the scouting functions to ensure that they do not become overly dependent on the support systems, but rather turn to them when they need assistance at critical points in the decision-making process.

Because *Disaster Control* simulates all the phases of an emergency simulation it tends to be highly complex. Such complexity can reduce a participant's ability to manipulate the simulation without prior training. Ideally, one would be able to produce digital simulations that are both complex enough to mimic the phenomena of real-world disaster scenarios and simple enough to learn to use by doing. Unfortunately, in most cases there will be substantial trade-offs between the complexity of the task and the simplicity of use. We have worked to ad-

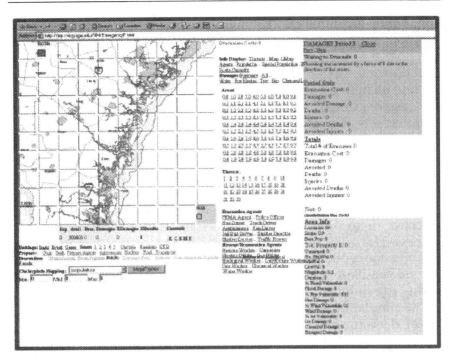

FIG. 9.2.   Damage control.

dress this issue in a number of ways. First, before beginning the simulation, participants can easily explore demonstration disaster scenarios that provide them with a basic sense of some of the key characteristics of a disaster. In addition, the simulation is divided into a series of specific learning objectives (Fig. 9.3) and tasks that build upon one another—tracking the sequence of the EM phases. This feature affords instructors and students with a degree of flexibility, allowing instructors to customize the focus of the simulation, and enabling students to successfully complete a specific learning task without having to learn the entire simulation application.

DISASTER CONTROL FEATURES

This section describes the features of *Disaster Control*, emphasizing how they might be used to help students understand the complex model of challenges faced by emergency managers. For a given disaster scenario, whether customized by the facilitator or student, deci-

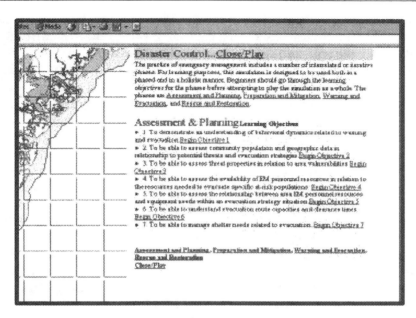

FIG. 9.3. Learning objectives for the assessment and planning phase.

sions in the simulation are made in relation to nine[1] characteristics that best mirror those of a real-world emergency situation. Since the simulation occurs across an entire coastal region, 100 *areas* are represented in the simulation environment. While each area has specific characteristics, they fall under five main categories: population, vulnerability, resources, evacuation capacity, and evacuation warning capacity. In an area, the population varies based on time of day or socioeconomic status. An area can have a particular vulnerability to a natural disaster, such as fire. It may, or may not, have on-site personnel and equipment to handle emergencies. It can have the infrastructure in place to enable easy travel for evacuation purposes such as large capacity roads and it could, or could not have, mechanisms in place that can be used to communicate warnings and critical information to the community such as large organizations and associations that have quick access to their constituents.

The simulation addresses the type and level of threat that might lead to an emergency situation such as a storm, fire, tornado, or ice.

---

[1]The nine main features are: areas, threats, personnel, skills and equipment, training, interagency agreements, warnings, transport, and emergency shelters.

The simulation also allows for human-made emergencies, such as chemical or biological situations. Each threat has a host of attributes that impact the type and speed at which a participant must make decisions. The direction of the threat or its magnitude and duration influence the way in which an emergency manager would need to respond to the threat as it unfolds. Most threats during a disaster represent various degrees of distinct types of destruction. A storm, for example, may correspond to varying levels of water, wind, ice, and chemical harm. Therefore, rather than telling the student how a manager should respond to a storm threat, the simulation helps the student understand the complexity behind the threat of storm and how responding to that threat can lead to a range of possible outcomes.

In *Disaster Control, personnel* fall into two basic categories, evacuation agents and rescue agents. Evacuation agents include police officers, bus drivers, truck drivers, shelter directors, doctors, traffic routers, jail bus drivers, van drivers, and ambulances. Rescue agents include rescue workers, carpenters, gas and electric utility workers, biological workers, workers to remove landscape debris, firefighters, chemical workers, and water workers. These personnel agents can be employed during their corresponding phase of the simulation. To simulate the real-life challenges faced by emergency managers during a disaster, agents in the simulation possess a variety of characteristics that make them more or less valuable in handling particular scenarios, including location, skill, contactability, autonomy, situational knowledge, and interpersonal relationship skills. Therefore, in the simulation the participant considers these various characteristics, and how they interact with each other, when determining which personnel to solicit for support and collaboration. The simulation reflects the manner in which a real emergency manager would solicit assistance from an agent on the ground. After choosing the type of agent to be deployed, whether for evacuation or rescue, the player can observe where agents are available at that time. Through the move personnel form (Fig. 9.4), the player moves one or more agents by checking the appropriate box on the form and supplying the coordinates for the agent's new location. The manager can then decide how to direct the agent, either by commanding or persuading the agent to the new location. The command–persuade option in the simulation, which is connected to the relationship that the emergency manager has with the agent's agency, provides the participant with a level of variability in the probability of a particular agent mov-

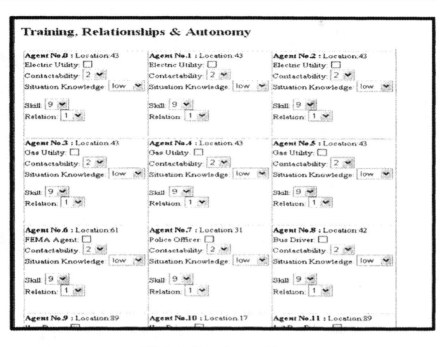

FIG. 9.4. Move Personnel form.

ing to the desired location. If an emergency manager commands an agent to a new location without having an established relationship with that agent's agency, the probability of the agent moving will be dramatically lower than if the emergency manager had previously established a relationship. This feature provides another opportunity for students to understand the complexity of EM by demonstrating the importance of building relationships and working with others to respond to a disaster. To further elucidate this understanding, participants can solidify good relationships with key actors through an *interagency agreement*, which provides the participant with greater ability to command agents. By expending resources in the relationship-building module, the interagency agreement module enables the participant to make these relations official, giving greater command over the agents. However, establishing sound relationships costs resources. Mirroring the complexity of real EM, participants are only able to make a limited number of agreements, requiring them to choose agencies strategically so they can effectively command agents to respond to the disaster scenario.

A responsibility of an emergency manager is to ensure that personnel are well trained and equipped to handle the emergency situation. The simulation allows a participant to choose whether to provide *training* to personnel. Training raises the skills of the personnel, thereby increasing their effectiveness on the job. However, as in real life, resources and time limit training opportunities. When a manager runs out of funds or preparation time, particularly when a disaster hits, training usually stops. The participant needs to weigh these factors when deciding whom to send to an emergency area. *Equipment* can impact the degree of effectiveness for a specific agent as well. EM agents who move with their equipment travel slower than those who can pick up equipment at the disaster site. However, unless there is already equipment in the area, it is generally necessary for agents to carry their equipment. When an emergency manager considers her personnel options, training and equipment issues are critical in the decision-making process.

Warnings represent a key action for emergency managers, as warnings result in the level of evacuation for an area. In EM, warnings need to be employed to the appropriate degree. Providing excess warnings may ensure against injury or death, however, they can also result in high economic losses. Similarly, providing less than adequate warning to a community can result in both economic and human loss. By enabling participants to weigh the strengths and weaknesses of warnings under the time constraints often associated with disasters, they learn to realize the importance of being able to pinpoint the area(s) that need warning in a timely manner and to set the level of warning so that it results in an appropriate evacuation rate. As with other components of EM, *Disaster Control* simulates warning characteristics, including type, style, location–use associations, and speed period. More so than deciding whether to provide a warning to a particular area, the participant needs to consider an area's characteristics to ensure that an effective warning is issued.

Transport is needed to allow agents to move special populations from a designated evacuation area. Transportation, such as buses, vans, jail buses, and ambulances, that is available within the specific area is automatically engaged when an evacuation event occurs. A participant can also call additional transportation to the area. The learning objectives outlined in the warning and evacuation phase help the participant understand the needs and characteristics of special populations and the available transportation to then calculate the remaining transport needs based on the maximum capacity for the buses, vans, jail buses, and ambulances.

The key facility in the simulation is the *emergency shelter*. As residents evacuate an area in reaction to a warning, an emergency manager identifies emergency shelter slots to provide these residents with adequate shelter and safety. If the shelters do not exist in the areas of high need, or if the shelters are not properly staffed, simulated injuries and associated costs occur. While a participant can open shelters in given areas, set the occupancy for these shelters or increase the occupancy of existing shelters, each slot that is opened represents a cost in resource units or dollars.

The agent-based adaptive simulation technology of *Disaster Control* helps to create a learning tool that approximates the learning an emergency manager would experience on the job. Agents represent independent software objects that adapt to changes in the environment by altering their behaviors, symbolizing the characteristics of natural complex systems, including unpredictability. Adaptability refers to the ability of the simulation to adapt to the skills of the individual player. Adaptive simulations identify the specific weaknesses of the player and provide a scenario that focuses on the skills and understanding that challenge the player the most.

Most EM situations tend not to be adaptive in this manner. Typically, they do not include the ability to change the underlying assumptions to allow the player to simulate any number of what-if disaster scenarios. Furthermore, they are often deterministic rather than naturalistic in that they do not include autonomous agents. Finally, they rarely adapt the nature of the challenge to the specific skills of the individual player. To date, no simulations on the market or under development attempt to model the aspects of disaster management in ways that replicate real-world circumstances using autonomous agents as the base technology for the simulation.

LEARNING THEORY SUPPORTING *DISASTER CONTROL*

Disaster Control implicitly acknowledges three barriers to learning within the field of EM. First, students of EM predominantly bias decisions that have a short-term impact on the disaster rather than considering the long-term effects of an alternative course. Second, students have difficulty understanding that the number and type of decisions addressed during a disaster are typically a direct result of the choices that were, or were not, made at the outset of the threat, or even before the emergency began (FEMA, 2002). Finally, while students may learn about the factors that impact decision making in their training courses and textbooks, this abstract manner of learning is disconnected from the reality of the emergency experience. When faced with the time pressure and threatening constraints of an emergency situation, students have difficulty incorporating these kernels of knowledge and facts into an effective response plan.

Disaster Control addresses these learning challenges by situating EM decision making in an authentic and safe context that scaffolds students' learning of EM and their understanding of its complexity. Learning occurs most effectively when students actively engage in constructing and manipulating their knowledge (Vygotsky, 1978). Furthermore, authentic and complex contexts that are relevant to the activity, the learner, and the culture of practice are integral to learning (Brown, Collins, & Duguid, 1989; Lave, 1988; Vygotsky, 1978). By role-playing in a real-world situation, students experience the time pressures, the stress, the rapid flow of information and data, and the innumerable variables that contribute to the progression of a disaster. This learning approach differs from traditional methods of teaching, such as teaching via lectures and textbooks, which, according to Brown et al. (1989), can impede students' access to contextual cues that enable learning. Although simulations come in a number of different forms, recent developments in computer science have made it possible to create digital simulations that more closely approximate real-life complexities and uncertainties (O'Looney, 2003). The context plays a critical role in the simulation, serving as the bridge that connects the conceptual understanding of decision making in EM to the practice of making decisions in emergency activities.

The *Disaster Control* simulation recognizes the role that generative learning plays in knowledge construction (Wittrock, 1990). Generative learning involves connecting new information to prior knowledge to construct more complex knowledge structures (Jonassen, Mayes, & McAleese, 1993). By enabling students to actively construct their understanding of the complexity of EM decision making, the simulation shapes the evolving mental model students use when interpreting actions taken during an emergency by helping them link their prior knowledge with new knowledge that is deeper and more realistic.

Moreover, the simulation's support tools, such as the damage reports and scouting features, act as scaffolding, providing support to students when they need it to help them integrate this new learning into their existing knowledge of the process. Scaffolding, key to Vygotsky's zone of proximal development learning theory and a method of cognitive apprenticeship, offers assistance to students that builds upon their own skills to enable them to engage in activities that would otherwise be too challenging (Collins, Brown, & Newman, 1989; Brown et al., 1989; Vygotsky, 1978). Scaffolding helps students navigate through the context by providing support when they have difficulty doing it on their own. In this way, students challenge and expand their own understanding of decision making in EM and develop a richer comprehension of its complex nature. The rich context of digital simulations, and the ways in which they scaffold learning can also help students transfer their new understanding into other situations (O'Looney, 2003).

The simulation dynamics, specifically the use of autonomous agents and the emergent behavior they display, reinforce that there is not an ideal solution to a particular emergency situation. As a result, players are not tested against a benchmark of excellent skill nor should students be compared against each other to determine who is more effective at managing an emergency. Given the multitude of factors at play throughout the EM process, the reality that there is no one right answer diverges significantly from traditional modes of teaching in which a specific problem has an appropriate solution. In the real world, and the case holds true for EM, there are often multiple solutions to the convoluted or murky problems that crisis scenarios create. *Disaster Control* maintains this level of reality in its simulations to facilitate the fog of disaster that exists in real emergency experiences. In this respect, students participating in a *Disaster Control* simulation have the opportunity to act in the capacity of explorers of complexity, attempting to identify heuristics rather than laws, which might help them to better manage dynamic events across multiple scenarios.

LEARNING GOALS

At the core of the *Disaster Control* simulation are nine implicit learning goals that address the complexity of the decision-making process associated with EM. Specific features and components of the simulation, as outlined in this section, embody these learning goals. However, they are not explicitly stated in the simulation. Rather, the simulation's instructions focus on more specific learning objectives that a participant needs to achieve, such as create interagency agreements and prepare for sheltering needs in a threatened area at each phase of the EM process.

We believe that in addition to helping students become effective emergency managers, learning these skills through simulated activity helps students incorporate this new knowledge into their existing understanding of the EM process, thus enhancing their development of the higher-order skills outlined in these learning goals. After working through the simulation several times and evaluating the outcomes of their decisions, students may see some improvement in their acquisition of skills even when they are not training to become managers. However, given the multiplicity of factors that influence the outcome of a disaster response, students begin to learn that increases in these skills do not necessarily change the range of key outcomes in both economic cost and human life.

Increase Ability to Balance Conflicting Goals

Participants learn to balance conflicting goals when making decisions in the face of a disaster. In EM, the need to protect the safety of citizens is juxtaposed with the need to result in the least economic loss for the community as a whole. While this econometric view has traditionally been outside the realm of EM, it has begun to take a more prominent role in the process. To scaffold this learning, underlying the simulation is an economic model that calculates the cost of an evacuation and compares this cost to what the disaster would have cost in dollar value of life and property damage had the evacuation not occurred.

Increase the Ability to Address Multiple Tasks
Under Time Constraints

The act of sequencing priorities and tasks is a critical learning objective within EM. The simulation helps students develop their understanding of the importance of appropriate sequencing of decisions and task processes. For example, when an area has been hit by a violent storm, if a manager sends in emergency medical personnel without having previously sent in a sufficient number of debris-clearing personnel, the medical personnel will likely be unable to reach the victims of the storm in a timely manner.

Understand Complex Threat Characteristics

Natural and human-made threats can take on any number of characteristics. Memorizing these characteristics fails to capture their complexity and the variability of their interaction with the community. Since real-world emergency managers need to understand how the different characteristics of a threat can result in varying degrees of harm and damage, the simulation enables an instructor to set specific threat characteristics so that the student can actively learn how these particular characteristics play out when confronted with a disaster scenario.

Understand the Impact of Different Communication Mechanisms and Their Timing

One of the major activities of EM is communicating warnings and orders for evacuation to the affected community. The ways in which information is disseminated to the public and the time at which these communications take place impact the evacuation behavior of the community. The simulation requires players to make warnings and prepare an evacuation plan during the threat scenario so that they can see how the timing of communication impacts later events in an unfolding disaster.

Understand the Impact of the Changing Environment on Evacuation or Rescue and Recovery Success

An emergency manager can order an evacuation and realistically expect a certain percentage of the population to evacuate the area. However, environmental conditions (e.g., a washed out road or too many people on small capacity roads) can result in an ineffective evacuation. *Disaster Control* incorporates a number of environmental variables and constraints against which players learn to contend and construct a viable plan to accommodate these factors. For example, a student will learn that upon ordering an East-West evacuation route a bottleneck develops in terms of the capacity of the road system to move a large number of people through a particular part of the region. The student will then have to devise a plan to mitigate the impact of this occurrence, such as moving up the timing of the evacuation warning to ensure that all the evacuees are able to leave the target area.

Increase Understanding of the Need for Preparation and Training of Emergency Personnel

This learning goal proved difficult to incorporate into the simulation. In this effort, we established a disaster preparation period in which players are allowed to use their capital resources to help shore up the gaps in their preparedness. In the simulation, players are asked to examine the capabilities of particular agents and can then choose to use some of their capital to upgrade capabilities of these agents. Players are also allowed to use their capital to create interagency agreements with certain agents to enhance their effectiveness at responding to a disaster. Interagency agreements result in a greater likelihood that an agent will react to the direction from the simulation player.

Increase Understanding of the Fog of Emergency Response

EM is often hampered by ignorance due to limited information and time constraints, among other factors. *Disaster Control* provides students with an environment that is data rich. Since in a real-world disaster, managers often need to make decisions based on limited information, the simulation also attempts to construct experiences where a player has trouble getting accurate information or in getting the agents to act in accordance with the decisions of the manager.

Increase the Ability to Effectively Match Resources to Tasks

Disaster Control requires players to think in terms of economic and logistical efficiency. The simulation accomplishes this by having the player direct agents and resources to a disaster area to complete a rescue or recovery task. If the player sends too few agents or resources, the problem may worsen. If the player sends too many agents or resources, the cost to taxpayers becomes greater.

Increase Knowledge of the Research on EM

Disaster Control scaffolds students' learning by offering them support tools to build upon their understanding of EM concepts. By answering multiple-choice questions at the beginning and end of each phase, students can enhance their understanding of EM by identifying key concepts in the process and applying them in a contextual and active learning environment.

EDUCATIONAL APPLICATIONS OF *DISASTER CONTROL*

The potential of *Disaster Control* extends beyond the training of future emergency managers. The simulation provides the greatest opportunity for learning when used within a classroom setting or among groups of students. The flexibility of *Disaster Control* enables students to work collaboratively, building scenarios for each other and identifying appropriate decision-making strategies. When used in a group setting, students can watch how their peers react to the challenges and then discuss how their strategies impacted the outcome of the disaster, offering each other alternative strategies to handling a given threat. Brown et al. (1989) argued that confronting ineffective strategies and misconceptions is a salient feature of group learning.

Furthermore, the simulation allows the facilitator to duplicate the settings for multiple rounds of the same scenario, providing several learning opportunities for students. A participant can run through the same scenario, making different decisions to see if she or he can achieve a more desirable outcome or pinpoint which specific decisions resulted in a particular outcome. Redoing a threat scenario also enables the participant to determine how alternative courses of action impact the development of a threat and its outcome. A group of students can also run through the same threat scenario. Observing how classmates make different decisions based on the same information, and comparing their results with peers to identify the most effective strategies, enables students to reflect upon their own decisions to better comprehend the complexity of the decision-making process in EM.

In this section, we highlight various social science fields in which educators can integrate the *Disaster Control* simulation as a learning tool into their curricula. By integrating a digital simulation into a course curriculum, educators provide students with a contextualized learning environment that creates opportunities for students to work through complex situations, generate and test problem-solving techniques in realistic scenarios, and hone higher-order thinking skills. Curricula that integrate technological tools, such as a digital simulation, promote knowledge networking, as well as the ability for students to transfer their newly constructed knowledge to different situations (Salomon & Perkins, 1996). To date, we have not evaluated whether transference to other settings outside of EM occurs as a result of using the *Disaster Control* simulation. However, we believe that in accomplishing the learning goals set forth in the simulation, participants will also improve over time on the higher-order decision-making strategies and be able to apply them in other knowledge domains.

History

A history curriculum provides one example in which *Disaster Control*'s educational application moves beyond the discipline of EM. By placing a disaster scenario in a historical context, whether a natural disaster such as Hurricane Andrew or the San Francisco earthquakes or a human-made disaster such as the Oklahoma City bombings or Exxon oil spill, students can digitally experience these real-life historical events. Integrating the simulation into a history course offers instructors the opportunity to emphasize the element of complexity required to interpret EM decisions. Furthermore, digital simulations provide students the ability to role-play past events to better understand the dilemmas faced by those who experienced them at the time.

Economics

An economics course represents another curricular area in which the *Disaster Control* simulation could be easily integrated. For example, students can apply their understanding of the concepts and theories applicable to a course on the economics of disaster, which typically addresses the costs of natural and human-made disasters either domestically or internationally, the existing policy frameworks and strategies for minimizing these costs, the ways in which these policies might be adapted around the world by experiencing a simulated real-world disaster, or all of the aforementioned. The economic model that underlies the *Disaster Control* simulation can help students understand the impact of economic costs and human loss on the affected community and how these factors play into the phases of emergency management.

Ethics

Ethics play a significant role in EM decision making. In fact, the FEMA Independent Study Program's course on decision making and problem solving in EM dedicates an entire unit to ethical decision making, as do many university level EM programs. Weighing conflicting goals, maintaining a community's trust and confidence in government, as well as upholding legal statutes and regulations are key learning principles associated with EM. The simulation can be used in conjunction with an ethics course as a case study. Students, whether studying EM or not, can use the simulation to understand how ethics play into managing emergency disasters and the types of ethical decisions and legal issues emergency managers face on the job.

Political Science

Incorporating the simulation into a political science course, particularly one on public policy, helps students understand the role of local, state, and federal government agencies in responding to natural and human-made disasters. The need to form interagency agreements and the myriad key actors responsible for managing and implementing an emergency response plan are represented in the simulation. When used in a seminar setting, students in the course can assume the roles of various governmental agencies involved in responding to a disaster and work through a disaster collaboratively. Moreover, by experiencing a disaster firsthand, students can develop a richer understanding of how public policy and legislation are shaped and implemented as they interact with: politics, society, economics, and the environment, among other spheres of society.

CONCLUSION

In this chapter, we present a digital simulation that helps students learn the skills and decision-making processes associated with EM. *Disaster Control* provides an authentic and safe environment for participants to explore their knowledge of EM, create and test problem-solving strategies, and develop a deeper understanding of the complex nature of decision making in the field as they devise a viable response plan to a real-world natural or human-made disaster scenario. By actively engaging in a disaster situation, participants experience the time pressures, the information overload, and additional barriers to making the most appropriate decisions in response to the disaster. We argue that for students to fully appreciate the complexity of the work accomplished by managers during an emergency, they need to personally experience the challenges of EM. However, due to the high risks associated with failure, real EM is potentially too dangerous for students to learn through practice on the job. Digital simulations, therefore, offer an ideal learning environment for students to act within real-world situations without the real-world consequences of human and economic loss.

While initially designed to train emergency managers, *Disaster Control* offers educational applications beyond the teaching of EM skills. By providing a context to test and manipulate theories and concepts, the simulation opens opportunities for meaningful, active learning that books and lectures alone cannot provide. When integrated into a suitable social science course curriculum, such as that of an Economics or Political Science course, *Disaster Control* serves as a learning tool to help students construct a healthy respect for the innumerable factors that comprise the complexity of decision making in EM. Knowing how decision making in EM connects across an array of disciplines facilitates students' ability to develop a deeper understanding of EM and transfer it to other domain areas. Furthermore, in a class setting students can work collaboratively, using peer interaction and feedback to better understand some of the complexities, such as the reality of multiple courses of action for the same disaster scenario and the role that misperceptions play in decision making.

Disaster Control was developed through a contract with a state agency that did not include funding for large-scale testing, integration, and deployment of the simulation. As a result, its impact on student learning has not been scientifically validated. Further funding and resources would be needed to integrate the *Disaster Control* simulation into educational contexts to evaluate its influence on students' understanding of the complexity of decision making in EM. However, the advantages of digital simulations—enabling students to become active participants in learning, providing constructive experience with decision making, offering immediate feedback, and challenging students to test their knowledge in new ways—prove promising for the future role of *Disaster Control* as an educational tool.

REFERENCES

Brown, J. S., Collins, A., & Duguid, P. (1989). Situated cognition and the culture of learning. *Educational Researcher, 18*(1), 32–42. Available: http://www.ilt.columbia.edu/ilt/papers/JohnBrown.html

Collins, A., Brown, J. S., & Newman, S. E. (1989). Cognitive apprenticeship: Teaching the crafts of reading, writing, and mathematics. In L. B. Resnick (Ed.), *Knowing, learning, and instruction: Essays in honor of Robert Glaser* (pp. 453–494). Hillsdale, NJ: Lawrence Erlbaum Associates.

FEMA Independent Study Program. (2002). *Decision making and problem solving.* Available: http://www.fema.gov/emi/ishome.htm

Jarrell, J. D., Landsea, C. W., Mayfield, M., & Rappaport, E. N. (2001). The deadliest, costliest, and most intense United States hurricanes from 1900 to 2000 (and other frequently requested hurricane facts). *NOAA Technical Memorandum NWS TPC.* Available: http://www.aoml.noaa.gov/hrd/Landsea/deadly/

Jonassen, D., Mayes, T., & McAleese, R. (1993). A manifesto for a constructivist approach to technology in higher education. In T. Duffy, D. Jonassen, & J. Lowyck (Eds.), *Designing constructivist learning environments* (pp.). Heidelberg, Germany: Springer-Verlag.

Lave, J. (1988). *Cognition in practice: Mind, mathematics, and culture in everyday life.* Cambridge, UK: Cambridge University Press.

Naidu, S., Ip, A., & Linser, R. (2000). Dynamic goal-based role-play simulation on the web: A case study. *Educational Technology & Society, 3*(3), 190–202.

O'Looney, J. (2003). Using technology to increase citizen participation in government: The use of models and simulations. *IBM Endowment for The Business of Government.* Available: http://www.businessofgovernment.org/pdfs/OLooneyReport.pdf

Rappaport, E. N. (1993, December 10). Preliminary report: Hurricane Andrew. *National Hurricane Center*. Available: http://www.nhc.noaa.gov/1992andrew.html

Salomon, G., & Perkins, D. (1996). Learning in wonderland: What do computers really offer education? In S. Kerr (Ed.), *Technology and the future of schooling* (pp. 111–130). Chicago, IL: University of Chicago Press.

Vygotsky (1978). Interaction between learning and development. In M. Cole, V. John-Steiner, S. Scribner, & E. Souberman (Eds.), *Mind in society: The development of higher psychological processes* (pp. 79–91). Cambridge, MA: Harvard University Press.

Williams, R. J. (1996). An emergency management demonstrator using the high level architecture. *Proceedings of the European Simulation Symposium EES 1996*. The Society for Computer Simulation International, October 24–26, 1996, Genoa, Italy.

Wittrock, M. (1990). Generative processes of comprehension. *Educational Psychologist, 24*, 345–376.

10

Immersive Virtual Environments and Education Simulations

Jim Blascovich
University of California, Santa Barbara

Jeremy Bailenson
Stanford University

The multitude of methodologies described in this volume and elsewhere demonstrates the value placed on the creation and use of simulations (i.e., synthetic or artificial situations) for education and training and associated research by members of a wide spectrum of disciplines. The notion of educational and training simulations is undoubtedly ancient. The ideal toward which creators of such simulations aspire, fidelity to the actual situations represented, is unchanging. However, the tools used to create and implement simulations change constantly.

In this chapter, we focus on one such tool, immersive virtual environment technology (IVET). The chapter is divided into three sections. The first provides conceptual and background information regarding immersive virtual environments (IVEs) and the tools or technologies (IVETs) used to create them. The second discusses possible advantages and disadvantages of IVETs for educational and training simulations and research. The third provides an illustration of an IVET simulation.

IMMERSIVE VIRTUAL ENVIRONMENTS VERSUS IMMERSIVE VIRTUAL ENVIRONMENT TECHNOLOGY

As the heading here suggests, the products—IVEs—and the tools—IVETs—used to create them are not equivalent. We have argued elsewhere (Blascovich, 2002) and continue to argue here that humans have experienced virtual environments, including immersive ones, from the beginning. We also describe how modern technologies allow us to create powerful virtual environments relatively cheaply.

THE CONCEPT

The term virtual environment[1] refers to an organization of sensory information (e.g., the simulation) that leads to perceptions of a synthetic (artificial) environment as nonsynthetic (real). Hence, from a phenomenological standpoint, perceptions need not differ in virtual environments from those in analogous nonsynthetic ones, though virtual environments may be created without direct nonsynthetic analogues. Such phenomenological equivalence provides the criterion or ideal toward which developers of virtual environment-based educational and training simulations strive.

One must note that virtual environments can be created on the basis of organized information via any sensory channel or combination of sensory channels including vision, audition, touch, olfaction, and taste. Sensory information—for example, light waves, sound waves, tactile pressure, chemicals—mediates our experience of objects, movements, and other aspects of environments, whether virtual or physical. Hence, the reception of exactly the same sensory information whether generated via a virtual or natural environment can result in equivalent phenomenological experience in perceivers. More specifically, providing that they remain unaware or unconscious of information about how the environment came to be, perceivers should not be able to distinguish sensory information transmitted naturally from the same information transmitted artificially.[2]

The term IVE refers to a virtual environment that creates a psychological state in which the individual perceives himself or herself as existing within it (i.e., as being immersed or having presence in it). The interaction of various characteristics of the person and the sen-

---

[1]The terms virtual environment and virtual reality are used in common language interchangeably. Indeed, virtual reality is probably more common. However, the academic community generally prefers the former, probably because of the apparently oxymoronic juxtaposition of the terms virtual and reality.

[2]Observation of many computer game players suggests many in this category experience a great deal of immersion.

sory information contained in the environment determine the level of immersion. At an extreme, we can imagine an individual receiving nothing but virtual sensory information with no conscious knowledge that the information is artificially produced (e.g., the movie character Truman that Jim Carrey played in *The Truman Show*). Such an individual should be totally immersed in that environment save bouts of daydreaming. Somewhat less extreme, we can imagine an individual receiving nothing but virtual sensory information, but with knowledge that the information is artificially produced (e.g., the movie character Morpheus that Lawrence Fishburne played in *The Matrix*). The immersion that such an individual experiences varies as a function of consciousness of that knowledge. To take a less or even nonextreme case, we can imagine an individual simultaneously receiving virtual and natural sensory information accompanied by conscious knowledge of which is which (e.g., viewers of an IMAX movie). Such an individual would likely experience less immersion because the natural and artificial environments are intertwined.

Whether or not they label it as such, many educators and researchers have proven masterful creators of IVEs. In our own field of social psychology, several of these virtual environments have proven intellectually, as well as historically significant over the years. For example, in the late 1950s and early 1960s, Milgram used immersive virtual teaching laboratories to investigate obedience (e.g., Milgram, 1963). In these studies, Milgram assigned participants the role of teacher. The participants had no knowledge that the teaching laboratory was a simulated or virtual one (relative to the real purpose of the study). The teacher's task was to administer increasingly painful shocks to a learner when the latter answered questions incorrectly. Participants became so immersed that many exhibited extreme emotional responses including frustration, guilt (toward the learner), and anger (toward the experimenter) because they believed their actions physically harmed other people. Milgram received severe criticism (e.g., Baumrind, 1964) for failing to judge the severe consequence of the immersion on participants. Indeed, Milgram's studies led to current government restrictions on what human participants must know about experiments in which they agree to participate (i.e., informed consent). Hence, the depth to which human research participants can be immersed in virtual environments (i.e., without their being informed and made consciously aware of the fact that the environment is virtual) is actually federally regulated.

A decade later, Zimbardo and colleagues created an immersive virtual prison in the basement of Jordan Hall at Stanford University (Haney, Banks, & Zimbardo, 1973). He used this IVE to study inmate–staff interactions by randomly assigning students to the role of prisoner or guards. Like Milgram's, Zimbardo's simulation proved dangerously immersive. After a few days, the guards were so immersed that they mistreated the prisoners who, like the guards, were so immersed that they, in turn, became submissive and depressed. Indeed, the immersion proved so strong that Zimbardo himself terminated the study after only the first of the two initially planned weeks for the study.

Not all such research IVEs have become infamous. In fact, several have had more positive impacts. For example, Latane and Darley (1969) developed a number of virtual environments to investigate prosocial behavior. These environments, such as a room filling with smoke, helped them discover processes underlying bystander apathy in the face of potential danger to bystanders, themselves, and others.

In sum, the concept of virtual environments is by no means a new one. Under different labels (e.g., simulation), academics, educators, playwrights, moviemakers, and others have used virtual environments for one purpose or another. Virtual environments differ as a function of their contribution to participants' or inhabitants' phenomenological experience of immersion. Presumably, the level of immersion determines to some degree the generalizability of important aspects of the virtual experience (e.g., learning) to analogue physical environments.

TECHNOLOGY

In the previous examples (Milgram's teaching environment, Zimbardo's prison, Darley and Latane's smoke-filled room), researchers created convincing IVEs concretely using millennia-old tools and materials such as hammers, saws, nails, wood, paint, etc. Many museums exhibit concrete virtual environments to depict, for example, historically significant habitats (e.g., cave dwellings, Native American sweat lodges, slave ships) and workplaces (e.g., the White House oval office, turn-of-the-century stores, airplane cockpits). Other virtual environments are used in educational settings, for example, mock courtrooms and classrooms. However, despite their advantages, concrete hammer and nail virtual environments or simulations carry distinct disadvantages for simulation and research, the most important of which include space, expense, construction time, and nonportability.

The advent of modern computers brought with it the possibility of creating virtual environments and IVEs digitally. Sutherland, the inventor of computer graphics and the person who coined the term virtual reality, foresaw this possibility as early as 1963, building a prototype head mounted display (HMD) for rendering visual stimuli similar in principle to state-of-the-art HMDs used today. Sutherland realized that digital computers could display graphic visual stimuli from any point of view relatively quickly. Unfortunately, in Sutherland's time, computer-processing speeds permitted the quick rendering of only relatively simple graphic visual images. However, with computer processing speed doubling every 18 months for nearly four decades this limitation no longer presents serious problems. Here, we divide our discussion of IVET along major functional lines: creation and implementation.

IVE Creation Technology

At the end of the scene in *The Matrix* in which the character Morpheus demonstrates computer-generated IVEs to the character Neo, the latter asks rhetorically, "You mean we're inside a computer program." This description captures the essence of digital IVEs. Developers build digital environments or worlds via computer programming code, which when properly implemented envelops users or participants in the IVE. By far, most of this effort has been directed toward the creation of visual aspects of digital worlds, sometimes coupled with auditory aspects, though haptic and olfactory aspects can also be included. Developers use both software and hardware tools in their IVE creation endeavors.

Software. Like improvements in other software applications (e.g., web page creation), high-level programming tools (e.g., languages, run-time libraries) and software standards (e.g., virtual reality modeling language, VRML) have evolved to ease the development of digital IVEs. These tools include both model creation and scripting software. Programmers use the former to create the boundaries of the desired digital world (e.g., walls, floor, and ceiling for a virtual classroom; ground, sky, and geologic features of the horizon for a virtual park), the objects in it (e.g., chairs, desks, lights, people for the virtual classroom; vegetation, walkways, benches for the virtual park), and artificial physics (e.g., gravity, lighting, wind).

Programmers use scripting software to animate digital worlds via logical operators such as conditional or if–then statements. Scripting software is used to render movements of objects, including human representations, virtual machines, etc., once the IVE is actually operating. For example, if a participant kicks a virtual ball to another participant, scripting software can be written to allow the ball to move to the other participant, bounce off walls if misdirected, etc. If a participant smiles or frowns, his or her digital representation can be programmed to smile or frown accordingly.

Hardware. Special hardware devices help developers create realistic looking objects that they want to include in their virtual environments. Typically, these devices capture a physical object translating it into its own database. One type of device is a three-dimensional scanner. Such scanners can be used similarly to the two-dimensional scanners and copy machines with which most of us are familiar but for three-dimensional objects including both inanimate (e.g., chairs, tables) and animate (e.g., animals, persons) ones. Less expensive model creation systems utilize two-dimensional information to produce (via specialized algorithms and software) three-dimensional digital objects, such as the creation of photographically realistic three-dimensional human heads from digital snapshots of a person's face and profile. Of course, once a digital model of a three-dimensional object is created, it can be archived and ported to any other digital virtual environment without the need to build it over and over again.

The final product of digital IVE creation is a database analogous to the dimensions and size of the specific world created. For visual information, one can think of the database as containing pixels filling in a three-dimensional space. Every pixel in the digital database would correspond to the visual information at the corresponding point in the phenomenological environment the creator wants to develop. The number of pixels contained in the database is a function of the resolution of the IVE and processing and storage capabilities of the computer on which it is stored.

IVE Implementation

In our view, little difference exists between the phenomenological experience of participants in concrete simulation or virtual environments (e.g., Zimbardo's prison) and ones created digitally, providing both are equally detailed and have similar restrictions or lack of restrictions governing participant behaviors especially movements.

Nevertheless, concrete hammer and nail virtual environments or simulations preclude an important technical problem against which digital IVE developers must struggle; that is, making sure participants sense (e.g., see) what they should sense by virtue of their physical position, head orientation, and gaze in the immersive virtual environment (e.g., stimuli within their field of view) including the position, orientation, and behaviors of objects and others sharing the environment. For IVEs, we label this process tracking and rendering. In a concrete simulation environment, tracking and rendering are not a problem. Participants sense what they are supposed to sense no matter their position and orientation because the concrete IVE physically surrounds them (e.g., a mock courtroom).

The discovery of, and the technology to generate and transmit, electricity heralded an economic and social revolution of an unparalleled magnitude near the end of the 19th Century and provoked a plethora of amazing inventions. Although most of us do not think of it as such, one of these inventions, the telephone, represents the first application of electronic technology to the creation of virtual environments. Individuals using Bell's invention heard each other speak not because they could hear the other's actual voice, but because the telephone electronically tracked the other's voice, transmitted it across telephone lines, and rendered a version to the listener. As long as directionality of sound does not matter to the social interaction, tracking the conversants' head orientation is unnecessary. Arguably, telephones are immersive because we rarely allow our conscious knowledge of how the device actually works (if we even have such knowledge) to interfere with our false but compelling assumption that we actually hear the other person.

Tracking and rendering visual information, however, proves much more difficult because directionality is generally more critical to the role that visual information plays in guiding our behaviors. For example, unless our visual attention is focused directly on an individual snatching a purse from pedestrian, we are unlikely to even notice the crime much less be able to identify the perpetrator. An important type of visual directionality for social interaction involves eye contact. Mutual gaze, or lack of it, strongly influences social interaction. For example, sincerity is associated with eye contact; insincerity is not. Because ordinary television does not permit mutual gaze, this medium (e.g., video teleconferences) has proven largely unsatisfactory and less immersive for social interactive virtual environments than the simple telephone.

Because an individual's visual point of view changes constantly as a function of ordinary dynamics of body position, head orientation, and eye movements, it is necessary to track such movements in order to identify appropriate visual information to display or render to the individual within the IVE. If an IVE participant gazes left, he or she should immediately be able to see the part of the IVE in his or her changed field of view. If he or she then looks right, he or she should immediately be able to see the part in the new field of view. If he or she approaches an object in the IVE, the object should subtend a larger arc of his or her retinas. If he or she distances him- or herself from an object, the object should subtend a smaller arc of his or her retinas. If he or she stands on his or her tiptoes, the object should appear lower, if he or she crouches, the object should appear higher.

Fortunately, with appropriate peripheral devices, computers can track these movements very precisely and control the display of graphic visual information rapidly and appropriately. Hence, computers can be used to track, store, and render visual information in digital IVEs. Of course, appropriate audio information can be coupled telephonically relatively easily with visual information providing information via two sensory channels. More difficult, but still possible, is the inclusion of olfactory and haptic (i.e., touch) information. The basic components for handling sensory information such as visual information in IVEs consist of tracking, storage, rendering, and display devices. Each may include several subsystems, each of which, in turn, can include multiple devices.

Tracking. As previously mentioned, the problem of tracking the frustum of participants' gaze in digital IVEs proved relatively difficult. One solution involves so-called cave automated virtual environment (CAVE) technology, a technique that in its original form basically presented visual information in a manner completely analogous to a concrete IVE. In this form, a complete CAVE consists of a rectangular box with six back-projection screens forming four walls, a ceiling, and a floor each with a computer projector behind it. Computers synchronize and drive the projectors so that the visual information of the IVE appears on the walls. At a stationary point inside the room, participants wearing special 3-D shutter glasses experience immersion in the environment. Participants can change their gaze direction (i.e., frustum) at will and view the IVE in a naturalistic manner because they are inside a three-dimensional 360° panorama constantly back-projected on the CAVE sides. More complex CAVEs also track participant translation (i.e., left–right, front–back, up–down) movements so that participants can walk around three-dimensional objects that appear visually to be inside the physical dimensions of the CAVE. Though it works well, this technology has severe impediments and limitations for IVE implementation. It is very costly in terms of equipment ($1 million plus) and space (typically requires a room three times the size of the CAVE itself in all three physical dimensions to accommodate the back-projection distances necessary, such that a 3 m³ CAVE would require a 9 m³ building to house it). Furthermore, visual stimuli pertinent to only a single point of view at a time can be projected making it necessary to have multiple CAVEs for live virtual social interaction inside it, a prohibitively expensive proposition for most educational and behavioral investigators.

Researchers, including ourselves (see Loomis, Blascovich, & Beall, 1999), have overcome the challenges posed by CAVEs by developing a much more cost-effective tracking technology. Figure 10.1 depicts a simple configuration of the type we use in our work. Participants wear headgear that contains devices for tracking their movements and gaze direction. A small light-emitting diode (LED) sits on a small cube atop the participant's head. This light is monitored via a video tracking system that includes two tiny inexpensive cameras each mounted in an upper corner of the room in which the IVE experience takes place. There are no special requirements for this room other than any lighting needs to be dimmed. The video image of the light against the background of the physical room is transmitted to a video capture board that provides information to a software algorithm that locates the three-dimensional coordinates of the light in the physical space within a millimeter. Hence, at any given moment, the system knows where the top of the participant's head is located in the physical space that itself corresponds to the lo-

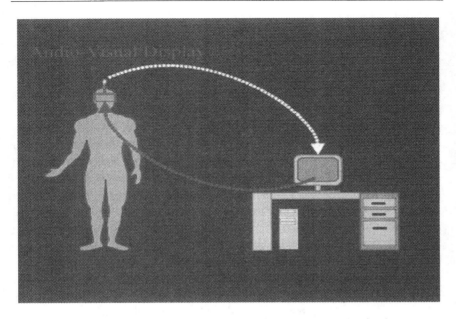

FIG. 10.1. Simulation participant using an alternative to CAVE technology.

cation of his or her head in the virtual space. This measurement is called translation. In order to track which direction the participant is facing (i.e., where his or her nose is pointed), a small inertial tracking device is located just under the light (i.e., the cube). This device provides information directly to the computer indicating the orientation of the head in three dimensions (i.e., roll, pitch, and yaw).

Coupling the orientation and translation information, the computer can monitor the direction the participant faces in real time. Generally, this is sufficient to establish the participant's field of view at any given time. Nonetheless, even greater specificity of the participant's field of view can be obtained by adding eye-tracking equipment to monitor eye movements independently of where the participant's head faces.

Storage. As previously described, digital IVEs are saved or stored as computer programs that include a database of the visual and other information contained in the virtual world, as well as a script that provides instructions to the computer to run the world. Since very large amounts of inexpensive computer memory and storage have become available over the last decade, digital storage capacity does not pose a problem. The programs underlying IVEs can be run from various media including CD-ROMs, DVDs, hard disk drives, local area networks, and even the Internet.

Rendering.   The computer that tracks participant movements and stores the digital IVE also can be used to render appropriate visual and other sensory information for the participant. Given the data stream generated by tracking the participant, the computer rapidly determines the visual information necessary to fill the participant's field of view or frustum. Because each eye has a slightly different field of view from the other, the computer can simultaneously render both, thereby permitting binocular or stereoscopic visual displays (see the following section) that permit three-dimensional perception.

Rendering time or lag consists of the period between participant movements (e.g., body, head, and eyes) and the actual display of rendered information. The amount of time the computer takes to determine what visual information in the field of view to render is critical to rendering time. If the lag is perceptible, participants will be negatively affected physiologically, creating the possibility of cybersickness, an undesirable malady not unlike seasickness. The time the computer takes is a function of the complexity of the visual information in the IVE database, the size of the field of view, and the processing speed of the computer. Increasing complexity (indexed by polygon count), field-of-view size, or both, slows rendering speed; increasing processing speed quickens rendering speed. As processing speed has increased generally for computers, rendering time has become less of an issue in rendering digital IVEs. As long as rendering speed stays under 40–50 milliseconds, the time lag in tracking and rendering remains imperceptible.

Display.   In order to display audio information, simple headphones typically suffice. In order to display visual information, we use HMDs attached to participants' headgear (see Fig. 10.1). The HMD consists of two miniature computer display screens (e.g., liquid crystal displays or LCDs), one for each eye with appropriate optic lenses that help focus displayed information on the participants' eyes. As previously mentioned, slightly different renderings are displayed to each eye, resulting in the experience of stereoscopic or binocular vision.

An Added Note.   Once a digital IVE has been developed and a participant wears the equipment necessary for tracking and rendering, the stage is set for the participant's immersive experience. Much of the quality of this experience depends on the quality of the sensory information in the digital world itself. However, much also depends on the freedom of participants to move (e.g., walk, run, jump, kneel) in a naturalistic fashion. Being able to do so provides kinesthetic feedback from the muscles and body structures that is the same as that in naturalistic settings and concrete IVEs.

THE VALUE OF IVET FOR EDUCATIONAL AND TRAINING SIMULATIONS AND RESEARCH

Given that digital IVET is still in its infancy, its ultimate value for simulation-based educational research will prove itself one way or the other in the future. However, several advantages are apparent already.

Elimination of the Experimental Control–Mundane Realism Trade-off

Methodologists have long recognized an important problem in laboratory-based experimental behavioral research for many decades. Specifically, the greater the investigator's control over the experimental environment, the lower the mundane realism of that environment. Figure 10.2 depicts this trade-off. Because experimental control provides the basis for causal inferences from the results of experiments and mundane realism provides the basis for the generalizability or external validity of experimental results research, experimental investigators typically could not claim both.

However, the inverse relationship between experimental control and mundane realism is not a matter of firm scientific principle or logic. Rather, it is based on the typical way in which most experimental psychologists and others choose to control (or not control) extraneous variables in experimental situations. Those interested in strong causal inferences have controlled cues associated with unwanted variables by eliminating them, freezing or making them static, or all of the aforementioned, if they could not be eliminated entirely. For example, rather than study a participant's learning and memory in an actual classroom filled with students and a teacher and other distractions, many experimentalists bring individuals into

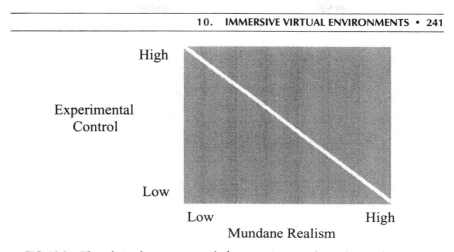

FIG. 10.2. The relation between control of an experiment and mundane realism in experiments.

stark windowless laboratories in which little distraction exists and in which experimental variables can be precisely controlled. On the other hand, those interested in generalizability have conducted research in mundane settings such as actual classrooms but at the expense of drawing weak theoretical inferences.

The reason for either alternative has been practical. One cannot control all aspects of a mundanely or ecologically realistic experimental environment easily, especially if that environment is one in which other humans (e.g., a teacher, other students) are present. One cannot be sure that the actions of the other humans (i.e., confederates) will occur in precisely the same way experimental session after experimental session.

However, digital IVET makes it possible both to create ecologically realistic experimental environments (e.g., classrooms, courtrooms, airplane cockpits) and to control every aspect of that environment including the actions of other human representations within it. Hence, there is no loss in experimental control and strength of causal inferences and generalizability or external validity remains high. Figure 10.3 depicts this new relationship.

Facilitation of Exact Replication

Replication in many of the behavioral sciences, including social psychology, has proven difficult. Hence, many findings stand on the basis of relatively few replications and even fewer replications across

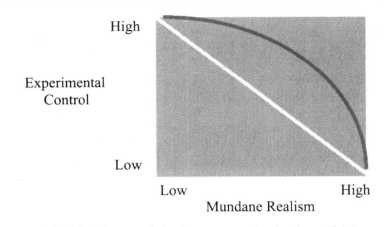

FIG. 10.3.   The new relation between control and realism with IVE.

laboratories. The replication difficulty arises for several reasons. First, experimental environments differ in both nonsubtle and subtle ways from laboratory to laboratory, and university to university. Regarding the former, the physical environments are unlikely to be the same or even very similar. The personnel (e.g., confederates) interacting with experimental participants differ both nonsubtly (e.g., gender) and subtly (e.g., stature). Although methods and procedures sections of research articles can guide a replication, they do not typically report enough detail (e.g., the vocal tone of taped instructions) to permit an exact replication. These problems conspire to make exact replications impossible, thereby lessening the probability of a replication and, more insidiously, providing rationalizations based on lack of procedural similarity for failures to replicate, thereby increasing the longevity of findings or phenomena that might actually be artifactual.

Digital IVET-based experimental environments, however, eliminate these problems. Once inside a digital IVE, experimental participants in any laboratory can experience the exact experimental scenario as anyone else in the world with the same digital IVE. The only caveat is that they use the same display hardware system. Hence, nearly all physical laboratory differences become irrelevant, confederates (actually digital computer agents) are exactly the same, and exact methods and procedures are transmitted via the computer program scripts. Failures to replicate can no longer be explained away in terms of differences in implementation of the replications. Furthermore, disparate investigators can carefully modify digital IVE software to manipulate additional independent variables of theoretical interest without affecting the general paradigm, thereby providing a better basic for replication and extension experiments.

Provision of Unobtrusive Measures

Campbell and his colleagues (Webb, Campbell, Schwartz, & Sechrest, 1999) pioneered the identification and use of unobtrusive dependent measures, arguing that such measures are not susceptible to experimenter bias or experimental demand characteristics. Unobtrusive measures are made without the awareness of those being measured; for example, time spent reading particular articles in a magazine as a measure of the individual's interest in a particular topic; food packaging found in garbage cans to determine an individual's eating and brand preferences; the distance people maintain between themselves and others as a measure of intimacy. Digital IVET makes a plethora of unobtrusive measures available to researchers more or less automatically.

Tracking and rendering requirements of IVET systems include many measures that can be used as unobtrusive measures in research experiments. These measures can be categorized as temporal, spatial, temporal-spatial, and auditory. In and of themselves, unobtrusive measures are intrinsically interesting. However, their more informative value lies in their justification as measures of theoretical constructs; justification that must be provided by the individual investigator.

Temporal unobtrusive measures include reaction times, latencies, and durations. Reaction time is defined as how quickly an individual responds to an action contingent on the appearance of a specific signal or stimulus; for example, pressing the accelerator of an automobile when a traffic light turns green. Latency refers to the time interval between events; for example, the length of the period between an individual seeing another person smile and smiling back. Duration is the time spent at a particular task; for example, the length of time an individual spends writing an essay. All three of these measures can be included in digital IVE scripts; for example, how quickly an individual reacts (i.e., reaction time) to a virtual traffic hazard by pressing the brake on a virtual automobile, how long it takes (i.e., latency) an individual to determine whether he or she has seen a virtual object or person before; the length of time (i.e., duration) an individual plays blackjack in a virtual casino. Again, however, these measures need theoretical and conceptual justification to be useful.

Spatial unobtrusive measures include location and orientation information; for example, where an individual places himself or herself and where he or she gazes after approaching a virtual human representation. Figure 10.4 illustrates final location information for research participants who have approached a virtual human representation who gazes (panel A) or does not gaze (panel B) at them while they approach. Similarly, we could record the frustum of a research participant's gaze toward others in the IVE.

Temporal-spatial unobtrusive measures include recordings of paths and movements. Similarly, we could determine the velocity of such approaches, as well as whether or not participants accelerated or decelerated their approaches to the virtual human representation.

Providing a Platform for Previously Impossible or Very Difficult Manipulations and Controls

In a digital IVE, investigators can control the appearance of any representation with or without their knowledge. Hence, an individual's physical identity can be changed even in ways that alter his or her social identity. For example, the sex, race, ethnicity, or stature of a participant can be changed. This feature has enormous implications for educational simulations and research. Members of nonstigmatized groups can be given a stigmatized identity in an IVE and vice versa. Individuals can walk a mile in someone else's shoes and experience the social world from a quite different perspective.

Using digital IVEs, investigators can alter the actions or behaviors of representations without their knowledge enabling what we have labeled transformed social interactions (TSIs). For example, a leader making a presentation to a group of individuals within an IVE, or a teacher conducting a class in an IVE, can appear to gaze directly at each of the participants or pupils up to 100% of the time, a TSI we call non-zero sum gaze. This may increase the impact of what she or he has to say to members of the group or students in the class.

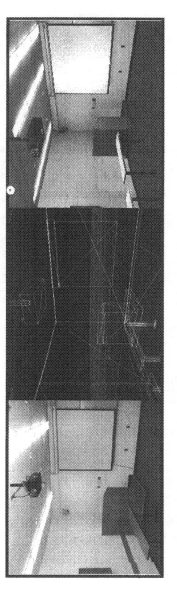

FIG. 10.4. Photograph of the crime scene (left), the virtual model of the crime scene without texture (middle), and the texture-wrapped virtual model of the crime scene (right).

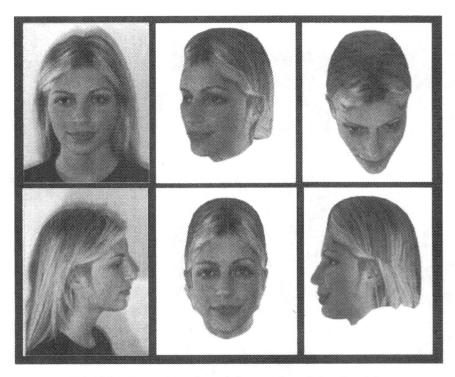

FIG. 10.5. Comparison of actual photographs and virtual models.

This same functionality enables investigators to control many aspects of research participants heretofore typically uncontrolled (see previous experimental control–mundane realism discussion). Hence, investigators using digital IVET can assure control over stature (e.g., height, girth, eye level) and appearance (e.g., skin color, eye color, hair color and style, clothing) of participants.

ILLUSTRATION OF AN IVET EDUCATION AND RESEARCH SIMULATION: EYEWITNESS IDENTIFICATION

We can illustrate the application of IVET-based simulation by describing one designed to educate participants about eyewitness identification, perhaps in the context of a criminal investigation. More specifically, this simulation involves identifying a suspect in the context of a police lineup. Toward this end, we review some of the substantive background literature, and describe how IVET can be used advantageously to create a lineup-type identification procedure.

Background

Eyewitnesses exhibit two major shortcomings when attempting to identify criminal suspects they previously witnessed committing a crime. They make too many false positive, or false alarm, errors (i.e., incorrectly accuse innocent people), and they are overconfident in their ability to recognize perpetrators. The research literature documents the shortcomings of eyewitness identification accuracy and, more importantly, from a societal point of view, raises the negative implications of those shortcomings (Loftus, 1975; Wells, in press; Wells & Loftus, in press).

Cognitive and social psychologists have produced a substantial corpus of research reporting investigations of the processes that occur when eyewitnesses attempt to recognize criminal suspects. The objective of much of this research involves the development and validation of tools that can be used to quantify and objectively measure the accuracy and, hence, fairness of police lineups (Brigham, Meissner, & Wasserman, 1999) so as to reduce false positives in which the eyewitness incorrectly identifies a foil as the suspect.

Research has demonstrated a variety of conditions that increase and decrease the accuracy of eyewitness identification. These include: the race and sex of the suspect (Bothwell, Brigham, & Malpass, 1989; Brigham & Barkowitz, 1978), the visual presence of weapons on the suspect (Tooley, Brigham, Maass, & Bothwell, 1987), the number of foils (i.e., the people inserted into the lineup as distracters for the eyewitness) contained in the lineup (Malpass, 1981), the manner in which the people are presented to the eyewitness during the lineup (Lindsay, Lea, & Fulford, 1991; Lindsay & Wells, 1985), the level of visual similarity of the foils to the suspect (Laughery, Jensen, & Wogalter, 1996; Luus & Wells, 1991), and the contextual or background surroundings that the eyewitness experiences during the lineup (Krafka & Penrod, 1985; Malpass & Devine, 1981).

In the illustration here, we focus on this last factor: lineup contextual cues. We propose that IVET can increase contextual realism for eyewitness identification procedures and therefore greatly improve our understanding of the impact of contextual factors on eyewitness identification accuracy. Such understanding should help educate people, including designers of identification procedures such as police lineups; witnesses and defendants involved in such procedures; and consumers (e.g., lawyers, juries, judges) of the information generated by such procedures.

Furthermore, improving the contextual realism of eyewitness identification procedures should increase the generalizability of research findings. As Malpass and Devine (1980) concluded, "to evaluate the generalizability and utility of (eyewitness testimony) laboratory studies, it is important to determine whether their results and related theoretical analyses survive the transposition to more realistic contexts" (p. 347).

Simulating Lineups Using IVET

Here, we illustrate how one might use IVET not only to simulate police lineups but to bring contextual realism into the process. In particular, we focus on how IVET improves environmental context realism for a lineup in terms of the actual crime scene, the realism of digital representations of criminal suspects and foils, and reconstruction of the viewing conditions during the actual witnessing of the target event.

Environmental Features.   Previous eyewitness identification research focused on the role of contextual cues from crime scenes in maximizing eyewitnesses' recognition accuracy. Techniques investigated included providing phrases and textual descriptions in order to bring the witness back to the mental state in which he or she was in during the occurrence of the crime (Cutler, Penrod, O'Rourke, & Martens, 1986; Hershkowitz, Orbach, Lamb, Sternberg, & Horowitz, 2001), showing witnesses photographs of the original crime scene (Cutler, Penrod, & Martens, 1987), showing witnesses objects from the environment (Krafka & Penrod, 1985), and conducting the lineup at the original crime scene (Davies & Milne, 1985). Accuracy for identifying faces in particular is augmented by background context. Indeed, Memon and Bruce (1983) demonstrated that the background context of a photograph can have a greater impact on recognition than the features of the face itself.

Of course, IVEs can improve lineup contexts in many ways by producing realism that goes far beyond photographs or videos in terms of social interaction, amount of information portrayed, and perceptual realism. Furthermore, it is often easier to construct computer models than to reconstruct a physical crime scene, arrange a physical on-site lineup, or both. Moreover, certain sites such as crowded streets or private property may be unavailable to us, and subtle ambient characteristics such as lighting and fog are extremely difficult to match without IVEs. Finally, a virtual lineup is mobile, can be reused, and can even be brought into the courtroom for demonstrations. Figure 10.4 illustrates how photographically realistic these virtual contexts can be. One can conduct a police-type lineup in such a contextually realistic IVE.

Realism of Digital Representations of Suspects and Foils. The value of digital IVE-based police lineups depends most critically on the realism of the digital representations of the suspect and foils. This includes what we call photographic realism but also extends to what we call behavioral realism. As Fig. 10.5 illustrates, virtual representations of humans can be constructed to behave quite realistically. These representations can also be animated realistically so that they can turn their heads, exhibit facial expressions, etc. Furthermore, the representations of suspects and foils can be dressed identically, wear the same eyeglasses, sunglasses, jewelry, etc.

In Fig. 10.5, the two leftmost panels depict actual photographs of a person. By using photogrammetric software designed to instantiate three-dimensional models from two-dimensional images, it is possible to create relatively realistic virtual reconstructions of a person's head and face. There are many advantages to creating such a model. One advantage, shown in Fig. 10.5, is the ability to closely examine the head from any angle, including novel angles for which there is no original photograph. In other words, it could be the case that a witness saw a criminal perform some action from a very specific angle. Given a virtual model of a head, it is not necessary to have photographs of the suspects and the distracter foils from that exact angle. All that is necessary is the existence of the virtual model, which then can be rotated to any desired angle.

More importantly, perhaps, the resemblance between and among the suspect and foils can be precisely calibrated psychophysically. For example, a digital representation of an anchor foil, by definition innocent, and a digital representation of the suspect can be used via morphing techniques to produce an appropriate number of equally spaced foils along a psychophysical gradient. Hence, one can quantify exactly how close to the suspect or the foil any witness identification is.

Reconstruction of Viewing Conditions. The prototypical police lineup takes place in a specially constructed suite consisting of a well-lit room in which suspects and foils stand aligned side-by-side, viewed from another room via one-way glass by witnesses. The viewing conditions; for example, the distance between the witness and individuals in the lineup, are determined by the physical constraints of the lineup suite, not by the original viewing conditions; for example, the distance at which they originally witnessed the perpetrator. Viewing conditions can be reconstructed more precisely using IVET. For example, the actual distance, viewing angle (e.g., from a third-floor balcony to a street), the lighting, and opacity of the air (e.g., clear, foggy, smoky) can be recreated with little difficulty thereby increasing the realism of the eyewitness identification procedure.

One of the benefits of developing IVE simulations is the ability to reuse that simulation. As Blascovich and colleagues (2002) describe in detail, IVE simulations allow a vast number of individuals to experience the exact same sensory experience. In other words, a researcher or instructor can ensure that his or her research participants or students all receive the exact same audio and visual information by donning the same equipment and going through the same IVE simulation. Along the same lines, once a research or training simulation is developed, there is little to no cost to reusing that simulation.

ON-LINE ADDENDUM

As an addendum to this chapter, we have developed a World Wide Web simulation in which a student witnesses a videotape of a person pilfering a wallet, and then participates in one of four different types of lineups. These lineups vary along one of two dimensions. First, the lineups either consist of all photographs (for both the suspect and the numerous distracters) or of all virtual models of heads. This dimension is important to examine because the student can experience the difficulty of performing accurately in the lineup procedure, as well as draw his or her own conclusions concerning the potential of using these virtual heads as substitutes for photographs. Second, the models can be presented simultaneously (i.e., all at once such that the witness can compare among the options) or presented sequentially (i.e., one at a time to avoid direct comparisons). Research by Wells (2002) demonstrated powerful differences between these two presentation methods. Specifically, sequential lineups tend to produce fewer false alarms (which result in wrongful incarcerations) than simultaneous lineups. However, until experiencing the differences in these presentation modes, it is difficult for a student to grasp the shortcomings inherent to the simultaneous presentations.

CONCLUSION

The advent of IVEs has made possible a wide array of digital decision simulations not possible before. There are many reasons to think that improvements in the technologies and techniques associated with IVE will revolutionize the world of decision simulations, and will lead to learning effects heretofore only dreamed about. The psychological research is only beginning to understand some of the reasons why students would be expected to learn more in such environments, but to the extent that having students able to suspend reality in order to effectively play their roles in a given simulation, then IVE facilitates this process.

REFERENCES

Baumrind, D. (1964). Some thoughts on ethics of research: After reading Milgram's "Behavioral study of obedience." *American Psychologist, 19*(6), 421–423.

Blascovich, J. (2002). Social influences within immersive virtual environments. In R. Schroeder (Ed.), *The social life of avatars* (pp. 127–145). New York: Springer-Verlag.

Blascovich, J., Loomis, J. M., Beall, A. C., Swinth, K., Hoyt, C., & Bailenson, J. (2002). Using immersive virtual environment technology as a methodological tool in social psychology. *Psychological Inquiry, 13*, 103–124.

Bothwell, R. K., Brigham, J. C., & Malpass, R. S. (1989). Cross-racial identification. *Personality and Social Psychology Bulletin, 15*, 19–25.

Brigham, J. C., & Barkowitz, P. (1978). Do 'they all look alike'? The effect of race, sex, experience and attitudes on the ability to recognize faces. *Journal of Applied Social Psychology, 8*, 306–318.

Brigham, J. C., & Malpass, R. S. (1985). The role of experience and contact in the recognition of faces of own- and other-race persons. *Journal of Social Issues, 41*, 139–155.

Brigham, J. C., Meissner, C. A., & Wasserman, A. W. (1999). Applied issues in the construction and expert assessment of photo lineups. *Applied Cognitive Psychology, 13*, S73–S92.

Cutler, B. L., Penrod, S. D., & Martens, T. K. (1987). The reliability of eyewitness identifications: The role of system and estimator variables. *Law and Human Behavior, 11*, 233–258.

Cutler, B. L., Penrod, S. D., O'Rourke, T. E., & Martens, T. K. (1986). Unconfounding the effects of contextual cues on eyewitness identification accuracy. *Social Behavior, 1*, 113–134.

Davies, G., & Milne, A. (1985). Eyewitness composite production: A function of mental or physical reinstatement of context. *Criminal Justice and Behavior, 12*(2), 209–220.

Haney, C., Banks, W. C., & Zimbardo, P. G. (1973). Interpersonal dynamics in a simulated prison. *International Journal of Criminology and Penology, 1*, 69–97.

Hershkowitz, I., Orbach, Y., Lamb, M. E., Sternberg, K. J., & Horowitz, D. (2001). The effects of mental context reinstatement on children's accounts of sexual abuse. *Applied Cognitive Psychology, 15*(3), 235–248.

Krafka, C., & Penrod, S. (1985). Reinstatement of context in a field experiment on eyewitness identification. *Journal of Personality and Social Psychology, 49*(1), 58–69.

Latane, B., & Darley, J. (1969). Bystander "apathy." *American Scientist, 57*, 244–268.

Laughery, K. R., Jensen, D. G., & Wogalter, M. S. (1988). Response bias with prototypic faces. In M. M. Gruneberg & P. E. Morris (Eds.), *Practical aspects of memory: Current research and issues* (vol. 1, pp. 157–162). New York: Wiley.

Lindsay, R. C. L., Lea, J. A., & Fulford, J. A. (1991). Sequential lineup presentation: Technique matters. *Journal of Applied Psychology, 76*, 741–745.

Lindsay, R. C. L., & Wells, G. L. (1985). Improving eyewitness identification from lineups: Simultaneous versus sequential lineup presentations. *Journal of Applied Psychology, 70*, 556–564.

Loftus, E. F. (1975). Leading questions and the eyewitness report. *Cognitive Psychology, 7*(4), 560–572.

Loomis, J., Blascovich, J., & Beall, A. (1999). Immersive virtual environment technology as a basic research tool in psychology. *Behavior Research Methods, Instruments, and Computers, 31*, 557–564.

Luus, C. A. E., & Wells, G. L. (1991). Eyewitness identification and the selection of distracters for lineups. *Law and Human Behavior, 15*, 43–57.

Malpass, R. S. (1981). Effective size and defendant bias in eyewitness identification lineups. *Law and Human Behavior, 5*, 299–309.

Malpass, R. S., & Devine, P. G. (1980). Realism and eyewitness identification research. *Law and Human Behavior, 4*(4), 347–358.

Malpass, R. S., & Devine, P. G. (1981). Eyewitness identification: Lineup instructions and the absence of the offender. *Journal of Applied Psychology, 66*(4), 482–489.

Memon, A., & Bruce, V. (1983). The effects of encoding strategy and context change on face recognition. *Human Learning: Journal of Practical Research and Applications, 2*(4), 313–326.

Milgram, S. (1963). Behavioral study of obedience. *Journal of Abnormal and Social Psychology, 67*, 371–378.

Tooley, V., Brigham, J. C., Maass, A., & Bothwell, R. K. (1987). Facial recognition: Weapon effect and attentional focus. *Journal of Applied Social Psychology, 17*(10), 845–859.

Wells, G. L. (2002). Eyewitness testimony. *The encyclopedia of crime and punishment*. Great Barrington, MA: Berkshire Publishing.

Wells, G. L., & Loftus, E. F. (in press). Eyewitness memory for people and events. In A. Goldstein (Ed.), *Comprehensive handbook of psychology* (vol. 11). New York: Wiley.

11

Current and Future Trends
in Digital Role-Play Simulations

Carolyn Thorsen
Boise State University

In the social sciences, we are most frequently dealing with situational simulations, those simulations that deal with the behaviors and attitudes of people or organizations in different situations. Situational simulations are the least commonly available educational simulations because they are difficult to develop since they reflect complex human and organizational behavior (Alessi & Trollip, 2001). These kinds of complex social situations requiring complex knowledge representation rely heavily on developments in the field of artificial intelligence (AI), perhaps more so than on faster CPUs and larger memories.

Although there is much to be said for the use of complex technologies in simulations, virtual reality being an example, much can be done with the technology that exists. What seems to limit us more than computer speed and power are methods for using the computers that we have to present effective digital simulations for the social sciences. Although virtual reality technology provides hands-on learning, new knowledge in the social sciences most often results from the give and take of ideas and concepts. While an airline pilot may need to feel the airplane and hear the sounds of the engine, the student of the social sciences will profit more from interaction that is most often verbal and conceptual. This student needs both to encounter life-like agents in plausible social situations and to work through complex decisions and consequences.

The *Crime and Punishment* simulation (presented in chapter 5), powerful as it is, does not require sophisticated equipment to produce the intended learning outcome. Rather, it relies on asking an elegant question using words and graphics that are stark in their simplicity and powerful in the amount of information internal to the viewer that it evokes. The Miller and Read simulation designed to teach safe sex could easily have been done, technically, in 1990 or so with videodisc. Its effectiveness springs from the compression of a life experience into highly evocative, emotionally charged video and dialogue that compress an evening and all of its decisions and consequences into half an hour. These examples point to the areas of development that will provide the infrastructure for more complex and realistic representations of social problems.

A further area of development that will play a large role in the future development of educational simulation is developments in pedagogical techniques and theories for building simulations. Current areas of research and development that must be expanded include building and using stories as a basis for simulation (Schank, 2000), using role playing (van Ments, 1999), and the development of pedagogically sound simulations as a method for teaching (Joyce, 2000).

A final area of development that will provide for the creation of more simulations than now exist will be the development of an authoring environment that subject matter experts and instructional designers as well can use without spending large amounts of time (years) learning how to be computer programmers. People have envisioned the computer as a teacher for a very long time. Tenczar and Bitzer assisted by Ozzie (Ozzie, 2003) developed an intelligent terminal to host a teaching environment called PLATO as early as 1974. Another vision, though never implemented on a large scale like PLATO, was suggested by Merrill of Utah State University (Merrill, 1990). His idea is that learning can be broken into transactions that can be programmed into shells, which then can be filled by subject matter experts or instructional designers, resulting in tutorial software for learners. One early implementation of this theory is called TICCIT.

To summarize, the future of computer-based simulations lies in expanding our knowledge and expertise in multiple areas:

- Developing a science of simulations;
- Creating multimodel simulation environments;
- Developing realistic, interactive delivery models;

- ○ Defining and creating psychologically plausible agents;
- ○ Increasing our understanding of how to convey complex meaning in concise verbal and graphical representations (Smith, 2002);
- • Refining current pedagogical models and·developing new ones for use in simulations;
- • Developing authoring environments that will allow subject matter and pedagogical experts to write simulations.

With significant advances in these areas and more importantly, subject matter and pedagogical experts who understand and can apply these advances to problems in the field, simulations will provide significant learning experiences to students at the highest levels of Bloom's taxonomy.

DEVELOPING A SCIENCE OF SIMULATIONS

Issues about research on games and simulations raise basic questions. Chief among them are how should researchers describe what they are working on? Should the emphasis be on defining features of games and simulations and examining how each feature influences use and learning? For instance, in this volume, several authors have noted the difference between role-play simulations, where users participate in the simulation, and simulations that require users to set parameters and then send them on their way. Is this a profound distinction that researchers should examine and use to develop a theory of simulations? Will research along these lines lead to a science of simulations that helps teachers use these tools?

At the moment there are few clear answers. At some point there will almost certainly be robust taxonomies and typologies for instructional science as there are in advanced sciences like physics, biology, and chemistry. In chemistry, for instance, atoms are clearly understood as being different from molecules. Research in chemistry (as well as in physics and biology) has been able to exploit these basic distinctions to create new knowledge in their fields.

In the use and development of simulations, the temptation is surely to develop taxonomies. Some simulations are multimedia, some are not. Some are multiplayer, some others involve just one person. These distinctions may turn out to be essential for developing a science of simulations and for considering what simulations are appropriate for teaching certain concepts and groups of students. However, the distinctions also may be misleading. The caveat offered here is to be on the alert for false distinctions. A program like *Crime and Punishment* may not seem to have a pedagogical model like *Virtual Sex* (see chapter 7). The *Virtual Sex* simulation uses a feedback model to help users learn to make safe decisions about using condoms. Mentors are used as well: they pop-up to (positively or negatively) reinforce decisions. There is a clear reliance on learning theory and instructional design. In short there is an easily identifiable pedagogical model. However, does the absence of these features in *Crime and Punishment* mean there is no pedagogical model? At face value it is easy to look at *Virtual Sex* and *Crime and Punishment* and think a key difference is that one uses a pedagogical model and the other does not. Yet that distinction may vanish when you take a closer look. *Crime and Punishment* offers students a structured judicial experience that emphasizes the latitude sentencing judges have in making decisions. This does not seem to have been built in by accident. It is part of the overall learning model. Likewise video is used to emphasize the personal characteristics of the felons and attorneys. All these features feed into a carefully designed class-based debriefing that helps students understand complexity. In the case of *Virtual Sex* and *Crime and Punishment*, the pedagogical model distinction might not be as clear-cut as it first appears. It might be more useful as a heuristic; it reminds you to search for the pedagogical framework and think about why certain design decisions were made.

The distinction between role-play based simulations and simulations that require users to set parameters and observe results may also begin to melt under close inspection. *SimCity* is a simulation (or is it a game?) that straddles the fence on this distinction. In *SimCity*, students can decide on basic initial features of a town (population growth, tax rate, ecosystem), start the simulation, and watch how the town changes. They can play god. However, is god a role? The distinction gets a bit dicier if we see students begin to play the role of town mayor and make changes to the initial conditions they set. It seems when this happens the students are shifting from observer to player. Part of the distinction depends not on the simulation but on the disposition of the student. It may be that play-god simulations can become role-plays, but not the other way around.

Again, the caveat is to be looking for false or weak distinctions. There is a learning ecology that serves as home for the simulations. It includes the minds of teachers and students. At the moment it is challenging to defend many of the distinctions given the flexibility of this learning ecology. Flexible rubrics for describing simulations might prove more effective for capturing the character of the simulations and the experience of the people that use them. Features may be hidden. It takes careful scrutiny on the part of researchers and teachers to fully describe the simulations they develop and use.

CREATING MULTIMODEL SIMULATION ENVIRONMENTS

Technically, the state-of-the-art in academic simulations now is largely visible in simulations for research. Social scientists who wish to set a process in motion have developed software that, once variables have been set and the program is run, will simulate some social process. Having the software engines (interfaces that make this fast and easy for nonprogrammers) to do this is one piece in the puzzle of building simulations for pedagogical purposes. Digital simulations of the future for pedagogical purposes will have to be built with smart, flexible, and dynamic software engines. Now, each of these simulations is based on one simulation model.

One characteristic of digital simulations that we will see in the future is the ability of the simulation engine to support multiple simulation models. What does this mean? Currently, even the best software represents knowledge only one or two ways. It may represent its knowledge with a neural network, with rules, or using frames, scripts, or a semantic network. Consequently, a program may be very smart about one small domain, but very dumb about the rest of the world. For example, a simulation based on the queuing model (Gilbert & Troitzsch, 2002) can tell one about how many counters and clerks should be available to minimize both the customer's average waiting time and the clerks' idle time. It might even be given some pedagogical kind of interface that would help a student learn how to think about such a problem. Yet, if that student also wanted to learn how to work with other elements of the organization to supply clerks when needed or what to do with idle clerks, the simulation based on the queuing model could not provide that flexibility.

Minsky (1992) suggested that AI-supported software of the future will not depend on just one kind of reasoning (like the queuing model based program previously described), but will match the reasoning algorithm with the problem. The situation is this: There are trivial problems and intractable problems. Trivial problems are composed of a few causes with minor effects. Typically, these can most often be solved with one kind of reasoning that he calls ordinary qualitative reasoning. At the other end of the continuum, there are problems with many causes and large effects. Solutions to these kinds of problems require many kinds of reasoning: ordinary qualitative reasoning, statistical reasoning, fuzzy logic, neural networks, etc.

Currently, social scientists write simulation software that uses one AI technique. In *Simulation for the Social Scientist* (Gilbert & Troitzsch, 2002) we see many example simulations. Each of these simulations is based on one of six different models:

- Microanalytical simulation models;
- Queuing models;
- Multilevel simulation models;
- Cellular automata;
- Multiagent models;
- Learning and evolutionary models.

Each model is supported by general-purpose language programs or software designed specifically for the model. Each of these models has strengths that make it useful for modeling different social problems. None, however, can take on problems other than those for which it is designed.

Although Minsky saw both the problem and the answer years ago, software with integrated reasoning systems is still not readily available especially for content area experts who are more interested in building a simulation than in programming. When it is, simulation developers will be able to represent large problems with many variables involved (the prototypical social decision) with fewer resources than they do now.

DEVELOPING REALISTIC, INTERACTIVE DELIVERY MODELS

Participating in a simulation involves one of the same skills that we call up when we watch a play or read a science fiction novel, the willing suspension of disbelief. The writer of the digital educational simulation must decide how much disbelief the user of the simulation can suspend and still learn what the simulation has to teach. It is clear that a good simulation must in some way provide a context real enough to allow the user to gather and retain information that transfers to the real situation. Current simulations achieve this verisimilitude in two ways. First, they use video of real people. Examples of these kinds of simulations in previous chapters include the safe sex for gays simulations, and the simulation based on the burn victim, Dax. Second, they create rich contexts. Examples of these kinds of simulations include the *Crime and Punishment* simulation on the influence of gender, race, and age on sentencing decisions about the guilt and innocence of defendants.

There are two especially important techniques that will be key to the development of future simulations: increased insight into how to write and create psychologically plausible agents and increased understanding of how to convey complex meaning in concise verbal and graphical representations. Interest in these two techniques and research in these areas is moving forward rapidly in the gaming industry. Game developers write simulations, though not necessarily of the real world. Nevertheless, many of their objectives are the same as developers of digital educational simulations. They must field interesting, realistic characters, and they must compress time by displaying as much information as possible in each snippet of dialogue and in each graphic.

Psychologically Plausible Agents

Many simulations require interpersonal interaction with another character in the simulation. Current techniques for providing this interaction include building simulations that include multiplayer (Asal simulation) simulations, using video scenes to provide a participant a third-person view into the unfolding of the simulation problem with choice points, and animated or graphical characters programmed to behave in determined ways with choice points throughout the program. In all of these cases, the character(s) with whom a simulation player interacts have a predetermined number of representations that they can display that elicit choices from the user. These characters typically cannot react to changes in the simulation environment themselves but rather are limited to giving the player a basis for reaction. Because each choice point in the simulation must be built in by hand, the simulation is limited by both the number of situations the simulation creator can devise and the budget for the simulation.

What if simulation creators could build characters capable of displaying many shades of behavior in reaction to changes in the simulation environment caused by the player of the simulation? The gaming industry is actively pursuing the research and development of these kinds of characters. One recent example of software that supports such characters is *Black and White* (Molyneux et al., 2002). In this game, the player chooses a character as a partner. When this character is first chosen, it knows very little. Instead, it is given the capacity for belief–desire–intention (Evans, 2001). This capacity is then developed by the player of the game who trains the creature to be helpful during the different problem-solving episodes presented by the game. Evans (2001) called this creature a "semi-autonomous helpful agent" (p. 48).

Evans, who was the AI director for *Black and White*, believes that based on this model person-like agents are possible. In order to be person-like, he said, agents need to have an infinite number of goals (like people), and an infinite number of ways of satisfying these goals. The advantage is this:

> They would give us an indefinite amount of flexibility in possible behavior. Even with a finite number of different animations the agents can play, these additions would enable an indefinite number of different ways of sequencing these animations. (Important parallel: There are only a finite number of words in a language, but an infinite number of possible sentences.) (p. 48)

Evans' second suggestion for future direction in characterization is empathic agents. By this he means that agents should form models about other agents' (including the player of the game) minds. They will use these models to understand language and for planning (Evans, 2001). Currently we communicate with agents–characters in simulations and games with a limited list of expressions. Though computationally expensive, we can expand this list of expressions by developing agents who not only have beliefs, desires, and intentions, but who also can develop models of the beliefs, desires, and intentions of other players in the simulation or game. Agent-helpers in

Black and White have been given a limited ability to develop such a model. The helpers collect data about the player of the game whom they are helping. If the player consistently performs cruel acts such as destroying villagers, their towns and animals, then the helper will spontaneously commit similar acts. On the other hand, if the player of the game is consistently kind, the character also performs kind acts.

One way to look at how a simulation of the future might use the plausible agent is to review a current state-of-the-art simulation and make some observations on how it might change. Schank (2002) in *Designing World Class E-Learning* relied heavily on the use of simulations. He provided a number of examples of simulations that have been used successfully by large business. The simulation we look at is one that he developed for Cutler-Hammer. The problem is teaching managers, who are busy and disinterested, to do performance evaluation interviews of the people that they supervise.

The design of Schank's software includes video vignettes giving the trainee a number of choices. The opening screen provides the following choices on which the trainee may click to see a scripted video of an actor playing an employee.

Choices include:

- Meet the previous manager
- Pictures of three employees with the following choices
    - Tell me more about Marie
    - What should I know about Luis?
    - Could you give me some background on Barry
- How is the department working toward its initiatives?
- Review employee files
- Performance development toolkit
- Go to next meeting.

After the trainee finishes with this screen, the actual interviews start. As the boss, the trainee works through several meetings with each employee with branching that provides successful and unsuccessful strategies. There is a final meeting in which there is a "tough conversation" (Schank, 2002, p. 135). All of these meetings are done featuring a brief video segment in which the employee speaks, and the trainee may then choose responses displayed as bulleted text items.

In a simulation of the future using psychologically plausible agents, the look and execution of this simulation would be different. The employees could be programmed as animations with expressive facial features and beliefs, desires, and intentions. Because these agents can react and respond to the user of the simulation, the experience would provide more shades of understanding and interaction than a simulation with a fixed set of branching pathways. Furthermore, these agents could develop a model of the trainee, based on interactions with the trainee.

Interviews could take place in real-time episodes unlike the current simulation that does not require the trainees to think on their feet. In fact, there could be two modes, one which is not real time, allowing novices to learn the fundamentals of what to expect in a performance review, and one which is real time for trainees who feel they are ready for a more realistic experiences.

Just how would this work? The answer to this question takes us to the next area for research that must mature—the use effective use of narrative in simulations.

Conveying Complex Meaning in Concise Verbal and Graphical Representations

Communication in the simulation environment for the social sciences is problematical. Unlike the science simulations in which the user–student often sets numbers in panels and clicks to go see what happens, creators of social science simulations frequently find themselves in a verbal rather than numerical environment. Most of the simulations presented in this volume involve verbal interaction between the user and simulation.

Yet, there is even more to the verbal element of the simulation than choices. There is the story itself. "What makes us intelligent is our ability to find out what we know when we need to know it. What we actually know is all the stories, experiences, 'facts,' little epithets, points of view, and so on that we have gathered over the years." Schank went on to say that each of these is like a computer screen with a label, and to find them we must find the label. Our intelligence is based on being able to react to the real world, finding relevant labels and applying the information to which these labels point to new situations. He said, "[i]n the end all we have, machine or human, are stories and methods of finding and using those stories" (Schank, 2000, pp. 15–16).

Simulations are stories that we hope will provide our students some context for future decisions. The next question is how best to represent those stories. The story of a simulation is not the same as a movie or a book. Nevertheless, one who has played a simulation can tell a story about it. Aarseth (2001), Editor-in-Chief of *Game Studies*, after asserting that many games are simulations said, "[games] are not static labyrinths like hypertexts or literary fictions. The simulations aspect is crucial: it is radically different alternative to narratives as a cognitive and communicative structure. . . . they can't be read as texts or listened to as music. They must be played" (p. 2).

Given that we learn by hearing and remembering stories (Schank, 2000), and that simulations are stories, though not in the traditional sense, the simulation of the future will profit from research and development in the representation of narrative in a simulation context. The question is, what direction will this research take and how will it change simulations as we know them now.

The purpose of narrative in any medium is to:

- Establish character attributes;
- Illustrate how characters interacted with each other before we met them;
- Provide a history of the world in the game or simulation (Smith, 2002).

However, gamers are often impatient with narratives in games. This may also be true of those who use simulations. The first challenge is to discover how much narrative is enough, pedagogically speaking. The second challenge is to pack as much information into as little dialogue as possible to overcome the impatience and move the story–simulation forward.

One area of study that will contribute to the future of simulation is the study of scripts. A script is "a set of expectations about what will happen next in a well-understood situation" (Schank, 2000, p. 7). For example, there are scripts that help us understand what will happen in a restaurant or at a stop light, what we say and do during an introduction, or how we relate to a person who is ill. One way to work with narrative so that it is compact is to use scripts to provide information without stating it. From another perspective, simulations may in fact, be about scripts that should be altered (for example, the *Crime and Punishment* simulation in chapter 5).

Refining Current Pedagogical Models and Developing New Ones for Use in Simulations

There are two current pedagogical models upon which current electronic simulations are modeled: role-playing and the physically based or human-mediated simulation. Although these two models have existed for many years and have been effective with a narrow range of problems, they should be examined in a formal way and translated to the electronic environment.

Teachers who are learning how to run simulations in their classrooms learn a model for using them. Aside from the simulation itself, the teacher learns that for the simulation to be maximally effective, it must be explained, refereed, coached, and discussed (Joyce, 2000). In future electronic simulations, could some of these functions be implemented by a computer? Refereeing and coaching would be good places to start.

There is much that we do not know about electronic refereeing and coaching. Following are some questions that will be answered and which will be a part of the interface of future simulations:

Coaching:

- Should the student ask for the coach or should the coach appear at some point where the student is having difficulty?
- For a given problem, how many possible misconceptions are there? Should they all have a coaching solution?
- When is it appropriate to provide the student with an answer and move on?
- How should coaching be written? What kind of narrative–explanation is most effective? How much information should the student receive? Should the student have a choice of how much information to ask for?

Refereeing:

- In simulations students often work in teams. The computer will sense friction among team members and resolve it?
- Simulations are conducted according to rules. The computer will sense a broken rule and apply proper referring tactics to resolve the problem and keep the participant in the game.

Role-playing is considered a subset or kind of simulation. It is "a kind of simulation that focuses attention on the interaction of people with one another. It emphasizes the functions performed by different people under various circumstances" (van Ments, 1999, pp. 3–4). Van Ments discussed the most serious problems with current electronic role-playing implementations. They include:

- When a student participates, the student's discourse is written meaning that is more considered and more permanent than in face-to-face situations. This situation reduces spontaneity.
- In face-to-face situations, the flow of the simulation is evenly paced. In electronic simulations because of time zones and the nature of the medium, the pace is unpredictable, sometimes frenetic and sometimes inactive.
- Body language is nonexistent.

Despite these handicaps, van Ments believed that there is a significant future for electronic role-playing. In a "Looking into the Future" (1999, p. 185) section, he provided examples of two role-plays, one for human resources managers on hiring and one for international marketing. These suggested role-plays have some common themes that include:

- Using the Internet as a data storage device for large amounts of information and graphics including physical layouts of offices. The example that he used was determining the strategy for conducting a meeting between two people in a set of offices housing a third person who should not know about the meeting.

- Because the role-play is not face to face, the tutor may play the parts of an unlimited number of other people providing participants with surprises and challenges not possible in traditional face-to-face role-plays. With the development of intelligent agents, the computer may take the place of the human tutor in role-plays.
- All conversations take place against a graphical, multimedia backdrop, or both, providing the participant a clear picture of the virtual environment in which they are working.
- Participant meetings that use chat may be monitored by other players.

Van Ment's role-playing vision looks at the near future. Some role-playing simulations exist that look very much like what van Ments described. To look at digital role-playing for pedagogical purposes further out into the future, one can envision an interface like the game *Everquest* (Everquest, 2003). This is an Internet-based role-playing game with 242,046 currently registered users. Though it is not pedagogically oriented, it does provide a model for those who would develop role-playing simulations using the Internet. It has the vast amounts of graphics and data that van Ments described, as well as individual and team pursuit goals. No one has yet developed a simulation this complex for teaching.

Development of Authoring Environments

Although some simulations will always be built line-by-line by teams of programmers, instructional designers, and subject matter experts (SMEs), other simulations could be built by SMEs themselves. PLATO is an example of an authoring environment for instruction. The language itself, called TUTOR, "was designed to have the power of a general-purpose language such as BASIC or PASCAL, but it had additional capabilities to support instructionally important features such as interactive vector graphics and real-time online transaction processing capabilities such as free-response answer analysis and feedback" (Foshay, 2002, p. 1). TUTOR influenced other subsequent instructionally oriented courseware authoring systems, Authorware being an example.

Instructional software that was developed using these authoring languages is primarily tutorial in genre. A concept or concepts is explained and then supported by interactive exercises and tests. For an instructor or instructional designer using these authoring systems, the joy is the prebuilt functions including such devices as:

- Templates for designing tutorial screens;
- Multiple-choice questions;
- Drag-and-drop questions;
- Matching questions; and
- Structures for judging short answer questions.

For the nonprogrammer who was primarily interested in automating the teaching of some content or finding a way to teach it better, these authoring environments made the difference between having instructional software or not. In many (perhaps most) cases it was not showy, but it served a purpose.

An authoring system for SMEs who wish to build simulations is a path that future simulations may take. We have previously referred to research that needs to be done in the area of building characters and writing narrative. Such an authoring system would provide the building blocks for believable characters. Additionally, it would be intelligent enough to prompt authors to write appropriate narrative. Furthermore, it would provide authors with strategies for structuring the simulation. It would do for the simulation what TUTOR and Authorware did for tutorials.

Virtual Reality

Simultaneous with the growth and development of knowledge in the field of simulation will be the growth of knowledge and improvement of hardware for virtual reality, a branch of simulation research upon which we have not yet touched. Virtual reality is another simulation technique but is different than the ones we have discussed in that it is hardware driven. If we add virtual reality to the tools we have discussed, we may find a simulation of the future in which the participant speaks with or views more realistic representations of people than they do now.

The Blascovich discussion of virtual reality in chapter 10 opens a window onto the possibility of a most engaging tool for educators. While his focus is on the use of virtual reality as a research tool, he also discusses it as a tool for teaching. To amplify on Blascovich's insightful comments on the use of virtual reality as a tool for education, we need only review a common current educational philosophy (constructivism) and a commonly used pedagogical technique (inductive learning). Virtual reality is a tool that provides teachers and professors another avenue to implement these teaching strategies that have proven so effective with lesser resources.

Constructivism does not describe just one school of thought, but there are some common elements of a constructivist perspective (Woolfolk, 2000). These include:

- Complex, challenging learning environments and authentic tasks
- Multiple representations of content
- Understanding that knowledge is constructed
- Social negotiation and shared responsibility as a part of learning. (p. 334)

Using Blascovich's description of the advantages of virtual reality for research, we can see that those same advantages apply to education–training. His description of the virtual reality environment described it as "ecologically realistic experimental environments (classrooms, courtrooms, airplane cockpits)" (chapter 10). This statement encompasses the first two of the four previously mentioned bullets. These two bullets are among the most difficult elements of a constructivist approach to implement in a classroom environment effectively and safely.

A second element of virtual reality noted by Blascovich as he discussed its advantages for research is the ease with which many kinds of data are collected. This feeds into the third previously mentioned bullet item, as well as the inductive model of teaching (Joyce, Weil, & Calhoun, 2000), articulated by the late Taba, a curriculum theorist and specialist in the teaching of the social sciences. Taba's view of learning is that "thinking is an active transaction between the individual and the data" (Joyce et al., 2000, p. 131). If students are using data of many kinds gathered from a virtual reality simulation that have historically been unavailable to them to construct their knowledge, then we have in virtual reality, a tool unlike any other in the history of education.

To conclude, we may see Dax's pain more graphically or view the defendant in a trial with more realism using virtual reality. We may engage in a simulation on international policy making a visit (by way of virtual reality) to the war-torn countries whose fate we hold in our hands. We may stand side-by-side with virtual soldiers who are fighting and dying in the wars we have created or are trying to stop. We may visit the starving people for whom we are trying to negotiate a trade treaty. Perhaps the greatest challenge that the educational community faces is the development of the resources that are necessary to create and implement good virtual reality simulations that are available to many students.

CONCLUSION

In the short term, future simulations will continue to be the creations of subject matter experts who find intriguing and difficult to teach problems in their content areas. They will be assisted by programmers who must build each simulation from its beginnings. However, as more and more of these kinds of simulations are built (the kinds of simulations that you have read about in this book) a body of knowledge about building simulations, simulation techniques, and about what works and what does not will grow. At some point, someone will be able to do a meta-analysis of the body of existing simulation work and derive those elements that are common to simulations and build a simulation engine. At this point, digital simulations will become a powerful force in education and training.

REFERENCES

Aarseth, E. (2001). Computer game studies, year one. *Game Studies: The International Journal of Computer Game Research, 1*(1), 2.

Alessi, S. M., & Trollip, S. R. (2001). *Multimedia for learning: Methods and development* (3rd ed.). Needham Heights, MA: Allyn & Bacon.

Evans, R. (2001, August). The future of AI in games: A personal view. *Game Developer*, pp. 46–49.

Everquest. (2003). *Alakhazam: Your online community.* Sony Online Entertainment. Available: http://everquest.allakhazam.com/

Foshay, R. (2002). The history of PLATO. *Plato: Roadmap to Success, 2*(1), 1.

Gilbert, N., & Troitzsch, K. (2002). *Simulation for the social scientist.* Philadelphia: Open University Press.

Joyce, B., Weil, M., & Calhoun, E. (2000). *Models of teaching.* Needham Heights, MA: Allyn & Bacon.

Kozma, R., & Bangert-Drowns, R. (1987). Design in context: A conceptual framework for the study of computer software in higher education. ERIC Document ED287436.

Merrill, M. D. (1990). Second generation instructional design (ID2). *Educational Technology, 30*(2), 7–11.

Minsky, M. (1992). Future of AI technology. *Toshiba Review, 47*(7). Available: http://web.media.mit.edu/~minsky/papers/CausalDiversity.html

Molyneux, P., Webley, M., Barnes, J., Giles, J., Chatelaine, J., Purkiss, O., Barnet-Lamb, T., & Hutchens, J. (2002). *Black and White.* Redwood City, CA: EA Games.

Ozzie, R. (2003). *Ray Ozzie's weblog.* Available: http://www.ozzie.net/blog/stories/2002/08/04/who.html

Schank, R. (2000). *Tell me a story: Narrative and intelligence.* Evanston, IL: Northwestern University Press.

Schank, R. (2002). *Designing world class E-learning.* New York: McGraw-Hill.

Smith, G. M. (2002). Computer games have words too: Dialogue conventions in Final Fantasy VII. *The International Journal of Computer Game Research, 2*(2), 11.

van Ments, M. (1999). *The effective use of role-play: Practical techniques for improving learning.* London: Kogan Page Limited.

Woolfolk, A. (2000). *Educational psychology* (8th ed.). Boston: Allyn & Bacon.

Author Index

Subject Index

A

B

C

Printed in the United States
by Baker & Taylor Publisher Services